30th Emmerdale Anniversary

Lance Parkin

GRANADA

The author wishes to thank: Gavin Blyth, Lisa Bowerman, Roseanne Boyle, Kathryn De Belle, Tim Fee, Steve Frost, Jim Greenhough, Karen Grimes, Roland Hall, Estelle Hind, Gillian Holmes, Mark Jones, Simon Kingsley, Luke Knight, Kevin Laffan, Mike Long, Sarah Mattingley, Helen Pannett, Nicky Paris, Katy Prout, Keith Richardson, Nicky Storey, Kaarina Suvanto, Michelle Tiruchelvam, Susan Trim, Janice Troup, Susanna Wadeson

Emmerdale is a Yorkshire Television Production

First published in Great Britain in 2002
by Granada Media, an imprint
of Andre Deutsch Limited
20 Mortimer Street
London
W1T 3JW

In association with Granada Media Group Limited

Text copyright © Granada Media Group Limited, 2002

A catalogue record for this book is available from the British Library

ISBN 0 233 05068 X

All photographs © Granada Media Group
Special photography by Lisa Bowerman
Design: Simon Buchanan
Managing Art Director: Jeremy Southgate

Printed and bound in Dubai

10 9 8 7 6 5 4 3 2 1

CONTENTS

KEVIN LAFFAN

Kevin Laffan created Emmerdale Farm in 1972, and continued as the main writer on the programme for the next thirteen years. A former actor, Kevin had written for the stage, radio and television, and continued to do so both during and after his time on Emmerdale. From 1973 – 1977, he also wrote Beryl's Lot for Yorkshire TV. His first novel was published in 2001.

Emmerdale started when Donald Bavistock, the Head of Programmes at Yorkshire TV, approached my agent about me writing a twice-weekly programme. Peter Willes, the Head of Drama, didn't want to do a twice-weekly programme and my agent didn't want me to do it, because I was a play writer. Peter Willes and my agent took me out to dinner to persuade me not to do it, and Donald took me and my wife out to persuade me that I should. So to satisfy both parties, I agreed to do it under another name, and I wrote twenty-six scripts, as a twenty six-episode play, then I forgot about it. When it went out, my name was on it, and that was it.

It was the start of television in the daytime, and they wanted something for lunchtime, and the idea was that it would last thirteen weeks, two episodes a week. It was a hit and I was asked to do another twenty-six ... then another. After that I started to take on other writers.

It's set in Yorkshire because Yorkshire TV were making it! They wanted something rural, and I wanted to do something set outdoors. I'd written a serial before then, the first part of one, and I was promised that it would have location filming, it was set in a fishing village, so I intended to show them fishing. But in the end there was only one episode where they filmed outside. I also wanted to write about an earth mother and her family. As I wanted her to be dominant, she couldn't have a husband, so I started with his funeral. There was a meeting where I was told that it would be a real switch off, but I told them I'd written it that way, and that was that. It worked really well. The first thing Annie says is 'I don't think he's going to come', and, you see, that's the hook for the audience – who does she mean? She means her son, Jack, who watches the funeral from a distance.

It's set on a farm because the idea was to write about a rural community. What better than a family running a farm? There's nothing autobiographical about Jack, the thing was that I wanted to write an environmental play, and I could capitalise on the fact that Jack's reason for going was that he quarrelled with his father about how he was running the farm. His father left him the farm out of revenge, so that when he came back he had to run it himself. And of course it meant his siblings were angry because they had been running it up to then. Jack wanted to run the farm along organic lines – no battery chickens etc. And to emphasise that contrast, I introduced a millionaire industrialist, Henry Wilks, whose factory had once poisoned a lot of fish in a beck. It was a question of looking at the conflict. I also included Toke Townley, who played Sam, as an old farmer, who liked the old ways – practical but wanting his animals to be treated with dignity.

We didn't have a name for it until very late in the day. I didn't imagine it going on more than thirteen weeks, but as I was coming to the end of the scripts, I was asked to keep it open. So that thirteen weeks ended with Jack going back to Italy, and that meant I could kick things off again with him coming back to the village.

People think that when characters speak dialogue they have to do so to explain. The great thing about a family is that they try not to quarrel – the drama is them trying *not* to argue, they know they have to live together, and to do what they can to prevent that row. The drama is knowing that it would all eventually break.

When people talk to each other, they know what they are talking about, but people listening in don't. The secret is to put that over without saying, 'Let me tell you about Emmerdale Farm'. If you listen in to a conversation on a bus, it's wondering what people are talking about that holds your interest. There's no drama listening to dialogue that's just people explaining things to each other.

I don't know the secret of why *Emmerdale* caught on... it's probably because it's human. There was never any forced drama about it. I never thought of a story as a plot – you have characters, people, and you see what they are up to. If there's a plane crash, it's – whoomf – and that's it. But if Joe's not come home, and Annie's worried, that's something where people can get involved with the story. You're in a situation that you want to see resolved. I think the obvious story they could do now, it's open and shut, is the young Sugden boy trying to get the farm back. He doesn't have to succeed, the story is him trying to get it. I'm not saying they should do it, but it's what I'd do.

I don't know when I realised it was a running serial, but when it became one, we brought in other writers. We had about four, each writing six episodes at a trot. We'd all know some things that had to happen in those episodes, for example, 'Your episodes have to have him proposing to her', but that was it, and the writer put his own story together. It used to go out with my name on the front of the programme, but I didn't want my name on some of those episodes – or take credit from other writers – and I told them they could put it at the end instead. Everyone read all the scripts and discussed them, and we'd make suggestions, but never tell anyone what to do. I don't work with being told that I'm writing episode fourteen, and someone else writes fifteen and so on – I did it my way.

The television people didn't like that. I used to feel protective about *Emmerdale*, but never proprietorial. After a period of time, the people that hired me originally retired or died – Peter Willes died, Donald Bavistock died – and they were replaced by new people. This wasn't only at Emmerdale, obviously, this is quite common, I wasn't picked on or anything. I was never up in Leeds every day, I was up there every fortnight or something like that. I was never part of the empire at Yorkshire Television, I was a freelance. When Peter and Donald had been alive, I'd always had an authority over the programme, but it got to the stage where I'd say, 'I don't want that', and people didn't want to hear it. Your life as a writer on television is made up of rows – you fight your corner and when we had the final row, there were new people there who didn't want to be told what to do by me.

It's so long ago, but as far as I'm concerned I left because I wouldn't change a script. I was writing two scripts a week, and the row was about being asked to change a script, *not* the exact

change they were after – I've written hundreds of scripts, and I'd only change them if they were too long or too short, no other reason. But I can't remember the specific script, or the specific problem. I wasn't rowing with *people* – it was just with the producers. They told me they didn't like what was happening, and we had a verbal punch-up. I told them I don't alter the scripts. I also told them I wouldn't have any sex in it. I didn't mind them talking about it, and we had Joe's initiation into sex in the programme, but we didn't show it.

Television's a load of old rope these days, I think, a total waste of time. You used to get a phone call from someone asking you to write so-and-so, and you'd write it and then they'd start making it. Now, they ask you for a synopsis, then a treatment, then a longer treatment... I've never written a synopsis in my life. When you're writing something, you're on a voyage of exploration – you don't start off knowing someone's going to jump out of a window at the end, if you did, you'd just be finding a way to get him out of that window. I'm interested in people and how they live their lives. I did write a treatment once, for a friend of mine, and they came back and said 'Could you do it again but make it exactly three pages?' and I told them, only not quite as politely, 'No'. It's pointless and it all takes so long.

There wasn't even a treatment for *Emmerdale Farm* – I wrote all the scripts and handed them to Donald, and I didn't discuss them with anyone until the scripts were finished. Television isn't writer-driven now. If they commissioned you then, they trusted you. It's totally different, now.

I enjoy writing – but I don't do TV any more. I had my first novel published in 2001, I called it *Pendle's Disposal* when I wrote it, and for two years no publisher was interested. But when I changed the title to *Virgins Are in Short Supply* I had two offers in seven days - what a reflection on the business!

There are much better writers than me who've not had a break, and I'm grateful I know where my next meal's coming from. I've had thirty-five years of writing. The first four or five were bad, but since then I've been very lucky, you need luck.

Am I happy to still have my name on the end credits of *Emmerdale*? Well, you can't see any names these days, they're so small and on for so little time! It doesn't matter. Those who know my name, and there aren't many, know me for Emmerdale, but I think of myself as a playwright. I've written lots of things, television, theatre, radio, film... I don't mind being identified with *Emmerdale* or worry about leaving, good grief – I don't have sleepness nights over it. I'm delighted it's a success, I'm delighted anything I do is. But I honestly don't think about it.

Introduction

Looking back over the 30 years *Emmerdale* has run, the striking thing is how much it has changed. Watch the first episodes of *Coronation Street*, from 1960, and it's recognisably the same show as it is now, with the same settings and even the same actor playing Ken Barlow. The first episode of *EastEnders*, nearly twenty years old now, looks almost identical to the current programme – Pauline Fowler even seems to be wearing the same pinny.

Emmerdale is almost entirely different from the *Emmerdale Farm* that started in 1972. Jack Sugden is still there (played by a different actor), but it's hard to believe that one early storyline began, 'It is haymaking time in Beckindale but the labours of the week have ceased and the villagers slowly make their way out of church.' Nowadays, someone is more likely to be burning that church down, having their gay marriage blessed in it or conducting an illicit affair there.

There has always been snobbery about the term 'soap opera', but soaps provide loyal audiences, which tend to stay on the same channel after the show has finished to give the next programme a try. Advertisers like soaps. Soaps get reliably large viewing figures – the advertisers know that an advert on between *Emmerdale* and *Coronation Street* will be seen by the largest number of people watching television that week. Indeed the term 'soap opera' was coined in America in the thirties to describe the daily radio dramas that women listened to and enjoyed while doing the housework – and so were sponsored by the companies that made cleaning products, like Procter and Gamble and Colgate-Palmolive.

Perhaps because of those commercial origins, until the eighties soap had always been the preserve of ITV, except of course, for *The Archers* on Radio Four. However, seeing the advantages in securing a guaranteed evening audience, both the BBC and Channel 4 launched soaps, *EastEnders* and *Brookside*. Until then, *Coronation Street* had been the only enduring evening soap that ran all year round, now there were rivals. *EastEnders* and *Brookside* changed the rules completely, gaining a reputation for high production values and 'hard-hitting' storylines. By the end of the decade, Australian imports *Neighbours* and *Home and Away* had proved that there was also a younger audience for the genre than had been assumed. *Emmerdale* went from a drama serial with seven regular cast members and about as many scenes per episode to a fast-paced soap with about fifty regular cast members at any given time.

Some people – including the programme's creator, Kevin Laffan – don't like the changes to the show, but change has always been a

Emmerdale village today.

Sam Pearson leads the beating of the bounds – an ancient tradition still being performed in the nineteen-seventies.

Main Street, Emmerdale.

theme of the programme. Right from the start, it was about a way of life that's changing. It's not been a simplistic fight between evil townies and bucolic locals, neither has it been about issues that don't affect people living in towns. Every part of the country has seen changes to the way people live and work. *Emmerdale* has documented that. It could be argued that the real life Walfords and Weatherfields have changed immeasurably more over the last few decades than the real Emmerdales. The soaps set in inner cities have, on the whole, failed to reflect the endemic social problems, the changes to the ethnic mix, or even the broader changes to society. *Emmerdale*'s been ahead of the game in some ways – noticeably green issues. It's odd to see episodes from the late seventies discussing organic farming, and Jack Sugden's been against battery hens since the day the series began. While the *Emmerdale* office often get letters criticising the 'lack of Yorkshire accents', it's merely reflecting the way small rural villages are no longer insular farming communities. The world has moved on.

Emmerdale's the soap most people would most like to live in, but the village has never been a cosy idyll. The rural crisis that has affected the country has recently seen Jack Sugden forced to sell up. It's never been an ideal place to live, there have always been villagers who've been jealous of the opportunities and anonymity of city life.

Off-screen, *Emmerdale* has changed, too. In 1972, *Emmerdale Farm* wasn't shown in every ITV region, it was shown during the day, and it was watched by about two million people, twice a week, with six-month breaks between series. Now, *Emmerdale* is shown five nights a week, at seven in the evening. Every weekday it opens the ITV ratings war, and every day around twelve million people tune in, over half the number of people watching television at that time. While 'the big two' soaps are *EastEnders* and *Coronation Street*, *Emmerdale* is never far behind, despite a lack of hype and tabloid front pages. Its fans are the most ferociously loyal of any soap.

As we'd expect, a lot has happened in 30 years, and we've learned a lot about the village and the people that live there. Making a programme like *Emmerdale* is hard work – writing and recording five episodes a week, week in week out, plus hour-long episodes, plus spin-off videos, to BAFTA-winning standard is unparalleled in British television. It owes its success to the work of thousands of talented people over the years, and any history of *Emmerdale* should declare that from the outset.

As Emmerdale reaches its thirtieth anniversary, there's a great deal to celebrate.

Emmerdale

TOUR OF THE VILLAGE

CHAPTER ONE

Emmerdale village may be small, but almost every
building has a long history and its share of secrets.

Emmerdale is a small village in Yorkshire, 39 miles from Bradford and 52 from Leeds. Its current population is around three hundred. The village sits on the banks of the River Emm, and consists of a few dozen properties built from grey Yorkshire sandstone with blue/grey slate roofs. As well as couple of dozen or so houses, there's a church, two pubs, a village hall, a post office and shop, a bed and breakfast, a small antiques shop, a vet's surgery, a restaurant and a cricket pavilion. Emmerdale is picturesque, but on the surface there is little to distinguish it from many other Dales villages of its type, and as it lies just off the main Hotten Road, and is too small to appear on most road maps, little traffic passes through it. It's a little too far from Leeds to have become a commuter village, or to have attracted the attentions of property speculators, although, as with most communities in the area, there has been a steady influx of outsiders for many years and locals can find it difficult to afford property in their own home town.

Emmerdale sits in the heart of the Yorkshire Dales National Park, and is surrounded by beautiful countryside, dotted with small mixed farms. It's a good base for a walking holiday, and most years there's a thriving tourist trade. The village amenities reflect this – there's a bed and breakfast, tearooms and a village shop that sells maps and postcards.

There are many excellent walks through and around Emmerdale, including one through Sparrow Wood, and one over the steep hill The Struggle – at the top, it's possible to look down over Hotten and, it's claimed on a good day, as far as Bradford or York Minster.

There is evidence that the area has been used for agricultural purposes since Neolithic times. There have been some archaeological finds dating from the Roman occupation as well as from Saxon times. The original name of the village, Beckindale, suggests Viking settlement and Viking remains were once unearthed underneath The Woolpack pub in the village, but the first firm documentary evidence of the existence of a village is an entry in the Domesday Book. Although St Mary's Church was rebuilt in the sixteenth century, it still has vestiges of the original Norman building. Some of the older families in the village, like the Sugdens, the owners of Emmerdale Farm, claim they can trace their ancestry back at least that far. Many more, particularly farming families, have lived in the area – often on the same land – for centuries.

In the Middle Ages, Beckindale was the site of a hunting lodge and a nunnery (which stood on the site of the modern cricket pitch). From Tudor times until 1979, the local squires were the Verney family, and they were responsible for managing the village from the seat of their power, The Hall. Gradually, a community developed around St Mary's Church and the bridge across the Emm, until there was a small village serving the local hill farmers. There was a fortress on what is now Dingle land that was destroyed during the Civil War. The oldest building still standing, Tenant House, dates to 1676. The school house (now a restaurant) was built in 1826, and most of the buildings date from the nineteenth century. In the twentieth century, the cricket pitch and pavilion were built by the Verneys to serve the community, as was the village hall.

Development in the area is strictly curtailed because of its location in a national park. The last substantial development was during the Second World War, when the RAF built an airstrip on part of Home Farm land just outside the village. After the war, this site fell into disuse until the 1990s, when the new owner of Home Farm, Frank Tate, developed the site into a holiday village – a number of chalets around an ornamental lake.

On 30th December 1993 one of the worst tragedies in British aviation history occurred, when an airliner from Eastern Europe exploded and crashed into the village and the surrounding countryside. All on board were killed, as well as twenty people on

The foot bridge over the Emm, leading up to the village hall and old school rooms.

Emmerdale, seventies style, when outside filming took place in Arncliffe.

EMMERDALE FACT

Outside locations were filmed in Arncliffe for the first few years of the show's life. However, this was a long way from the Leeds studios where the interiors were shot, and the cast and crew needed to stay overnight in hotels there, making it expensive. In 1976, the decision was made to film in Esholt instead, a village far nearer the studios. Studio facilities, though, remained fairly limited with a maximum of four sets up at any one time, and the writers having to take account of the fact that if one set went up, another had to come down first.

In 1989, with the programme now networked and on twice a week all year round, Emmerdale moved to a larger studio in Farsley. It was purpose-built, converted from an old textile mill, and allowed all the interior sets to stand at the same time on two stages, making shooting episodes a lot faster and more flexible.

When the show went to three times a week, a larger studio was needed once again. The new studio was opened in January 1997 by then Prime Minister John Major, and at twenty-six thousand square feet it's thought to be the largest single television stage in Europe. A great many of the interiors of houses are actually studio sets, including the Woolpack, Home Farm and the post office. The old Farsley studios now host other YTV dramas like Heartbeat.

With the switch to three times a week, it was felt that a more controlled environment for location shooting was needed – tourists flocked to Esholt to watch the filming, and every time one wandered into shot or a flashbulb went off, shooting of the scene would have to start again from the top. In addition to this, the makers of Emmerdale were acutely conscious that even if there weren't any tourists, they'd be disrupting the lives of people in Esholt by closing roads, clogging car parks and so on.

The solution was an audacious one, dreamt up by line producer Tim Fee and designer Mike Long. A 300-hundred acre site was leased in the countryside about twenty minutes' drive away from the Leeds studio, and a new village was built from scratch in just eighteen weeks. As well as all the village exteriors (except for Home Farm and the vicarage), a number of interiors are based out at the village set, such as the Reynolds' house and the vet's surgery.

the ground. These included Mark Hughes, Elizabeth Pollard, Leonard Kempinski and Archie Brooks, who was caught in a fireball on a hillside. That hill was renamed Archie Rise. Many buildings, including the Woolpack and Home Farm, were heavily damaged. The disaster obviously had a devastating effect on the small community, but it was also a time for great acts of heroism and stories of human resilience. Local men Frank Tate and Vic Windsor saved Frank's wife Kim from burning stables. With the bridge into the village blocked, Jack Sugden and Frank Tate managed to set up a temporary bridge made from piled-up drainage pipes, which allowed the emergency services into the village. Many survivors were pulled from the wreckage, including baby Alice Bates. Tate's son Chris wasn't quite so lucky – he survived, but suffered spinal injuries that left him in a wheelchair.

To avoid their village becoming synonymous with death and disaster, and to symbolise a new beginning (and in recognition of the role the Sugdens had played in village life over many decades), the villagers opted to change the name of Beckindale to Emmerdale in 1994. Nearly a decade on, there are many people that still vividly remember the night of the plane crash, but the villagers rarely talk about it, preferring to refer to it simply as 'the accident' when the subject comes up.

EMMERDALE

There are two streets, Main Street and Church Lane, both off the main Robblesfield Road which, just outside the village on the other side of the bridge, connects to the Hotten Road.

EMMERDALE FICTION

As the Series Bible, a comprehensive set of character and historical notes drawn up in early 1990, puts it: 'The geography of Emmerdale is fairly fluid'. Over the years, it's never been entirely set in stone how all the fictional locations fit together, and there have been different indications as to, for example, the distance between Emmerdale Farm and the village, the size and location of the nearest town, Hotten, or the extent of Home Farm land.

A number of maps of the village have been drawn up, either for use in the series as maps referred to by the characters or for reference books on the programme. There's an illustration of the village in Emmerdale Farm – The Official Companion *(published in 1988) and another appeared as the endpapers of 1997's* The Emmerdale Companion. *The only thing any of these maps have in common is that none of them have much in common!*

Within the fiction, the plane crash in 1993 was responsible for the destruction of a number of features, like Demdyke Row.

With the construction of the purpose-built village set, a lot of the geography of the Emmerdale village itself has been pinned down, as has the general direction of the nearby towns. But the designers have been careful to leave properties that aren't assigned to characters currently in the series, and there are all sorts of nooks and crannies on the new set. There is plenty left open for future writers to discover.

VET'S SURGERY AND ZOE'S COTTAGE

The first building any arrival in Emmerdale sees is the vet's surgery on Robblesfield Road by the junction with Main Street. It consists of Smithy Cottage, one of the largest houses in the village, and a smaller single-storey annexe.

As the name suggests, Smithy Cottage used to be the home of the village blacksmith, rented from the Verney estate. The annexe was, until the 1920s, the village washhouse. The last blacksmith was Frank Blakey, who in 1973 married Janie, the sister of Jack Sugden's first wife, Pat. Frank Blakey was opposed to hunting, and refused to shoe horses from the local hunt. This led to friction with George Verney, exacerbated by Jack Sugden who suspected Verney of being behind a move to evict Frank (in reality, Verney knew nothing about it). In 1974, Blakey left the village with Janie to become a teacher.

In 1995, Zoe Tate bought the property to use as a home and as a surgery for her new vet's practice. Her lover Emma Nightingale, an interior designer, transformed the house with a scheme that retained the original features of the rooms while giving them a modern twist.

The vet's surgery consists of three rooms – a reception area, manned by an allegedly full-time receptionist (in practice, the likes of Linda Glover and Kelly Windsor didn't prove the most reliable employees – although Zoe thought enough of Kelly to allow her to stay briefly in the cottage), a small operating theatre and a recovery room, with cages for everything from rabbits to large dogs.

Zoe had been 'out' as a lesbian for a couple of years, but two women setting up home and businesses in such a prominent part of the village proved too much for some elements of the community. Smithy Cottage was daubed with graffiti by teenagers Scott Windsor and Roy Glover, and Zoe was almost raped by one of her clients, farmer Ken Adlington.

Zoe and Emma split up the following year. Zoe's new partner Sophie moved in briefly, but soon left the village.

In 1997, Zoe took on Paddy Kirk, Mandy Dingle's boyfriend, to help with the surgery. In 1998 he became a full partner in the business, choosing to invest his money in that, rather than helping the Dingles escape eviction. This led to Paddy and Mandy splitting up, and Paddy moving into the spare room at Smithy Cottage. Months later, Zoe engineered a reunion at the Vets' Ball. Soon after, Zoe bought Home Farm and moved in there, renting the cottage to Paddy and Mandy, who had become engaged. Mandy wasted no time in redecorating the cottage to her unique tastes.

Mandy's father Caleb was seriously ill, and Mandy started spending more and more time in Southampton, looking after him.

Smithy Cottage - owned by Zoe Tate, who rents it to Paddy Kirk and Emily Wylie. The annex is Zoe and Paddy's vet's surgery.

ZOË TATE
B.Sc.,B.V. M.& S., M.R.C.V.S.
VETERINARY SURGEON
SURGERY HOURS
(BY APPOINTMENT ONLY)
MON - FRI   9-10 AM
             5-6 PM
EMERGENCIES ONLY SAT. 9-10 AM

While there, she fell for her father's carer Neil. Paddy discovered this, and – after an emotional showdown in the cottage – Mandy left the village. Paddy continued to live in the cottage, and took on a lodger, his cousin Jason. Eventually, Paddy's new fiancée, Emily, moved into the house. Paddy and Emily have toned down some of Mandy's excesses, but her influence can still be seen.

A house in Esholt was used for exteriors until the move to the village, where an almost identical replica was built. The vet's surgery is slightly larger than the old location that was used. Zoe's house was a studio set originally, but was moved to the village in late 1998, when the decision was made to move the Dingle barn into the studio and space had to be freed up. Upstairs in the village, there is a (little seen) bedroom set.

MAIN STREET

OAK LEA AND MULBERRY COTTAGE

Cottages adjacent to the bed and breakfast at the head of Main Street. Currently, they are either unoccupied or the residents are never seen.

THE GRANGE - BED AND BREAKFAST
(TEL: 01756 993993, FAX: 01756 993994)

Emmerdale has always had a bed and breakfast, and it's proved useful for people staying a short time in the village, as well as those who've found themselves out on their ear. The B & B sits next door to the Woolpack, and has a large dining and lounge area. There are four bedrooms, all heated, with colour TV and tea- and coffee-making facilities.

In 2000, Viv Hope and Carol Wareing were rival bidders for the B & B, with Carol outbidding her best friend – and ruining the friendship in the process. Carol left the village soon afterwards, but Alan Turner, former landlord of the Woolpack and guest at the B & B, volunteered to run the place for her.

He continues to do so, with Rodney Blackstock as a resident guest.

13

Alan Turner, the B&B and his old haunt The Woolpack.

THE WOOLPACK

The social heart of the village is The Woolpack pub. It gets its name from a time when wool was transported across the countryside by packhorse to textile mills in the cities, with the Woolpack evidently being one of the stops on that route. However, the current Woolpack has only been in use since 1976 – the original building was abandoned following problems with subsidence (it was eventually sold and converted into a private house).

This move was overseen by the longest-serving landlord of the Woolpack, Amos Brearly, who moved to the village after the war and ran the pub from 1948 until 1991. At first he worked for the brewery, Ephraim Monk, but in 1973 Amos and local businessman Henry Wilks bought into the business. Their partnership continued for 18 years, until Amos decided to retire to Spain, shortly before Mr Wilks died from a heart attack.

Amos had always resisted change, claiming he was concerned to preserve the Dales way of life, but often it seemed it was because he just didn't like new things – it was 1977 before he even hired a woman to work behind the bar. Over the years, Amos had, however reluctantly, toyed with taking bed-and-breakfast guests and serving food. More typically, Amos would bemoan Mr Wilks's installation of a new gadget, like a microwave oven or a computerised till, or would show a salesman the door for daring to suggest his customers might want to buy peanuts. The Woolpack had a loyal clientele, and Amos knew that many of them were at least as resistant to changes as he was.

The next landlord, Alan Turner, made a concerted effort to move the pub upmarket by opening a gourmet restaurant and later a wine bar. Some changes proved unpopular – there was a walkout of customers when he briefly switched the house beer from Ephraim Monk to that of the rival Skipdale Brewery. But most of Turner's changes were for the good, particularly a decision to appoint a bar manager (originally Terry Woods and his wife Britt, then Bernice Blackstock) to concentrate on the day-to-day running of the pub, and the Woolpack is now a thriving business, with something for almost everyone in the village.

The Woolpack was heavily damaged in the plane crash, and was rebuilt in 1994. Following a fire in 1998, the Woolpack was refurbished again, and now it is every inch the archetypal English country pub, with a bar made from limestone and oak, a beamed ceiling and a roaring fire in the winter months.

Following a health scare in 1999, Alan Turner sold the pub to his bar manager, Bernice Blackstock. Under the aegis of the Woolpack's first landlady, it expanded its range of food, hired a full-time chef and is now a popular place for villagers to have an evening meal. While, unusually, it doesn't have a television set, so doesn't show football matches, there are frequent 'theme nights' and it has become a tradition for villagers to eat their Christmas dinner at the Woolpack, rather than cook for themselves. In 2002, Bernice left the village, and the pub is now run by her mother,

The first location used for the exterior shots of the Woolpack was the Falcon Inn in Arncliffe, the village that was originally used for almost all the outdoor filming for Emmerdale Farm. The inn doubled as a base for the cast and crew while filming. When location filming switched to Esholt in 1976, the Commercial Inn was picked as the new Woolpack, with the subsidence story explaining the move in the series. Seen on television for almost twenty years, and replicated in the new village, the landlord of the Commercial Inn changed the name of the real pub to the Woolpack, and it has become a magnet for fans of the programme.

For the new village, designer Mike Long made the building more imposing by making it a little wider and a little less tall, and also made sure the area at the front of the pub was flat enough to put pub tables outside. The upstairs rooms of the Woolpack and the back entrance hall are village sets, the downstairs rooms (including the bar itself) are studio sets. On the rare occasions when scenes are set in the cellar, they are shot on location in a real pub close to the studio.

Diane Blackstock.

Rumours that the Woolpack has a resident ghost have surfaced from time to time. In 1976, the thought that the place was haunted was almost enough to make Amos Brearly pull out of buying it. In 1990, the story resurfaced – this time because a misprint in a guidebook had suggested the Woolpack had a 'welcoming ghost', rather than 'host'. Over the years, the Woolpack has had a gypsy curse put on it and suffered a plague of rats. Bernice's attempts to Feng Shui the Woolpack resulted in a spell of bad luck when she misread Seth's compass and, so she reckoned, reversed the flowing positive energy.

In the past, the Woolpack had two public rooms: the main bar, with a dartboard and the only public telephone; and the taproom, opened up in 1990, catering to a younger audience in the evenings, and families by day.

Following a couple of devastating accidents, the current Woolpack has been extensively refurbished. Now there is one large public room, the bar, with a dartboard and a jukebox (one which is rarely fraternised). One side of the room is set aside at lunchtimes and in the evenings for diners. The walls are dotted with memorabilia and reminders of the Woolpack's past. Miraculously, the Butterworth Ball – the traditional prize for winning an annual cricket match – has survived the various catastrophes to befall the pub. In honour of its longest-serving customer (he once claimed he'd been a regular since before Amos took over – this would mean he was propping up the bar during the war), Seth's usual spot is marked with a small brass plaque.

The bar can be reached from the front entrance on Main Street (via a small entrance hall, where the doors to the public toilets are) and by a side door, which has a ramp for wheelchair access.

Rarely seen by the punters, the backrooms of the Woolpack are extensive. There's a storeroom immediately behind the bar, full of boxes of soft drinks, crisps and other supplies. There is a large cellar, with a door that can't be unlocked from the inside, which

The Woolpack Inn, for many years the centre of village life.

has led to a couple of unfortunate mishaps in the past. In the last couple of years, a large kitchen has been fitted as the restaurant side of business has expanded. Also downstairs, there is the 'backroom', the large living room, with a small kitchen in one corner. There is also a back door and entrance hall, with a staircase leading upstairs and a large window overlooking the car park.

Upstairs there are at least three bedrooms and a single bathroom, all sharing a common landing. In the past, one of the bedrooms was used for bed-and-breakfast guests, but that hasn't been the case for a while. One of the bedrooms is substantially smaller than the others – when Bernice accepted the job as bar manager it was on the condition that she didn't get the smallest bedroom, forcing Tricia to move into it.

PEAR TREE COTTAGE, 18 MAIN STREET

Pear Tree Cottage, an end terrace next door to the Woolpack, was bought in 1996 by Steve Marchant, a financial consultant whose earnings allowed him to refurbish the cottage until it became one of the smartest properties in the village.

(above) Main St, including Pear Tree and Edna Birch's cottage

(right) Jacob's Fold, home of the Daggerts

Steve quickly became involved with the Tates – both by trying to pre-empt land deals Frank Tate was planning and by attempting to seduce Rachel, Frank's daughter-in-law. When Frank was on remand for the murder of Kim (she'd faked her own death), he surprised his family by appointing Steve as acting company manager of Tate Holdings. Kim reappeared, literally scaring Frank to death, and Kim and Steve lost little time in mixing business with pleasure – tightening their grip on Home Farm and Tate Holdings, and becoming lovers.

Great minds think alike – on the eve of their wedding in May 1998, Kim and Steve both lost all their money in business collapses, neither told the other, and both planned to use the other's money to get out of trouble. When the truth was revealed, Kim was forced to move out of the splendour of Home Farm to Pear Tree Cottage. From there, Kim and Steve plotted a way to recover at least some of the money – they would steal their own racehorse, Orsino, sell it and also pocket the insurance money. They invited Zoe to the cottage as an alibi. Steve would steal the horse, Kim would keep Zoe downstairs, and a tape recording of Steve's voice would play over the baby monitor, convincing Zoe that Steve was upstairs the whole time. Disaster struck when Steve ran over Kathy Glover, putting her in a coma and making the police far more interested in the crime. As the net tightened, Kim framed Steve, but it still wasn't enough to avoid jail. The night before she was due to be sentenced, she fled to Venezuela with the money and her son James.

Chris Tate, always one for a symbolic gesture, especially where family is involved, bought Pear Tree Cottage and moved in. It was here he conducted his affair with Scottish lawyer Laura

Johnstone. Once the Tates had bought back Home Farm, Chris began renting out the cottage. It currently houses Scott Windsor and his girlfriend Chloe Atkinson.

WOODBINE COTTAGE, 16 MAIN STREET

Edna Birch's house. The garden features the grave of her beloved dog, Batley.

TUG GHYLL

The house between Woodbine Cottage and Dale Head Farm. It is not known who lives there.

DALE HEAD FARM

Dale Head Farm sits at the other end of the terrace from Pear Tree Cottage, on the same side of Main Street as the Woolpack. Whoever lives there (we've never seen them) also owns the barn next door.

GARAGE

In 1998, Lisa Dingle was looking to start a car-repair business, but couldn't find suitable premises. Her husband Zak discovered an empty workshop at the back of Main Street, between Dale Head Farm and its adjacent barn. It was perfect for the task – it even had an inspection pit and old petrol pump, and had clearly been the local garage at some point many years ago. Discreet enquiries revealed that the building had been derelict for quite some time. Lisa tidied it up and opened up shop there, with no one objecting – on the contrary, many villagers were grateful there was now someone locally who could fix their cars.

After the original owner was found and Lisa was forced out, Scott Windsor (who had been helping her out) took over the business.

MILL COTTAGE

The Mill started life in the nineteenth century, as its name suggests, as a water mill. It's now one of the largest and most valuable houses in the village itself, and is the only building constructed from coursed sandstone. By the 1970s, it had become derelict and was bought by the young Jack Sugden to be converted into a quiet retreat where he could pursue a writing career. Jack ran into problems with the conversion work, and left the village in the mid-1970s. The Mill was left empty for ten years until 1986. Jack had returned to the village, and ended up bidding against his own brother, Joe, for the property. Joe won the bidding, but paid £35,000 for it, £10,000 more than he had expected to. Joe and Phil Pearce, from Phoenix Developments, intended to develop it into holiday flats. This fell through, but the house was now a desirable property and it changed hands a few

There has been some confusion in the past as to where the Mill is located. Originally there were reference to it being on Emmerdale Farm land. It was said to have been demolished in the late seventies, but clearly wasn't because Joe bought it and started renovating it in the mid-eighties, when it was said to be in the neighbouring village of Connelton. When Chris and Rachel lived there it was just outside the village. Now it stands at one end of Main Street, on the edge of the village itself.

times in the 1980s. In 1991, Frank Tate bought it as a wedding present for his son Chris and his new wife Kathy. Chris mortgaged the property for £250,000 in 1993. His marriage lasted less than three years, finally ending after Chris had an affair with Rachel Hughes which led to her becoming pregnant. Chris and Rachel married in 1995, but again that marriage was short-lived – lasting less than a year. Rachel was awarded The Mill as part of her divorce settlement, and lived there until her death in 1999.

In 2001, Rodney had his heart set on buying Mill Cottage, but he was outbid by Ray Mullan.

MILL BROOK

Not to be confused with Mill Cottage, Mill Brook is a large detached house standing at the head of Main Street. It was bought from the Home Farm estate by Laura Johnstone, the Scottish lawyer handling Lady Tara's business affairs. Laura stayed to help run Tate Haulage, and because she was romantically involved with Chris Tate. When both associations ended, she left the

Mill Cottage, the largest and most desirable property in the village itself.

village. The house was rented out (presumably by Laura) for over a year, before Zoe Tate bought it to live in, following her sale of Home Farm to her brother.

THE POST OFFICE

Up until 1973, the post office and village stores was owned by the Verneys, and leased to a succession of postmasters. It occupies a prominent position on Main Street and, as the only shop in the village, for many years it was the only practical place to buy most provisions. It also takes produce from a number of local farms, and supplies the hikers and ramblers who pass through the village. In recent years, in common with many small and rural businesses, it's faced increased competition from big supermarkets. While it's handy to pick up the odd item, the villagers of Emmerdale are now more likely to buy their weekly shop at the out-of-town GK supermarket on the edge of Hotten.

The last of Verney's tenants was Amy Postlethwaite, who retired due to illness. Alison Gibbons, her assistant, entered a partnership with Henry Wilks and approached George Verney and asked to buy the freehold. Verney agreed. Alison moved to Jersey in 1974, and Henry Wilks bought her share of the business. He hired Liz Ruskin, the vicar's wife, to run the shop. Two years later, on the vicar's retirement, Liz was replaced by Norah Norris.

Life at the post office was clearly uneventful for many years after that. In 1988, when a Mrs Robson was running the place, that was to change. Armed robbers raided the post office and were foiled by Nick Bates, who took some of the money they'd dropped and fell foul of a blackmail attempt by Eric Pollard and Phil Pearce.

In the summer of 1993, the Windsor family – Vic, Viv, Scott, Kelly and Donna moved in. Vic Windsor had been made redundant from Ford Dagenham, and used the redundancy money to fulfil a dream of running a quiet country business, away from crime and violence. It was the second marriage for both Vic and Viv, and this led to tensions within the family. But these were nothing compared to adjusting to village life – Vic didn't win any friends with his habit of racing along the country roads in his beloved Ford Zephyr, frightening horse-riders, in addition to this, the family left gates open and got lost on the moors.

Trouble was never far away from the Windsors. Scott was bullied at school and ran away, returning to Essex, before being found. Donna was trapped under a tractor in an accident. Worst of all, Viv's first husband, Reg Dawson returned to the village after being released from jail. He was persuaded to leave, but returned in June 1994 with two accomplices, and staged a raid, in which he deliberately started an explosion. The raid went seriously wrong, with Alan Turner being injured. The raiders fled to Home Farm, with Viv and Turner's new wife Shirley as hostages. One raider died when he crashed his car, and Reg accidentally killed the other, mistaking him for a policeman. Shirley stepped in to prevent Viv being shot – and was herself killed. Police marksmen shot and killed Reg. Vic played his part in rescue efforts following the plane crash, though, and did persuade a depressed Joe Sugden not to kill himself in its aftermath.

The year after, the Windsors' marriage was rocked when Vic first suspected Viv of having an affair with his friend Terry, then the affair actually took place. This seemed to trigger a series of disastrous relationships with men for elder daughter Kelly – one with her teacher while she was underage, one with Chris Tate and one-night stands with a number of men, including Biff Fowler.

Vic Windsor was killed on Christmas Day 1998 when he came home from Christmas lunch at the Woolpack to interrupt Billy Hopwood robbing the post office. Billy hit him on the head with his shotgun, and Vic died a slow and painful death. The death of her father devastated Kelly, who reached a new personal best by sleeping with her half-brother Scott. When news of this broke, almost a year later, it split the family in two. Following a suicide attempt, Kelly left the village.

Viv now runs the shop with the help of Emily Dingle, and lives with her new husband, Bob Hope. In 2002, Viv converted the downstairs living area of the property into tearooms, Cafe Hope, spotting a gap in the market.

Emily Wylie, current assistant post-mistress.

Keeper's Cottage, home of Seth Armstrong and Betty Eagleton.

KEEPER'S COTTAGE, 19 MAIN STREET

Nineteen Main Street, Keeper's Cottage, was rented from the Home Farm estate by Seth Armstrong and Betty Eagleton in 1995. Previously, Seth had lived on Demdyke Row, destroyed in the plane crash, before seeking refuge with 'the widow Eagleton'.

Seth and Betty supplement their income by having a lodger in the spare room. Over the years, the lodgers have included Britt Woods's father Ronnie Slater, Biff Fowler, teacher Tom Bainbridge (who was having an affair with his pupil Kelly Windsor), Terry Woods, Paddy Kirk (twice) and, following an eviction, Lisa and Belle Dingle.

Seth and Betty were briefly threatened with eviction in 1998, when the new owner of Home Farm, Lady Tara, planned to dispose of much of the Home Farm property portfolio. At their time of life, and with their financial history, Betty and Seth couldn't find a mortgage provider who would lend them the money, but Biff Fowler stepped into the breach, buying the house. Although he has since left the village, he still rents it to them.

Betty never used to see much of Seth at home – he would either be in his secret gamekeeper's hut on Home Farm woodland, or (more usually) propping up the bar in The Woolpack. Since he bought an old computer from Zoe in 1998, Seth's spent more time at home, surfing the internet and getting under Betty's feet.

VICTORIA COTTAGE, 17 MAIN STREET

Seventeen Main Street, opposite the Woolpack, is a three-bedroomed cottage which was rented from NY Estates in 1984 by Caroline Bates who arrived in Beckindale with her teenage children Kathy and Nick. She had left her husband, Malcolm, and was starting a new life as secretary to Alan Turner, then head of NY Estates.

In 1988, on the eve of her wedding to Jackie Merrick, a burst pipe at the house ruined Kathy's wedding dress, perhaps a sign of things to come for a woman uniquely unlucky in love. Annie Sugden lent Kathy her wedding dress from her marriage to Jacob in the 1940s. Kathy married Jackie and they moved out to Demdyke Row.

By then, Caroline and Alan Turner were running the Home Farm fish farm from a room in the cottage (and storing some fish in the freezer!). They began a relationship that ended when Caroline had to move to Scarborough to look after her sick mother. Turner bought the cottage from NY Estates in 1989, getting it for half the £80,000 it was worth because Caroline was a sitting tenant. After Caroline left for Scarborough, Alan Turner lived in the house for two years before buying the Woolpack and moving in there. Caroline returned shortly afterwards and demanded compensation – she had been tenant of the cottage which Alan had sold.

When Turner bought the Woolpack, Elizabeth Feldmann became the new manager of the fish farm, and moved into the cottage with her son Michael. Elizabeth, against Turner's advice, began a relationship with Eric Pollard, and was angry that Pollard was soon using the cottage as a business address and for storing furniture. This didn't stop the pair from marrying in 1992.

Elizabeth attempted to rein in Pollard, who was involved in a

Victoria Cottage has been home to many villagers over the years.

number of crooked schemes, ranging from buying antiques for ridiculously low amounts to cheque-book fraud and selling stolen goods. When he tipped the police off that Elizabeth's wayward son Michael was responsible for writing bogus cheques, that was the last straw. Elizabeth confronted him and threw him out the house. That was on the night of the plane crash. Elizabeth died that night, a presumed victim of the accident. Pollard ensured she was quickly cremated, leading Michael to suspect that Pollard had murdered her.

Pollard persuaded Kathy Tate to enter business with him by opening tearooms in the old School House. He also opened a wine bar there. Pollard continued to live in Victoria Cottage after Elizabeth's death, and his third wife Dee joined him there in 1997. That year, he reached an arrangement with Kathy Glover to exchange it for the flat above the School House.

Kathy moved into the house with her niece Alice Bates. Following a bitter custody battle with Alice's mother Elsa, Alice went to Australia in 2000. Nearly two years later, Kathy decided to join Alice there. Alan Turner bought the house once again, and rented it to his granddaughter Tricia and her boyfriend Marlon.

CONNELTON VIEW
The home of Brian and Katie Addyman.

DALE VIEW
In 1999, Kelly Windsor set her heart on Dale View on Main Street, but it quickly became clear she and new husband Roy couldn't afford the property. It was bought by a Leeds businesswoman, Miss Curtis, as a weekend cottage – and she hardly used it. She did hire Kelly to clean the place. Realising that the owner was hardly ever there, and possessing the keys, Kelly moved in, dragging her reluctant husband Roy along. It all ended in tears when Kelly damaged items in the house and the owner arrived unexpectedly, catching Roy and Kelly together.

More recently, the house has been sold on, and has become the home of Nicola Blackstock, who rents it from its new owner.

JACOB'S FOLD
Cynthia Daggert moved to Emmerdale from Bradford, hoping to make a better life for her family. At first they stayed in the bed and breakfast, but they were thrown out by the owner Carol. After staying with Ashley at the vicarage for a while, they looked for a more permanent place to live. Unable to afford a house in Emmerdale, and with a paucity of suitable houses to rent, they squatted in an empty cottage, Jacob's Fold, next to Tenant Cottage.

The original owner came to light, and now the Daggerts rent the cottage.

CHURCH LANE

FARRER'S BARN
Farrer's Barn is owned by Eric Pollard, who runs his antiques business from the ground floor and lets out the first floor to local businesses. His first tenant was Mandy Dingle, who sold second-hand clothes, but Pollard soon took the chance to move upmarket when Scott Windsor and Richie Carter asked if they could rent the space for their new computer business. Mandy was summarily evicted, much to her irritation. Since Richie left the village, and the computer company was wound up, the upstairs area has been vacant.

Pollard has converted an area of the barn for himself to live in.

Farrer's Barn – as the sign says – houses an antiques business. Eric Pollard has converted part of the barn and lives there.

ANNIE'S COTTAGE
The oldest surviving building in the village, built in 1671, Tenant House is a three-bedroomed cottage that was bought by Annie Sugden in 1993, when she was reluctant to live in the 'new' Emmerdale Farm. She had found happiness with Leonard Kempinski, a wealthy retiree, but the relationship ended in tragedy as Kempinski was killed in the plane crash. Annie herself spent months in a coma and, shortly after recovering, retired to Spain.

Jack Sugden began renting out the cottage. The first tenant was Dave Glover, who began the tradition of using the place as a bachelor pad. The cottage hosted his simultaneous affairs with Kim Tate and Kathy Glover. When both relationships collapsed, Dave Glover took in a lodger, Sean Rossi.

The Sugdens lived in the house while work was being done on

Annie's Cottage - the oldest surviving property in the village, and currently the home of Jack Sugden and family.

so disgusted she attempted to keep the place clean.

In early 2002, the Sugdens were forced to sell up Emmerdale Farm. Jack, Robert, Andy and Victoria moved into Annie's Cottage, which proved to be cramped after the farmhouse, but convenient for Andy, as his girlfriend Katie lived next door.

THE OLD SCHOOL HOUSE

Built in 1826, Emmerdale's school, was looked after in the nineteen seventies by caretaker Seth Armstrong. Like many village schools, it was closed in the late 1970s, due to falling attendances and increased maintenance costs. The building was apparently left idle for many years, before Kathy Glover bought the property in 1995 with money she'd received as part of a divorce settlement from Chris Tate and converted it into tearooms (originally called the Old School Tea Rooms), with room outside for tables in good weather. Eventually, the building came to incorporate a wine bar for the evening trade, run by Eric Pollard, who lived in the first-floor flat of the property. Kathy bought Pollard out of the business when he lost his licence for selling to underage drinkers. She sought to capitalise on the obvious demand for a meeting place for teenagers, and redecorated the place in the style of an American diner. The business was successful, but Kathy sold up, and was bought out by Marlon Dingle, her chef, who – after toying with taking the place downmarket – decided that the gap in the market, and the best vehicle for his ambitions, was as a gourmet restaurant. *Chez Marlon* was opened, following a refit that was funded by Chris Tate and Rodney Blackstock. While it received good write-ups, the business struggled, not least because

The Old School Rooms - formely Kathy's Diner and the restaurant Chez Marlon.

the new Emmerdale Farm, and following that the Cairns family stayed in the house.

In January 1998 the house was empty, and Biff Fowler and Marlon Dingle started squatting there after being thrown out by their families. When Sarah Sugden found out, Kathy Glover persuaded her to rent it to them, rather than evict them, and a figure of £300 a month was agreed on. This seemingly cemented the purpose of the cottage as a home for men who'd been thrown out of their houses. Jed Outhwaite, Terry Woods, Roy Glover and Sean Reynolds were all temporary residents. The cottage is structurally sound, but the furniture was rather basic, and a succession of jack-the-lad tenants meant that the decoration ran to posters from lads' mags and carefully arranged beer cans. Kelly Glover, hardly one to do housework, moved into the cottage with Roy in 1999, and was before opening, Marlon had worked as a chef in the Woolpack, and convinced landlady Bernice Blackstock to introduce a range of good-quality, good-value meals there – many villagers chose to eat at the Woolpack.

In early 2002, *Chez Marlon* closed, and the building was put up for sale. It currently remains empty.

FORD COTTAGE

A large house standing about fifty yards from the village, on the other side of the ford across the river. It is not known who lives there.

> *The outdoor set includes a house built some way from the main village, which was simply put there for perspective – in the shots in which it appears, it makes the village look larger! In real life, the building is the base and storeroom for the gardeners who tend to the village set.*

VILLAGE HALL

The village hall is the perfect venue for a range of village events. In the past, these have included plays and pantomimes, *including Jack and the Beanstalk*, *The Pirates of Penzance* and an inadvertently hilarious *Dracula* (adapted by Amos Brearly). There have also been discos and small music gigs.

The village hall is the centre for many outdoor events, like summer fairs, antiques fairs and jumble sales. There are a variety of activities during the evenings, including dance and keep-fit classes, and a kids' club run by Ashley Thomas.

Village meetings are held in the village hall, usually to discuss planning or development issues. In the past, there have been angry gatherings to oppose the development of a nuclear dump, an open prison, mass evictions and, most recently, the erection of a telephone mast.

The village hall's finest hour almost certainly came in 1998, when it became the temporary Woolpack. An accident with a box of fireworks had gutted the bar of the real Woolpack, but a licence was granted that allowed it to continue in business while it was being refurbished.

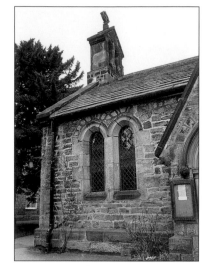

St Mary's Church.

The village hall was often depicted as being on Main Street, but it's now clearly on Church Lane, adjacent to the graveyard and on the opposite bank of the stream to the cricket pitch.

ST MARY'S CHURCH

There has been a church on the site since Norman times, and there's even been evidence of Saxon settlement, but the current church in the village dates from the late nineteenth century. St Mary's Church is, as in any community, a focal point for the village – the setting for baptisms, weddings, blessings, prayer services, memorial services and funerals.

For ten years from 1989 the village didn't have its own vicar, and services were taken by different curates and rectors, including Tony Charlton, and the reverends Jackson, Richards and Burns. Reverend Ashley Thomas was one of those occasional clergy since 1996, and at some point since then he became Emmerdale's own vicar, taking up residence in the vicarage.

In times gone by, every village wedding would have taken place at the church. Until recently, this was the case. Nowadays, many services take place in Hotten Register Office. The current vicar, Ashley Thomas, is more relaxed about marrying divorcees in his church (and he himself married Bernice Blackstock, a divorcee, in 2000). The memorial service for those killed in the plane crash took place in the church. In 2002 it was badly damaged in a fire started by Zoe Tate, who was suffering from a mental illness.

Inside the village hall.

The village set doesn't include a church or vicarage – any church scenes are still shot in St Paul's in Esholt, as are exterior shots of the vicarage. The interior of the vicarage is a village set in the Mill Cottage building. The graveyard is in the village, though – and uses headstones salvaged from an eighteenth-century East End graveyard that was redeveloped. Many characters killed off in the series have had special headstones commissioned.

The graveyard is the final resting place for many villagers ...

GRAVEYARD

Many of the past luminaries of the village are buried in the graveyard of St Mary's Church – no one in Emmerdale seems to opt to be cremated. The markers range from a large headstone for Frank Tate to a small wooden cross for Ben Dingle.

Until his death in 1989 the gravedigger was Tiny Watson. Seth and Archie took over his duties, but the only grave they dug was Tiny's, as they were sacked after that collapsed due to poor workmanship.

Kim Tate demonstrated her gift for the grand gesture in 1998, when she buried the money she'd got for stealing her own racehorse Orsino in Frank's grave. Frank's son Chris gave as good as he got, though – correctly guessing where Kim would have hidden the money, he dug it up and replaced it with a tape recorder with a message gloating that he'd outsmarted her. More recently, Chris made sure his secret half-brother, Liam, was buried next to their father, Frank.

VICARAGE

Next to the church is a large and well-appointed vicarage, dating from Georgian times. In the 1970s and 1980s, until the retirement of Reverend Hinton in 1989, it was host to a number of village fetes and other events (nowadays the village hall is the centre for such activities).

The vicarage has also had its fair share of lodgers over the years – Alison Gibbons stayed in 1973, working as a Woolpack barmaid and assistant in the village shop. Dolly Acaster stayed there in 1977, moving out when Donald Hinton arrived. Hinton's children returned to cause him problems – son Clive was arrested for gun-running in Athens, daughter Barbara Peters left her husband and stayed at the vicarage.

Ashley Thomas took over as the village vicar in 1996. It's unclear when he took up residence in the vicarage, but it was the

Sam and Amos spent much of their time at the allotments.

perfect place to romance Bernice Blackstock, who moved in when they married in late 2000.

OTHER BUILDINGS

ALLOTMENTS

There are allotments in the village, keenly tended over the years by people like Seth and Amos – who were, in their time, joint presidents of the Beckindale Horticultural Society. Seth rarely lost a competition, resorting to stealing flowers from the graveyard to beef up a floral display or filling a marrow with lead shot to make it weigh more.

THE BRIDGE

There has been a bridge across the Emm for centuries, the crossing point possibly even explaining the location of the village. The road bridge was blocked in the plane crash, and a new crossing had to be improvised by Frank Tate and Jack Sugden. Elsewhere in the village, there is a small footbridge and a ford.

The Emm flows down from Home Farm land – in 1984, Turner built a dam that completely blocked it off, making the stream dry up, but it was soon demolished.

CRICKET PAVILION

Emmerdale boasts a large cricket pavilion, donated to the village by the Verney family. Since 1903, Emmerdale has hosted a sports match, usually cricket, where they play against a team from nearby Robblesfield for the honour of winning the Butterworth Ball. The home team frequently win and when things are looking unfavourable, and Lady Luck doesn't intervene, Seth Armstrong has often managed to swing things to Emmerdale's advantage.

DINGLES' FARM

Five hundred yards or so up the hill from Emmerdale, on Robblesfield Way, off the main Robblesfield Road, is Wishing Well Cottage, the home of the Dingle family. The Dingles have had a reputation as local yobs and thieves for many years. While they've only been a prominent part of village life since the mid-1990s, Zak Dingle claims to have been born in the property, so

Inside the Dingle's farm

The cricket pavilion - scene of Joe Sugden's sporting triumphs.

before that they were clearly better at keeping their heads down. The smallholding is a pig farm, and gains its name from the old Woolpack well, salvaged from the 1995 refurbishment of the pub by Zak, who gave it to his wife Nellie as a Valentine's present and renamed the house in its honour.

The Dingle farm was previously part of the Home Farm estate, the nearest part of the old estate to the village. The dilapidated barn and outbuildings had been sublet free to the Dingles for over twenty years by a Home Farm tenant farmer, Holdgate. The Dingles were not popular in the village, and at one stage only seemed to appear there to have fights with the villagers, including one where Luke McAllister apparently killed Ben Dingle –

although it was later revealed that Ben Dingle had a pre-existing medical condition which caused his death.

In 1995, Frank Tate attempted to evict the Dingles so that he could rent their farm to the Glovers, but was surprised to face concerted opposition from not just members of the extended Dingle family, who flocked to help Zak (this was the first time Mandy Dingle had been seen in Emmerdale), but also other villagers. Frank conceded defeat, started charging the Dingles nominal rent, and moved the Glovers into the adjacent Holdgate's Farm.

The following year, Mandy developed a taste for building work when she converted an outbuilding into a self-contained flat. The first occupant of the flat was their Uncle Albert, but Mandy moved in herself when Albert left. When Mandy moved into Smithy Cottage with Paddy, Butch installed his girlfriend Emily in the flat.

In 1998, the buildings were declared unsafe, and Lady Tara Oakwell, then the majority shareholder of the Home Farm estate, had them repaired. Shortly afterwards she put most of the estate property, including the Dingle farm, up for sale. Facing eviction once again, unable to raise the £6000 the barn was worth, the Dingles were resigned to their fate. Indeed they left the family home – Zak and Butch taking Rachel Hughes's offer of a temporary place at Mill Cottage, Lisa and Mandy moving in with Betty and Seth. Mandy saved the day: Paddy's mother was horrified at the thought of Paddy marrying her, and offered to pay Mandy the money if she would marry someone else. Having fallen out with Paddy, Mandy jumped at the chance, but the only candidate for husband was Mandy's own cousin, Butch. She duly married him, and the Dingle clan returned to their home, Zak worried that he was becoming too middle class now he was a homeowner.

Lisa Dingle gave birth to baby Belle in one of the pig stalls on Christmas Day 1998. Lisa hadn't even realised she was pregnant, and the Dingles set about making their farm safe for a young baby.

The Dingle barn was the only building already in existence at the village site. At first the interior scenes were also shot at the village, but with the arrival of Zak's and Lisa's baby, Belle, the set was moved to the studio, which was much more safe and warm (not to mention rat-free!) than the real barn.

THE TAT FACTORY

Recently, the old Dingle barn was bought by Pollard to house his 'tat factory', a workshop where 'genuine Dales artwork' is created, assembled and shipped out to gift shops. It consists of an office for Pollard and a fairly cramped working area,

The Dimgles' farmhouse and yard

essentially just enough room for a large bench.

The factory has proved profitable, mainly because Pollard keeps his overheads down by hiring the likes of Sam Dingle and Betty Eagleton as his 'craftsmen'.

HOLDGATE'S FARM

(Full address: *Holdgate's Farm, Robblesfield Way, Emmerdale, W Yorkshire, HT3 8AP, Tel: 01756 924378*)

The property adjacent to the Dingles' is Holdgate's Farm, a large farmhouse named after an old tenant. Holdgate's was part of the Home Farm estate until 1995, when Holdgate died, with the Dingles' place actually being the outbuildings from the main farmhouse, which Holdgate had been subletting to the clan. The Holdgate farmhouse is a big four-bedroomed property with a large front lawn and a thriving vegetable garden at the back. It's about five hundred yards from Emmerdale village itself just off the Robblesfield Road.

Following Holdgate's death, Frank Tate originally wanted to let the outbuildings to the Glover family, tenant farmers. He failed in his bid to oust the Dingles, and eventually settled for letting out Holdgate's Farm itself to the Glovers. Ned Glover set about running the mixed smallholding, and was particularly proud of his vegetable crop.

The Glovers, though, struggled with debts throughout their time in Emmerdale, and suffered tragedy after tragedy. Linda Glover had a relationship with minor local aristocrat, Danny Weir, and when she attempted to abort their child herself she ended up in hospital. Dave Glover, the eldest son, started an affair with Kim Tate, Frank Tate's wife. Frank Tate was both the Glovers' landlord and employed Dave as assistant farm manager at Home Farm.

Lady Tara Oakwell, as part of a plan to sell off much of the

Holdgate's Farm - home to the Glovers, then the Reynolds family.

Home Farm estate, evicted the Glovers and put the property on the market as a large private house. The house was bought by Sean Reynolds and his family, and they moved there in 1999.

HAWKINS FARM

This large house was bought by incoming village GP Bernard McAllister. His wife Angharad became the deputy head of Hotten Comprehensive. The McAllisters' time in the village was brief – they left after their son Luke was involved in the death of Ben Dingle at a rave, and Bernard was pursued by Kathy Tate, who virtually stalked him when her second marriage broke up. The luck of the McAllisters' children didn't improve when their parents left. Their daughter Jessica had a fiery relationship with Biff Fowler, and Tina Dingle jilted Luke at the altar, after faking a pregnancy, which led to Luke dying in a crash. Betty Eagleton, hired as a housekeeper by the McAllisters, found it difficult to keep up with the gossip.

THE MALT SHOVEL

There is a rival pub to the Woolpack in Emmerdale, the Malt Shovel. In the 1970s, the landlord was Bill Appledore, who was rumoured to be living there with a young woman who he wasn't married to. Soon after that, though, old Ernie Shuttleworth took over as landlord, and ran the pub with the help of 'his Doreen', who had an unexplained, unrequited passion for Mr Wilks. The Malt Shovel is on the Robblesfield Road just outside the village, and Woolpack regulars dismiss it, claiming the beer is flat (although it also serves Ephraim Monk ale, and Seth was happy to frequent both pubs in the 1980s). There's a traditional, usually friendly rivalry between the two, which most often manifests itself in a sports match – either cricket or rugby. Amos claimed that while the Woolpack was an 'inn', the Malt Shovel was a mere 'public house', but was unable to explain the distinction, or come up with any difference between the facilities offered. One of the

attractions was Ernie Shuttleworth's talking dog, although Amos was sceptical: 'It doesn't talk, Mr Wilks, I've always said that.'

In 1989, the Malt Shovel started longer opening times to steal business from the Woolpack, which led the two pubs into an escalating series of gimmicks to win customers. Amos eventually joked that he would get strippers in – and Seth booked them. Eventually Amos and Ernie called a truce – the customers were getting their own way, and that would never do.

> *The Malt Shovel has been mentioned a lot over the years, but only rarely seen, and there isn't a Malt Shovel building in the new village set. It's usually mentioned when someone tells the landlord of the Woolpack that they're taking their business elsewhere. In the 1970s, story synopses refer to the name as one word: 'Maltshovel'.*

SKIPDALE ROAD

Eric Pollard once arranged a house clearance for 14 Skipdale Road, only to have Sam Dingle carry out the clearance on number 40.

DEMDYKE

About four hundred yards from Emmerdale, between the village and Emmerdale Farm, is the hamlet of Demdyke. The main feature, the terrace Demdyke Row, was destroyed in the plane crash. Before that, it had provided cheap housing for young locals and newly-weds – the houses were two-bedroomed, with a living room and small kitchen. Three Demdyke Row, in particular, was popular. It was bought by Joe Sugden in 1977, and was the home, over the years, of Jackie and Sandie Merrick and the Bates family. Kathy lived there until her marriage to Chris, and in 1990 it was worth £65,000.

Seth Armstrong lived at 6 Demdyke Row from at least 1978. Seth's little-seen wife Meg died at the house in February 1993. The end of the year and the plane disaster saw the destruction of the house and the death of Seth's beloved dog Smokey.

In 1996 Frank Tate hoped to develop Demdyke Quarry, which was profitable but losing out because of poor access.

> *Demdyke is rarely, if ever, referred to now. Demdyke Row was destroyed in the plane crash, and the characters that lived there moved into the village itself.*

EMMERDALE FARM AND SURROUNDINGS

EMMERDALE FARM

Emmerdale Farm itself was the home of the Sugden family from around 1850, as tenant farmers for the Verneys until the 1930s, when Joseph Sugden bought the freehold (for many years, it was the only freehold farm in the area). Over the years, Joseph's son Jacob and Jacob's sons Jack and Joe bought up and sold off adjoining land, as their means dictated. Currently, the farm is around 450 acres, mostly sheep and cattle, but also barley and kale, and a few chickens and geese.

The farmhouse of Emmerdale Farm is about a mile from the village. It's within walking distance, but most people drive. Emmerdale has a common boundary with Home Farm, and possibly with the holiday village. Many other farms have been said to be neighbours of Emmerdale over the years. Some outlying fields of Emmerdale land are nearer the Woolpack than the farmhouse. The smell from a proposed pig unit at Emmerdale would have affected the Woolpack. Underneath Emmerdale land are valuable limestone deposits, but the farm would have to be turned into a quarry to reach them.

The farmhouse is actually the third Emmerdale Farm in recent years. The first served until 1993, when it was found to be suffering from subsidence. The second, Hawthorn Cottage, served until 1997, when it was demolished to make way for an access road. The Sugdens lived in the current farmhouse, formerly Melby's Farm, from 1997 to 2002.

The current farmhouse has four bedrooms. In 1997, it cost Jack £170,000 at auction. After a number of years of financial difficulty, Jack was forced to sell up, the farmhouse was sold to Ray Mullan, the best land to Chris Tate.

HAWTHORN COTTAGE

The farmhouse of the neighbouring farm to Emmerdale, a 30-acre smallholding, Hawthorn Cottage was bought in 1972 by Henry Wilks, who outbid Jack Sugden when Harry Jamieson sold up. The name was coined the following year by new tenants Matt and Peggy Skilbeck after a small wood on the land. Peggy died suddenly, and the farm passed to Joe Sugden and his new wife Christine. That marriage was also short-lived, and Joe lived there alone until 1977, when he sold it – by which time he'd acquired another 20 acres of land.

Jack Sugden bought the run-down cottage in 1993 from Bob

Joe, Matt and Peggy feed the sheep at Emmerdale Farm.

Thorley, and refurbished it to become the new Emmerdale Farm. Four years later, the Sugdens sold up and the cottage was demolished to make way for an access road to Demdyke Quarry. The Sugdens moved into the former Melby's farmhouse.

WOODSIDE FARM

Originally bought by Jack Sugden in January 1997 to serve as the third Emmerdale farmhouse (the second was demolished to make way for an access road), the Sugdens never moved in, after

The current Emmerdale Farm.

The fields around Emmerdale.

discovering that it would need underpinning. Jack nevertheless managed to sell it to the Cairns family for £50,000 more than he paid for it. The Cairns did the necessary work, and moved into the property in November 1997. They lived there for less than a year as Tony Cairns accepted a new job in Germany, and the family left the village.

EMMERDALE WOOD

A 20-acre wood planted as saplings by Jack on Emmerdale land in the late 1980s in protest at the Home Farm estate felling many of their own trees.

PENCROSS FELL

Rough moorland, used as common grazing by Emmerdale and Home Farm, the Fell is a hilly area close to the village, the site of a disused lead mine. It is owned by the Ministry of Defence. In 1987, the government planned to dump nuclear waste in the old mineshafts, leading to a concerted, and ultimately successful, campaign in Beckindale against the scheme.

INGLEBROOK

A large house, bought by Henry Wilks, a wealthy wool merchant who retired to Beckindale in 1972. It was close to Mill Cottage, shared a border with Emmerdale land and a footpath ran past Emmerdale to Inglebrook. The property burnt down in April 1973 after a spark fell from an open fire onto a carpet.

HOME FARM AND SURROUNDINGS

HOME FARM

The local squires, the Verneys lived in a large manor house situated in extensive grounds about a mile from the village on a hillside known as Miffield Rise. On most maps, it's referred to as Miffield Hall, although it was more often known simply as Verney's or The Hall, and these days is invariably known as Home Farm. It was built in 1681, and extensively rebuilt in the nineteenth century. It is now a Grade II listed building, with ten bedrooms and a self-contained 'nursery flat', originally for servants. While the feudal system has passed, whoever owns Home Farm is the most powerful person in Emmerdale – the only significant landlord and employer. For the day-to-day running of the place, the owner usually employs an estate manager, a coveted job with great powers of patronage and influence.

Today, Home Farm is still easily the largest building in the Emmerdale area (although it is dwarfed by stately homes a little further afield like Thornfield Hall and Oakwell Hall). Outside, there is a long drive and extensive lawns, rose arbour, stables and a courtyard, a walled garden, a hard tennis court, walkways, a pond and even a small boathouse.

Historically, the Verneys were masters of all they surveyed. Over the years, following money problems, the payment of death duties and a degree of mismanagement, the Verney estate shrank in size. Even so, by 1978, and the death of the last lord of the manor, George Verney, the estate still consisted of many hundreds of acres and included dozens of tenant farms, as well as many residential and commercial properties in and around Beckindale.

Verney retired to Cannes in 1973 after his marriage to Laura collapsed, and the manor house was used for a few years as a teacher training college. In 1978, George Verney died, and his nephew sold the property to NY Estates. Since then it has been known simply as Home Farm. NY Estates had a far more commercial and unsentimental approach to farming, one that often put them at odds with their tenants and the other villagers, but one that was extremely lucrative. One of the canniest decisions was made in 1979, when Seth Armstrong was employed as gamekeeper to solve a problem with poachers. Seth's knowledge of the local countryside is unrivalled and as he was responsible for most of the poaching in the first place, his appointment ended the problem. Another coup was hiring Joe Sugden as assistant manager. The younger Sugden brother was ambitious, and keen to try new farming techniques that his brother Jack was loath to try at Emmerdale.

However, Joe was disappointed not to be appointed estate manager in 1982. Instead, the job went to Alan Turner, a businessman inexperienced in farming, who rode roughshod over the village at first. Turner went off the rails, drinking, gambling and launching into a series of disastrous affairs. Joe Sugden eventually bypassed the estate manager job by becoming the NY Estates regional manager – Turner's boss. However, Joe's decision to buy Hotten Market proved lucrative for all concerned.

In 1987, NY Estates pulled out of Home Farm. Joe Sugden and Alan Turner teamed up to buy the plum parts of the estate – the shoot, the fish farm and 250 acres of farming land. Their venture wasn't as profitable as they hoped, and Turner soon sold his shares to the unscrupulous Dennis Rigg, who was trying to establish a new quarry in Beckindale. He continued as estate

manager, but discovered that the estate had been sold from under him …

In 1989, the estate, consisting of Home Farm, 250 acres of farmland, 250 acres of woodlands, a number of smallholdings and the 150-acre Whiteley's farm, was purchased for a million pounds by businessman Frank Tate, a property developer and haulier. Tate was a self-made man who owned a Skipdale haulage company. He had ambitious plans for the estate, shifting it away from agriculture to more profitable country pursuits. These included a fish farm, a game farm and a stud farm, but mostly concentrated on tourism. While plans for a museum of rural life and a golf course fell by the wayside, Tate did open the holiday village. Tate invested a great deal of money, and at first saw little return. This led to a number of evictions, as outlying property on the estate was sold off, and resentment from the village.

The business began showing a profit in 1992 when the holiday village opened, and the villagers came to respect Frank Tate a great deal more after his heroism during the plane crash in late 1993. It became clear that Tate saw himself as lord of the manor

Home Farm is a large property in extensive grounds, with a large adjacent stable block.

– and recognised that such a position meant that he had duties and obligations, as well as power and influence. Tate Holdings thrived, even after Frank Tate's death in 1997, although infighting between members of the Tate family meant a controlling interest fell out of their hands, and into those of Lady Tara Oakwell. Lady Tara was facing mounting debts following her father's death. She began a swingeing series of evictions and sell-offs. It was testament to Frank Tate's business skills that when Home Farm itself was auctioned off in 1999, it was worth £2.1 million (and lottery winner Stella Jones actually paid a million pounds more than that, because her proxy bidder, Eric Pollard, got caught in a bidding war with Chris Tate).

Even after the mass sell-offs initiated by Lady Tara, the modern estate is around 650 acres, which includes arable land, grazing, stables, a stud farm and a number of smallholdings. Home Farm land reaches down to the outskirts of Emmerdale itself, and the estate still includes a number of village properties, usually let out to tenants.

Home Farm is the traditional starting point of the Demdale Hunt, an occasion marked by the annual Hunt Ball. It has also been the venue for large events such as weddings, game shoots and society parties.

DALE PARK HOLIDAY VILLAGE

Situated close to Home Farm, about three quarters of a mile from Emmerdale itself, the holiday village was opened in 1992 by Frank Tate as one of the keystones of his plans to develop the commercial potential of the area. It consists of around a dozen chalets, as well as support buildings, all set in woodland around an ornamental lake and swimming pool.

Visitors are offered horse-riding, pony-trekking, orienteering, a driving range, access to a heritage farm and other outdoor pursuits. Since 1994 there has been a country club offering drinks and meals to visitors to the holiday village. This puts it in direct competition with the Woolpack, which has led to tensions over the years. Farmers such as Jack Sugden have also been less than impressed by holidaymakers crossing his land without following the Country Code – on one occasion, a gate was left open and organic sheep roamed across non-organic fields.

But the holiday village has been a valuable source of employment for villagers, particularly youngsters looking for summer jobs.

When Home Farm left Tate hands in 1998, the holiday village was sold to new owners, who kept it running for two years, without much contact with the villagers. The foot-and-mouth epidemic of 2001, and the downturn in tourism, forced them to sell up. Chris Tate entered a partnership with Rodney Blackstock to invest in the holiday village. Rodney hired Maggie Calder to manage the site, and she brought her partner Phil Weston and their children from their previous marriages. The country club reopened successfully for Christmas 2001.

FISH AND GAME FARM

Home Farm has a shoot. NY Estates used it for important customers and executives. When they withdrew, Joe Sugden and Alan Turner bought it and started running it as a commercial operation, with sportsmen or, more often, companies buying a day's shooting. Turner also added quail and guinea fowl – not for shooting, just for the table.

The fish farm rears trout in tanks for the table, and has a long-established clientele in amongst local restaurants. This is a year-round enterprise.

Neither have been mentioned for a number of years, so we can perhaps speculate that the fish and game farms were sold off by Tara as part of her asset-stripping in 1998.

FILLEIGH WOOD

Part of the Home Farm estate. Seth has a small shack hidden here, a secret hideaway. In 1989 he was attacked by badger baiters in the wood.

FIR TREE PLANTATION

A small area given over to the cultivation of several hundred Christmas trees.

Frank Tate opens the Holiday Village

HAZEL SPINNEY

Another part of the Home Farm estate, a small wood which seems to share a border with Emmerdale Farm. In 1977, an old lady, Mrs Venables, lived in a caravan in the wood. Several years later, Mr Wilks prevented NY Estates from using it as a rubbish tip because it was a valuable habitat for wild birds and animals.

BICKLE SPINNEY

Another wood on Home Farm land.

PRIMROSE DINGLE

A narrow valley on Home Farm land which was completely spoiled when it was all but filled in with rubble by NY Estates. On NY Estates' maps it was known, rather more prosaically, as HF7.

PUDDLE TOP PATH

A right of way that NY Estates ploughed over and blocked off in 1981.

OTHER FARMS

BULL POT FARM

A small farm that bordered Emmerdale and was owned by Arthur Braithwaite.

HOLLY FARM

Home of the tyrannical Jim Gimbel, his wife Freda and children Martin and Davy in the mid-1970s. Holly Farm adjoins Emmerdale Farm. Joe Sugden dated Kathy Gimbel for a while after she had walked out on her husband Terry Davis, whom Jim had forced her to marry when she fell pregnant (she miscarried soon after the wedding). Jim violently objected to Joe and Kathy moving in to Demdyke Row together. When Jim hit his younger son, Davy, Freda walked out on him, and Jim killed himself with a shotgun. This devastated Kathy, who left the village soon afterwards.

The farm was later rented by Winn and Nick Groves. Some years later, it was bought by NY Estates, along with the rest of the Verney estate.

KELLER BOTTOM FARM

A 100-acre smallholding that was part of the Home Farm estate, rented by the Feldmanns in the early 90s. It's three miles from Emmerdale, 'on the tops'. It's mainly poor-quality land, suitable for sheep. Frank Tate sold half the land for housing soon after

A view of the back of the village.

buying the Home Farm estate (it has spectacular views of Connelton). He sought to turn the rest of the farm, somewhat against the Feldmanns' wishes, into a farming museum.

LOWER HALL FARM

The tenant farm of Clifford Longthorn in the early 1980s, sited near Demdyke. Clifford lived there with his wife Peggy and their children Carol and Andy. The Longthorns were evicted in 1986 by NY Estates, and 30 acres of the land was bought by quarry owner Harry Mowlem.

TOLLY FARM

A tenant farm owned by NY Estates, a neighbour of Emmerdale Farm, and run by irascible Enoch Tolly. NY Estates was unhappy with Tolly's use of a dangerous pesticide, but Tolly only changed his ways when his family objected. Enoch Tolly died in a tractor accident in 1981, and his wife Grace and daughters Hannah and Naomi struggled to cope. They eventually sold up the following year.

WHITELEY'S FARM

The 150-acre tenant farm, rented by Bill Whiteley, who died in 1990. Lynn Whiteley, Bill's daughter-in-law continued to run the farm, and took in lodgers Archie Brooks, Michael Feldmann and Lorraine Nelson.

WYLIE FARM

A small mixed farm a short bus ride from Emmerdale, owned by John Wylie, the puritanical father of Emily Wylie, whom he had kept sheltered from the outside world following his wife's death. In 1999, Emily was forced to take a job at the post office shop in order to raise money for the failing farm.

Just before her interview, Emily was cheered up by Butch Dingle, who had seen her looking nervous at the bus stop. The two tentatively began a relationship, with Emily terrified of what her father would think.

John Wylie disowned Emily, forcing her off the farm. He couldn't run the place without her, though. In early 2000 he sold the farm and moved to Beckwith.

Many other local farms have been mentioned over the years, including WINSLOW'S FARM, the ADLINGTON FARM, HATHERSAGE FARM, a 40-acre freehold farm which borders Emmerdale, HESTON FARM, which the Sugdens sold some sheep to once and RIDGE FARM

GEOGRAPHICAL FEATURES

ARCHIE RISE

A hill named after Archie Brooks, who was killed there in the plane disaster. It appears to be between Emmerdale and Robblesfield.

BLACKRIDGE SCAR

A steep hill within walking distance of the village. Amos climbed it, but became trapped on his way down.

BURRUCK GILL

An area popular with potholers – a pair of Swedish tourists got trapped here in 1977 and had to be rescued by the Wharfdale Cave Rescue Team.

KELLER FELL

A nesting spot for peregrine falcons, presumably quite close to Keller Bottom Farm.

SPARROW WOOD

The location of one of the easier walks it's possible to take from Emmerdale.

THE STRUGGLE

Emmerdale sits at the base of this large hill. From the top – which, as the name suggests, is not an easy climb – there are spectacular views of the surrounding countryside. On a clear day, it's claimed you can see as far as Bradford, or even York Minster.

THE VIADUCT

Not far from Emmerdale is a railway viaduct (presumably part of the Hotten–Leeds line). In 1997, fearing he had Huntington's disease and had passed it on to his unborn child, Biff Fowler contemplated suicide there. He was talked out of it by Andy Hopwood.

The Cave Rescue Team hunt for missing potholers.

NEARBY TOWNS AND PLACES OF INTEREST

BLACKFELL
Rarely mentioned, Blackfell is a hamlet three miles from Emmerdale. Matt Skilbeck's aunt and uncle lived there in the 1970s.

BRIARDALE HALL
A stately home close to Emmerdale. In 1994, Pollard robbed the property, taking £150,000 worth of antiques and other goods.

BRASSINGTON
A nearby town, location of a pub called the Red Lion.

BURVIEW CRAG
A local beauty spot, popular with walkers. Graham threw Rachel off it when she realised he'd killed his wife.

CONNELTON
Connelton is just over three miles to the west of Emmerdale, in the same general direction as Hotten. It's a village larger than Emmerdale, with a population of about 1400, and has two churches, a primary school (the nearest to Emmerdale), a range of shops and pubs, a supermarket, a library and two small art galleries. Its most picturesque features are its canals, and there is also a large boatyard. It is also the location of the Feathers, a hotel and restaurant that people from Emmerdale have traditionally used for clandestine business meetings or secret liaisons.

HOTTEN
The nearest major town to Emmerdale is Hotten, about eight miles away. A market town, with a population of around 13,000, Hotten seemingly has every facility the people of Emmerdale need.

There's quite a large shopping centre, as well as a busy main street, Wool Exchange and Corn Exchange, a wholesaler's, estate agents, car dealerships, at least a couple of vet's practices, bridal shops, boutiques, a baby store ('Hotten Tots') and an auction house. In the last couple of years, a large out-of-town branch of GK Supermarkets has opened, which many village shopkeepers blame for a downturn in their trade. There is also a small industrial estate, Hotten Business Park.

Tate Haulage is based on the Emmerdale side of Hotten. The site was chosen because it is 'close to the motorway', but how close, and which motorway, has never been established.

Scott Windsor briefly worked for Think Tank Logistics, a computer firm based at the Business Park.

Entertainment available in Hotten includes pubs. The one seen most often is the Black Bull, by the market and the offices of the *Courier*. Young people prefer the Flag. There are Greek, Chinese, Indian and Italian restaurants, galleries, a weaving museum, clubs (including at least two catering for the gay community, the gay bar Steel and the lesbian club Sapphire), the Hotten Everyman Theatre, bowling, swimming baths and a cinema.

Hotten also has a football team, but it is not a league one.

Hotten Radio broadcasts to the surrounding area. Paddy Kirk was, briefly, a phone-in vet for the station, until he was usurped by Mandy Dingle, his wife, whose impromptu astrological predictions, as 'Mystic Mandy' proved more popular.

Hotten is also home to the local newspaper, the *Hotten Courier*. It's unclear whether it's a morning or an evening paper, but it makes for popular reading in Emmerdale and the other villages. It was established in 1760. The villagers of Emmerdale pick it up from the post office shop, and its coverage of local events and issues is comprehensive and completely unrivalled.

The annual Hotten Show sees agricultural exhibits from all the surrounding villages.

Emmerdale comes under the jurisdiction of Hotten Council, surely one of the most corrupt councils in the country – Eric Pollard has, over the years, colluded with crooked councillors Charlie Aindow and Daniel Hawkins, and in 2000 became a councillor himself. As far as Emmerdale is concerned, it seems that the only contact with the Council is when it cuts services (the primary

Joe Sugden brings his cows to Hotten Market - a few years later, he would be running the place.

school closed in the late 1970s, the mobile library service survived until 1990) or tries to push through a number of dodgy land deals – notably a 1990 attempt to build an open prison near Emmerdale, and the proposal for a nuclear dump. The Mayor of Hotten, though, is traditionally well-respected.

Since the 1970s, Emmerdale's policing has been run from the station in Hotten. There is a court (and solicitors' offices) and a register office. The town has its own bishop.

The nearest train station to Emmerdale is in Hotten, and there is also a coach station there.

The older children of Emmerdale attend Hotten Comprehensive. There is also a Hotten College of Technology and an agricultural college.

The people of Emmerdale are rather accident-prone. Over the years, Hotten District Hospital has treated a number of the villagers. It saw Emily Wylie marry Butch Dingle on his deathbed following his fatal injuries in a bus crash. More happily, Hotten also has St Mary's Maternity Hospital.

Most of the villagers in Emmerdale nowadays have cars, but there is a bus service to Hotten. This is fairly rudimentary, though – there is a school run (taking in a lot of the surrounding villages) in the morning and afternoon, and a few services during the day, but the last bus back from Hotten is no later than about nine o'clock, meaning that anyone going there for the evening needs either access to a car or faces an expensive taxi ride.

HOTTEN CATTLE MARKET

The cattle market was bought by NY Estates in 1986, but this proved to be an unsuccessful venture, and it was sold to the District Council in the late 1980s.

KELTHWAITE

A town ten miles from Emmerdale. Dolly Skilbeck had an on-off affair with Stephen Fuller, a timber consultant, from the town in 1988. Fuller died in an accident and was buried in Kelthwaite cemetery, the service was arranged by Dolly.

LECK FELL

Close to Pencross Fell, and also once the site of lead mining. The mineshafts were covered over when the mines were closed, but often only with wooden blocks, which have begun to rot away. Jackie Merrick once fell down one of the mineshafts on Leck Fell, and was rescued by the Fell Rescue Team.

LITTLEWELL

Eight miles to the north-east of Hotten, Littlewell itself is a tiny hamlet, but is notable for the Littlewell Nature Reserve.

OAKWELL HALL

Inheriting vast Oakwell Hall at a young age, Lord Alex Oakwell was one of the most eligible bachelors in the area, and one of the most attractive potential investors. He approached Kim Tate to run his stud farm, but mainly because he wanted to get Kim into bed with him.

Oakwell was engaged to posh Tara Cockburn, whom he married. The same year, after leaving a party to celebrate Kim's engagement to Steve Marchant, high on drink and drugs, he crashed his car, killing his passenger, Linda Fowler. He fled the country to avoid prosecution, and retribution from the Glovers – Ned Glover burned down Oakwell's stables.

In 1998 Alex returned, to steal some diamonds. Lady Tara had, by now, taken control of the Oakwell Estate and bought into the holiday village. Knowing that the finances weren't as healthy as they appeared, following her father's death, she quickly bought a majority shareholding in Home Farm and began a systematic asset-stripping – selling off most of the tenant farms and property owned by the Home Farm Estate in the village to fund her first priority, the Oakwell estate.

Alex Oakwell, meanwhile, was in London and had fallen in with some drug dealers. Roy Glover spotted his photograph in a newspaper and followed him down to London. Oakwell died in an ensuing chase.

Hit by mounting debts and a second set of death duties, Tara felt she had no choice but to marry Lord Thornfield. This sorted out her problems, and removed her from the scene in Emmerdale for a couple of years.

THE OLD BRIDGE
A restaurant, somewhere in the countryside, used by the villagers as an alternative to the Feathers.

INGLETON
A town close to Emmerdale, the location of a pub run (in the 1970s) by George Bailey.

ROBBLESFIELD
Three miles from Emmerdale, in the opposite direction to Connelton, Robblesfield is the great rival for the Butterworth Ball, the trophy for the winner of a sports match (usually cricket, sometimes football, once a game of bowls). Over the years, a couple of pubs have defended the honour of Robblesfield – the Millers Arms, a pub that celebrated its two hundredth anniversary in 1977, under landlord Fred Teaker and, a couple of times in the 1980s, the King of Prussia pub.

SKIPDALE
Further afield is the large market town of Skipdale, around fifteen miles away. This is a brewing town, home to both Ephraim Monk, the brewery (founded in 1778) who used to own and who still supply the Woolpack, and their rivals, Skipdale Breweries.

It has a cathedral where Donald Hinton once preached, with a number of villagers there to support him.

Frank Tate and his family originally lived in Skipdale, and the original Tate Haulage was based on a large industrial estate there.

Hotten town square.

REAL LOCATIONS

The people of Emmerdale often use HARROGATE for quality shopping or dining. Paddy Kirk's mother, Barbara, lived there until her death in 2002.

The nearest big city is LEEDS, and it's a day trip to go there – but one that a number of villagers over the years have made for special shopping trips or dates. A number of young villagers have studied at Leeds university. It's just possible to commute from Emmerdale to Leeds, but it makes for a long day, and most villagers soon tire of it and either move closer to their work or give up the job.

The nearest airport is Leeds/Bradford Airport – flat out, on a motorbike, on a day with light traffic, not paying too much attention to the speed restrictions, it's possible to get there from Emmerdale in just over an hour, as Biff proved when he took Ned Glover.

Henry Wilks was a textile mill owner, and his company, Wilks and Fisher, was based in BRADFORD. The villagers can also spend the day in YORK, and might possibly call in at the bar in St Helen's Square run by Terry Woods's ex-wife, Britt. Sarah Connolly briefly moved to York after a temporary split with Jack Sugden, and Eve Birch was sent there after disgracing herself in Emmerdale.

MIKE LONG

Mike Long is the Production Designer, the man in charge of designing and maintaining the sets. He's responsible for planning the new studio and village sets.

My job is many-faceted. With the studio and the village sets built, you might think my job was done, but we're constantly adding interiors to the village – there are very few buildings without an interior now. It's an ever-changing thing. We're in the process of redecorating – people move around, they come in, they leave. At the moment we're starting the inside of the new café, which is a studio set, but the exterior village set has to match up. We're redecorating Paddy's cottage because he and Emily have been in there for a while. We're doing a bedroom for Turner at the B & B – we have a bedroom there, but it was done for Carol, so it's completely inappropriate. I'm adding some new headstones to the cemetery.

There is a constant change of requirements, and a demand for maintenance. The village is four years old, and weather, the crews and so on all cause wear and tear. What's nice is that the landscaping is really starting to develop. Now we have to cut plants back, before we had to add to them. We do have to maintain it, and it takes constant looking after. In theory we've got one gardener, Alison Berry, who's there five days a week – she has to work weekends because it's often difficult for her to work during the week when they're recording. In practice we can call on some of the resources of the Harewood Estate to help out, and we need that in the summer when the grass needs cutting a lot.

We coped with going to five episodes a week, the sets can take the extra wear. The big difference is that the studio is in almost constant use, so it's difficult to get in there to do work – joiners and so on have to work during everyone else's lunch hour.

The village is unique. **EastEnders** seem to keep adding bits to their lot, but I'm not sure how that all fits together. We can shoot in any direction at any time, directors can aim their cameras wherever they want – the only thing they have to watch out for is that they don't shoot themselves or the production vehicles. The opening shot of the village, the aerial one, doesn't really do the village justice, because it looks more like a hamlet than a village, but at ground level it's fine.

The nicest surprise is that four years on I still see episodes where there's a view of the village we've not seen before. It's nice to know the directors haven't got bored of exploring it. I often regret that we don't use the village as an overlap between scenes – twitching curtains and people being nosy.

My favourite building is Zoe's cottage – either from the graveyard or there's a particularly good angle from the B & B, it's just an attractive shape, but it looks rather nice when you look back at it from the village. It sounds big-headed, but there's nothing in the village that worries me, or that I regret. I wish we could expand it a bit. I want to see animals in the fields around the village, because whenever I go into the Dales there are

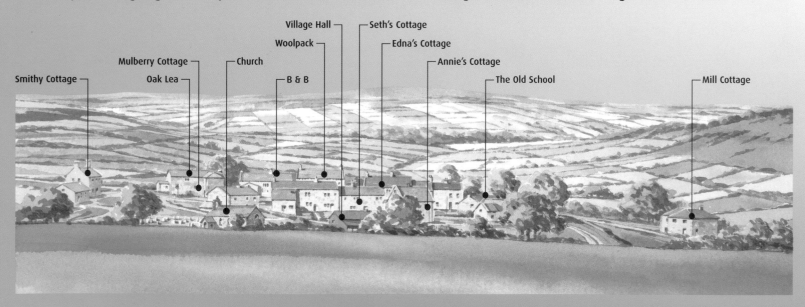

always sheep and some cows really close to where people live. We've got a wildflower meadow in, so it's very lush and green. It would be nice to do a country fair that got away from the centre of town and into the fields.

A lot of the details are down to the design team, I can't take the credit for that. I design all the sets, and I'm amazed how that's still a full-time job, but a new producer will come in and there will be a new input. We built the holiday chalet for the Calder-Westons, we moved Annie's Cottage out to the village, but that's coming back to the studio, greatly improved on what it was like before. There's a new Mill Cottage set which is far easier to shoot around. I'm proud of the studio, we're lucky the building was available and we've got such a large floorspace. I tried not to pile all the sets on top of each other, so there's plenty of space to work. The tidier the studio is, the more efficiently it can run. It means there's more time to make the programme. You don't want people tripping over things. It's conveyor belt television, and it has to be safe and fast. We're just moving into a new prop stores, and that also helps. Without the crews looking after it, though, the studio would quickly become a tip, so it's down to them.

We can do anything, really, I don't dread anything. This year we've had the Village in Bloom competition, and that's needed a lot of thought. It sounds simple, but in design terms it's really complicated. We film weeks in advance, so the flowers blooming in July on screen have to be ready in May. Worse than that, they film out of sequence, so the continuity is tricky – I've got a schedule that goes into a lot of detail as to when things should and shouldn't be around. The gardener Alison, Sue, my buyer, and I have discussed when people start putting out window boxes and hanging baskets, but it's too early, really. We're having to use a mix of real plants and artificial ones. It's going to be an expensive exercise. I tend to take scripts seriously.

Seth and Betty's cottage is full of knick-knacks.

Zoe's cottage, as seen from the B & B – a favourite view of Mike Long's.

on close ups anyway, so it was a lot of work for nothing. I hope the Village in Bloom doesn't end up like that, because it's a massive amount of work. But we'll have something for the directors to use if they want, and I'd rather have it that way.

I'd love to build the church. My latest idea is that we could have a new church in the old diner – even though it's based on an old school house it looks like a chapel, and if there was a story where the old church burned down, they could consecrate it. It would mean the vicar would live in the heart of the village. It wouldn't cost much to do the interior. So everything would be in the village.

Sometimes we can put a lot of effort in, but the value doesn't seem to end up on screen. When Viv's café was being converted, we liased with the writers, and had a set that over a couple of weeks looked like a building site, then it gradually took shape. The idea was that you could see the changes – in the end, there weren't that many scenes, and the builders were always on a tea break, or they weren't there. So you never saw any building work, and the directors concentrated

There are still a couple of sets I'd like to put my mark on. I'm going to improve the dining room and kitchen of Home Farm, which still looks pretty much the same as when Frank owned it, and I want to bring it a bit more up to date. The kitchen there is laid out so that you can't really do a scene where someone's cooking, which is a bit odd for a kitchen, I'm not sure why it was done like that. Now there's a housekeeper, they're playing up the Upstairs/Downstairs stuff, which is good, it means that instead of Chris sitting round the kitchen table, he eats in his dining room.

The only other major one is Marlon's and Tricia's cottage, and that's a tiny set. I'd like to redecorate that, but the characters don't have much money, and so it's difficult to do in terms of the storyline.

Emmerdale

YEAR
BY
YEAR

CHAPTER TWO

The last thirty years have been very eventful for the small village of Emmerdale – people have come and gone, and there's been plenty of death and disaster.

KEY EVENTS

Jacob Sugden dies, unexpectedly leaving the farm to black sheep of the family, Jack Sugden.

Henry Wilks and his daughter Marian move to the village.

SUGDENS

On 16 October 1972 the funeral took place of Jacob Sugden, the 56-year-old patriarch of the Sugden family, and the owner of Emmerdale Farm since before the Second World War. The family had seen turbulent times – they had struggled to modernise the farm, but it had declined in recent years. His wife Annie, father-in-law Sam Pearson, younger son Joe, daughter Peggy and her husband Matt Skilbeck had worked hard to keep the farm afloat – while Jacob preferred to spend time drinking in the Woolpack.

Jack Sugden, Jacob's and Annie's eldest son, had left eight

years previously after rowing with his father about farming methods. Jack had moved to London and written a best-selling novel, *Field of Tares*, and had little contact with his former life. He returned for the funeral (only showing himself after the service). Joe presumed that the farm would pass to him, as Jack had abandoned the farming life, but when the will was read, it became clear that Jacob had left the farm to Jack. Joe deeply resented the decision, feeling he deserved the farm after all his work. Peggy was also unhappy, but for a different reason – she had hoped to sell her share of the farm and move to town.

Jack, for his part, was reluctant to return, but saw Beckindale as a peaceful place to write his follow-up novel. A derelict water mill on the farm would be the perfect retreat, both to write and to keep some distance between himself and his family, and he began conversion work. This is the property that would eventually be named Mill Cottage.

WILKS

Wool merchant Henry Wilks arrived in Beckindale the same week as Jacob Sugden's funeral, settling down to rural retirement after the death of his wife. He had made his money running the textile firm Wilks and Fisher. He was accompanied by his daughter, Marian, and they moved into the large house of Inglebrook. They immediately fell into a dispute with the Sugdens over rights of

Emmerdale Farm opened with Jacob's funeral. At the time, it was intended to run twice a week for 26 weeks, and was shown in the early afternoon as part of what was then an experiment with 'daytime television', which also included Crown Court, General Hospital *and* Mr and Mrs.

The programme was not shown in all regions at first, and was screened at different times in different regions (it was as late as 1988 before the programme was 'networked' – shown in every ITV region at exactly the same time). Some regions fell behind the Yorkshire schedule – all dates given here refer to when an episode was first shown in the Yorkshire region. The first episode got 2.2 million viewers. Soon afterwards, this had built to a little over three million – helped by an omnibus edition at half past ten in the evening in the Yorkshire TV and Tyne Tees TV regions. The producer of the first twenty-two episodes was David Goddard.

way. Henry began using an old path across Emmerdale land, until Jack discovered that the path continued on and led through marshland to Inglebrook, and Wilks could be liable for the costs of draining the land.

Wilks quickly got his own back, bidding against Jack for the 30-acre Jamieson Farm. While researching that, Wilks found that, thanks to a technicality, the Sugdens hadn't actually ever bought the freehold on their land when Jacob had bought the farm from the Miffield Estate. He bought it for himself, becoming the Sugdens' landlord.

(Opposite) *The first line up of regular cast .*

(This page) *The Sugdens mourn the death of Jacob.*

KEY EVENTS

Partnership with Wilks brings some security to Emmerdale Farm.

Wilks moves into the Woolpack, forming a partnership with Amos Brearly.

Peggy Skilbeck gives birth to twins, but dies soon after.

SUGDENS

Although deeply resentful that Henry Wilks was now their landlord, the new arrangement gave Emmerdale Farm exactly the financial security and management skills it had been missing for the last few years. Henry Wilks set the farm up as a limited company, with himself, Jack, Peggy and Matt, and Joe and Annie as shareholders (they bought out Annie's father, Sam). Henry invested some of his own money in new equipment and livestock – but there were still disputes: Jack convinced the others not to allow Wilks to build an intensive pig unit.

Free from the day-to-day running of the farm, Jack ought to have been concentrating on his writing, but couldn't find the inspiration, and ran into problems trying to convert the water mill. He romanced Marian Wilks, but she left Beckindale within a few months of arriving. Jack was living in the unconverted water mill, and was joined by Trash, a tramp who had abandoned a former life as a librarian for life on the road. Jack was inspired by Trash's bohemian lifestyle, but Trash wasn't as carefree as he appeared, and killed himself in February.

Jack started a dangerous affair with Laura Verney, the young wife of George Verney, the lord of the manor. When Verney discovered what they had been up to, he horsewhipped Jack outside the Woolpack, leaving him with a scar on his cheek that he bore for quite some time afterwards. Laura left her husband, and Verney himself left the village for retirement in Cannes.

Peggy gave birth to twins, Sally and Sam in April 1973, and they moved out of Emmerdale Farm and into Jamieson's old farmhouse, which they renamed Hawthorn Cottage. But their happiness was to be short-lived – Peggy died in July of a brain haemorrhage. Matt sent the twins away to their Aunt Beatrice and Uncle Ben Dowton in Blackfell, and threw himself into his work. At first he was worried about his future – he wasn't a blood relation of the Sugdens, after all – but Annie soon made it clear that she considered him part of the family.

HENRY WILKS AND AMOS BREARLY

Henry Wilks also suffered a disaster, when Inglebrook burned down. Henry moved himself into Emmerdale Farm, a temporary measure, but one that cemented his friendship with Annie Sugden. His next move was also meant to be short term – he rented a room in the Woolpack from Amos Brearly. This became a permanent move in October, when the brewery put the pub up for sale, and

Jack Sugden returned to Beckindale, and didn't take long to fall for new arrival Marian Wilks.

The first major cast member to leave the series was Gail Harrison, who played Marian Wilks. She returned, briefly, in 1975. The character would appear again in the 1980s, played by Debbie Blythe.

Behind the scenes, Peter Holmans replaced David Goddard as producer in January. He produced the show until July, when Robert D Cardona took over. He would stay in the job for nearly three years.

The Blakeys lived in Smithy Cottage.

Twins Sam and Sally Skilbeck.

Henry helped Amos to buy it. This took up most of Wilks's retirement nest egg, but was to prove a fruitful and long-lasting partnership.

Henry was, by now, becoming a committed member of the Beckindale community, a churchwarden and a councillor. He also organised and acted in plays put on at the village hall. He became particularly interested in conservation and in preserving village traditions.

Amos briefly courted Annie Sugden, thinking himself a good catch and assuming Annie was lonely. He proposed marriage, but Annie gently declined the offer.

ELSEWHERE

Teenager Sharon Crossthwaite was raped and strangled in a ruined abbey near Beckindale. The event, naturally, rocked the small community. The perpetrator was discovered by Jack Sugden to be Jim Latimer, an unemployed factory worker from Hotten. Jack prevented Latimer from attacking Penny Golightly, and had him arrested.

Alison Gibbons arrived and started working in the village shop, taking it over when Mrs Postlethwaite retired. Henry Wilks helped her to take over the lease, having befriended her at church choir meetings. When Henry discovered Alison had been found guilty of shoplifting before moving to the village, he felt betrayed – but soon forgave her, and by the end of the year he'd even proposed marriage.

Village blacksmith Frank Blakey and Janie Harker married in March 1973 – Jack Sugden was the best man. Frank didn't approve of hunting, and refused to shoe horses used in the Hunt. Not long afterwards, they left the village when Frank decided to become a teacher.

1974

KEY EVENTS

Jack Sugden leaves for Rome.

Joe's marriage to Christine Sharp doesn't last long.

SUGDENS

In January, Jack Sugden left for Rome – he had been offered the chance to write the film script for his novel. One of the reasons he picked Rome might well have been that old flame Marian Wilks had ended up there.

With Peggy and Jack gone, Joe was now doing the farm accounts, a time-consuming and complicated business. He decided that the farm should try for accredited status – having the Milk Marketing Board test the herd to declare it disease-free, making the milk worth more. As this process began, Joe met and began dating Milk Marketing Board official Christine Sharp. They first spent a night together at her house after Joe's car had broken down. Within the year, she'd given up her job and moved into Emmerdale Farm. They married in September (Jack didn't attend his brother's wedding, but did send a telegram), and moved into Hawthorn Cottage on returning from honeymoon. But

Joe and Christine were happy here - but not for much longer.

cracks quickly developed – Joe finding it difficult to deal with Christine's use of credit cards and hire purchase as he had been brought up to pay cash and not to run up debts. Her taste for antique furniture also worried him. Christine left Joe after only five weeks of marriage.

SKILBECKS

Alison and Matt Skilbeck began dating, but soon came to realise that they were looking for support rather than romance. Alison was also courted by Amos Brearly, but only after he learnt that the brewery was more likely to sell the Woolpack to a married couple. Alison left for Jersey in September to open a shop of her own.

ELSEWHERE

Henry employed Reverend Ruskin's wife Liz to run the village shop once Alison had left. Amos had his own problems – he was pursued by the lascivious Ethel Ainsworth.

Another traveller, 'Dry', was befriended by the Sugdens. He proved to be a useful handyman, converting an attic into a bedroom for Joe. Dry was yet another suitor for Alison Gibbons, and also saw another villager, Diana Prescott, but left for Ireland later in the year – hotly pursued by a woman, Celia, whom he'd jilted at the altar some years before.

Andrew Burt, who played Jack Sugden, decided to leave the programme this year. He would return for a few weeks in 1976. It represented the first big change to the programme, as Jack had been perhaps the central character of the show. In the event, Jack's departure allowed others (particularly Frazer Hines, as Joe) to shine.

Diana Davis, who appeared in four episodes this year as Letty Brewer, would be cast ten years later as the long-running character Caroline Bates.

Rev. Ruskin, Amos and Mr Wilks have their peace disturbed.

1975

KEY EVENTS

The Sugdens feud with the Gimbels.

Rosemary Kendall moves in with the Sugdens.

Sixteen-year-old Rosemary Kendall moved in with the Sugdens while her mother was in hospital.

SUGDENS

Annie's cousin Jean collapsed and was admitted to a long term stay in hospital. Annie first sent some money up to Middlesbrough, where the Kendalls lived, then took in her sixteen-year-old daughter, Rosemary Kendall. There had been a long-standing feud between the Sugdens and Kendalls, but Rosemary melted Sam Pearson's heart and she helped Annie to run the farm. She remained in the village after Jean recovered, and had a crush on Joe, although he failed to notice.

Annie was coming out of her shell a little – this year she became a churchwarden and took driving lessons. Sam had a long-running dispute with the new vicar that threatened the harvest supper, but a compromise was reached.

The Sugdens were involved in a row with their neighbours, the Gimbels, over farming practice – Jim Gimbel was overusing fertiliser, and it was affecting Emmerdale land.

Matt Skilbeck met an old friend, Sarah Foster, who enquired about buying the stables at Hawthorn Cottage. She was having an affair with a married man, but realised it was leading nowhere at Christmas, when he spent it with his family. Instead, Matt invited her to Christmas lunch at the Woolpack with the Sugdens.

WILKS AND BREARLY

Henry Wilks decided to fly out to Rome in the New Year to see his daughter Marian – much to the chagrin of his friends, who had arranged for Marian to visit him. Amos Brearly saved the day by pretending he'd lost his voice after becoming choked on a piece of Christmas cake. Marian stayed for a week, but wouldn't tell anyone if she was seeing Jack in Rome.

Later in the year, there were rumours that Wilks had money problems. He certainly didn't seem as wealthy as he had been on his arrival in the village. The truth of his financial situation was never pinned down.

Once again, Amos was the subject of unwanted attentions from a widow, this time Norah Norris, who was looking for a new husband.

There was a five-month gap in the transmission of the show from the end of May to mid-October this year.

Lesley Manville, who played Rosemary Kendall, was the first wife of actor Gary Oldman.

Amos and Joe in the Woolpack.

KEY EVENTS

Joe's and Kathy Gimbel's affair scandalises the village.

Matt's twin children die in an accident.

Amos becomes a reporter for the **Hotten Courier**.

SUGDENS

Early in the New Year, tragedy struck the Sugdens. Matt's twin children died, along with their aunt, in an accident at a level crossing. Coming so soon after his father-in-law's and wife's deaths, Matt was unable to cope with the bereavement, and spent the night wandering alone on the moors. Reverend Ruskin and Sam Pearson tried their best to support him when he returned.

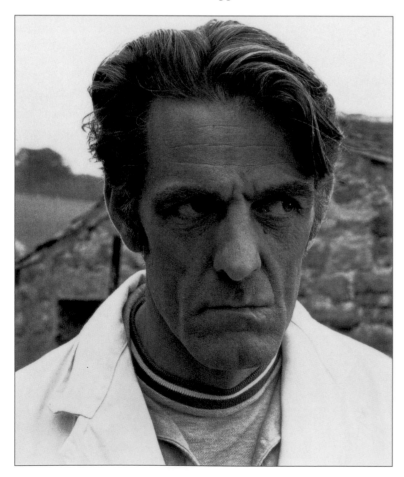

Matt inherited Peggy's share of Emmerdale Farm and, as he had after her death, threw himself hard into his work there.

Rosemary Kendall started to date Martin Gimbel. Martin's father Jim was a tyrant, expecting his twenty-year-old son to work on the farm for almost nothing. His mother was keen for him to get engaged to Rosemary, but Rosemary herself wasn't so sure. In the end, Martin ran away to join the army after a final row with his father. Rosemary continued to have a crush on Joe Sugden; Joe still failed to notice.

Instead, Joe fell for Martin Gimbel's sister Kathy. Both she and Joe had brief previous marriages under their belts – Kathy had married a local troublemaker Terry Davis under pressure from her father when she became pregnant, then miscarried and left her husband. Neither Joe nor Kathy were divorced, and the relationship scandalised the village. Joe's wife Christine returned in the autumn, hoping for a reconciliation. Instead, Joe filed for divorce. Now he was single again, Rosemary made a move on him – and returned, heartbroken, to Middlesbrough when he spurned her advances.

Christine's canny father, Robert Sharp, hired good lawyers who pressed for Christine to get half Joe's share in Emmerdale Farm – a move that would have effectively forced the Sugdens to sell up. Henry Wilks, no stranger to this sort of manoeuvre himself, advised Joe to counter-claim for Christine's share in her father's lucrative dairy business. The Sharps gave up their claim, and Christine was never seen again.

Jack Sugden returned to Beckindale for the first time in two years. He continued to have problems with his second novel, and had (perhaps unsurprisingly) been called back to England by his publisher, who was keen to see what progress had been made. The water mill had been declared uninhabitable the year before. The feud between the Sugdens and the Gimbels helped bring the two brothers together, and when Jack departed again, it was on much better terms with his family.

Sam Pearson proposed to old flame Nellie Dawson, who turned him down. He helped her fight eviction from her cottage.

WILKS AND BREARLY

Amos Brearly was by now a part-time correspondent for the *Hotten Courier*, a job he saw as legitimising his nosiness into what was going on in every quarter of the village. Wilks was

Jim Gimbel ruled his family with a rod of iron.

that Amos was so nervous about the ghost he was moving things himself and forgetting where he'd put them.

ELSEWHERE

PC Will Croft was the new policeman assigned to the village, and took a strict line. His insistence on the exact letter of the law rubbed Sam Pearson in particular up the wrong way.

Beckindale retained the Butterworth Ball in a cricket match against Robblesfield, thanks to Wilks and Joe Sugden.

Amos Brearley enjoyed his new job as a writer for the Hotten Courier.

The Woolpack subsidence story explained why the exterior location for the pub had changed. In reality, location filming had switched from Arncliffe to Esholt.

The programme once again had a long break between seasons, ending in mid-May and not starting again until the following January.

A new producer, Michael Glynn, took over in late 1976, and he would remain in the job for nearly three years.

annoyed that Amos wasn't pulling his weight at The Woolpack and began dropping hints that they should get a cleaner or a dishwasher.

The Woolpack was found to be suffering from subsidence, and had to be abandoned. Amos and Henry bought a new property, formerly a large private house, at the other end of the village and moved in, although Amos was alarmed to hear rumours that the new place was haunted, and kept insisting for several months after the move that a poltergeist was at work. Wilks's theory was

KEY EVENTS

Joe and Kathy Gimbel become Beckindale's
first live-in lovers.

Dolly Acaster becomes a barmaid at the Woolpack.

The villagers celebrate the Queen's Silver Jubilee.

SUGDENS

In a sign of the changing times, Joe Sugden and Kathy Gimbel became the first live-in lovers in Beckindale early in 1977, moving into 3 Demdyke Row after Joe sold off Hawthorn Cottage. The older generation in particular were strongly opposed to what they

saw as their immoral behaviour – Sam Pearson made his feelings very clear to his grandson. Henry Wilks – who had lent Joe some money to help buy the cottage – hadn't realised he was helping to set up a love nest.

Joe joined the volunteer fire service, and helped fight three or four serious fires this year, winning a medal for bravery.

Kathy's father, Jim Gimbel, was becoming increasingly violent – when he hit his son, his wife Freda walked out on him. Soon afterwards Jim killed himself. Kathy felt responsible for her father's suicide, and left Joe and the village.

The Sugdens had money troubles, and started taking lodgers. First were Ray and Sarah, a couple from the village whose cottage was demolished by a falling tree. When they left, Angela Read lived with them for a while as part of a church scheme supporting problem teenagers. Finally, Dolly Acaster began renting a room.

Tom Merrick, a former worker at Emmerdale Farm and the husband of Jack's old flame Pat, joined his brother-in-law Syd Harker in a spot of sheep rustling, selling the meat on at Hotten market. Syd was caught breaking into 3 Demdyke Row, and was arrested.

Sam briefly left to join Jack in Italy – his son-in-law had decided that his elusive second novel would be a fictionalised biography of Sam's life in the Dales. On his return, Sam confessed he'd missed Annie's home cooking.

AMOS AND MR WILKS

Wilks became increasingly annoyed by Amos's journalistic pretensions – he boasted he'd brought 'literary style' to the *Hotten Courier*. Amos was intensely proud of his work, and soon had a set of business cards printed with 'Amos Brearly – Reporter' on them. The way Amos saw it, he was now entitled to attend every local event, from balls and dances in local towns to every party anyone happened to throw in Beckindale.

Amos also secretly booked driving lessons with a P. Morphet, who he was shocked to discover was a woman. After she turned up in the Woolpack, revealing his secret, he dispensed with her services – and forced Mr Wilks to teach him instead.

An article he co-wrote with Sam mysteriously omitted Sam's name, much to Sam's irritation. But Amos was capable of sensitivity – he skirted over the more sensational details of

Dolly Acaster became the first of many Woolpack barmaids this year.

Matt Skilbeck joined the Cave Rescue Team and soon saw action.

Gimbel's death, and instead wrote a fair obituary.

The Woolpack was beginning to change with the times. Amos experimented with a dominoes and darts night, which was a huge success, and a chess night, which wasn't. After a request to sell 'pies, like the Malt Shovel does', Wilks bought up his rival pub's unsold stock at a knock-down rate, then sold them on the next day. Amos was horrified, and banned him from ever doing it again, although the customers didn't seem to mind. Due to a misunderstanding, Amos and Mr Wilks took a Swedish couple in as bed-and-breakfast guests. Asta and Olaf promptly got trapped by rising waters while potholing at Burruck Gill, and had to be rescued by the Wharfdale Cave Rescue Team. It provided a scoop for Amos and the *Hotten Courier*, and Amos was able to interview Matt Skilbeck, one of the rescue team.

Love was in the air for Henry Wilks, who met up with an old

The programme was now broadcast all year round. It had previously been seen as a strongly regional programme, but was being shown regularly by more ITV regions, and at more favourable times. Some regions who'd been slow to support the show were still catching up by broadcasting the previous year's episodes. The Yorkshire and Tyne Tees regions started showing it at 7 pm from April. By August, ATV, Southern, Ulster and the Scottish regions followed suit, and Granada and Harlech were showing it at 6.30 pm. The rest of the country saw it at 5.15 pm. By now, the programme was regularly getting around ten million viewers.

The location filming switched from Arncliffe to Esholt, which was nearer YTV's Leeds studios. Until now, the cast and crew had had to stay overnight at hotels in Arncliffe whenever there was location filming, which, of course, made it expensive to do. Market research and the ratings suggested that the viewers wanted to see more of the countryside in the programme, rather than studio interiors.

The character of Angela Read is most notable for who played her – future The Singing Detective *star, movie star and (for seven years) wife of Val Kilmer, Joanne Whalley.*

Joanne Whalley as Angela Read.

49

girlfriend, Janet Thompson, in the nearby Littlewell Nature Reserve. It seemed as if they would have a future together, a prospect that amused and pleased the villagers, but instead the relationship fizzled out.

DOLLY

Against his better judgement, Amos hired the first woman to work at the Woolpack. Dolly Acaster arrived as part of a training scheme run by the brewery. Henry Wilks was instrumental in talking Amos round but as far as he was concerned, it was only necessary because Amos was spending so much time now writing for the *Hotten Courier*. Amos resented the new presence, becoming even more pompous than normal, but agreed when he realised she'd be on trainee wages (although he was astonished to learn she'd earn a pound an hour!). Dolly couldn't stand it for long, and left to run a pub in Leeds. Only a few months later, Amos was surprised to find Dolly in a senior role at the brewery when he went on a tour.

Later, Henry Wilks persuaded her to come back to work at the Woolpack, and she would remain there for a decade. Amos gradually grew to appreciate her. Dolly lodged at the vicarage at first, then at Emmerdale Farm, where she soon started dating Matt Skilbeck.

ELSEWHERE

Robblesfield attempted to nobble the cricket match for the

Like the rest of the country, Beckindale celebrated the Queen's Silver Jubilee with a street party.

Butterworth Ball by fielding former professional Phil Kitson. Beckindale were bowled out for 28 and looked doomed, but the fire siren was sounded, and the local auxiliary volunteers, who made up a big proportion of the team, and included Joe Sugden, were called out. The match had to be settled by tossing a coin. Beckindale won.

It was a year of change at St Mary's. Reverend Ruskin had retired the previous year. Beckindale got a new vicar, William Hockley, but he was quickly replaced by David Cowper, who in turn was replaced by Donald Hinton. Hinton's first contact with his new parish was meeting Sam in Hotten where he mistook him for a down-and-out. Despite beginning with that faux pas, Reverend Hinton would stay in the village for many years, until his retirement, and loved the village so much he refused to become archdeacon when the post was offered to him.

The Silver Jubilee was celebrated in style in the village, with almost all the villagers seemingly involved in organising the street party and other events. There was a procession through Beckindale, culminating in the planting of new saplings just outside the village.

1978

KEY EVENTS

Steve Hawker and Pip Coulter commit armed robbery.

Dolly and Matt marry.

NY Estates buy Home Farm.

SUGDENS

Teenagers Steve Hawker and his girlfriend Pip Coulter stole Joe's shotgun and robbed the Woolpack, leaving Amos and Mr Wilks locked in the cellar. They then headed for Emmerdale Farm, where they kept Sam Pearson at gunpoint. Annie supplied them with a getaway car to prevent further violence.

Jack Sugden's second novel, *One Man in Time*, was published. Sam Pearson had particular reason to look forward to it – the book was his fictionalised biography. But Sam hated the book and wrote Jack a letter telling him as much – although Donald Hinton was far more enthusiastic.

David Annersley, an old flame of Annie's, turned up. Twenty-five years before (so around seven or eight years after she'd married Jacob), she had a crush on Annersley, but had remained faithful to her husband. Sam was still angry with Annersley, and made it clear that the threat he'd made in the 1950s – to kill him if he ever set foot in the village again – still stood. Joe was amazed that his mother had a torrid past – she retorted, 'In them days I was as big a romantic as any of you. On the other hand, I'm born and bred a Yorkshire lass, and we know the difference between dreams and reality.' Annersley got the message and soon left the village.

Matt Skilbeck married Dolly Acaster, the first church wedding for a number of years.

Seth Armstrong debuts - and starts as he means to go on.

DOLLY/SKILBECKS

Dolly Acaster was happily in a relationship with Matt Skilbeck when her past reared its head. Her former boyfriend Richard Roper, the father of her illegitimate son, appeared in the village. After getting Dolly pregnant, it was revealed, he'd run off to South Africa. Now he wanted to find their son and settle down together as a family. Instead, this crystallised Dolly's feelings for Matt – and they were married in June. They moved into Emmerdale Farm.

HOME FARM

George Verney, who'd been living out his retirement in Cannes, died this year. His nephew, Gerald Verney, inherited the estate, and death duties of £600,000. Gerald was forced to sell up. As he put the sale into motion, he discovered that the Sugdens had been farming a 20-acre field, known as Top Twenty, that was actually part of the Miffield Estate. The Sugdens were forced to buy it. The manor house and the rest of the estate were bought by NY Estates, property developers and a big agricultural corporation, with its head office in Lincoln. From now on, the most important person in the village would be the estate manager of the Hall – which now became known as Home Farm. The first person to be appointed estate manager was Trevor Thatcher.

This was perhaps the single biggest change to affect village life for centuries – the feudal system, with a lord of the manor and deferential tenants and workers, had given way to a purely commercial operation, one where the agenda was one of maximising profits. Some, like Sam Pearson, would mourn the passing of the old ways. Others, like his grandson Joe Sugden, would learn to thrive in an environment that presented many opportunities for advancement and innovation. He reckoned that 'big combines with brass win every time, hands down'. NY Estates quickly started pulling up hedgerows to consolidate the size of their fields.

SETH ARMSTRONG

Trevor Thatcher quickly had Sam Pearson arrested for poaching, although the actual culprit was Seth Armstrong, the school caretaker and boiler stoker. Seth was secretly taught how to read and write this year by new teacher Antony Moeketski, who was also teaching Seth's teenage son, Fred. Sam Pearson, suspicious of Moeketski because he was black, worried that he was teaching Seth 'subversion'!

Seth entered the village vegetable competition for the first

time in a number of years –
he'd previously had his carrots
poisoned by 'that Nathan
Curry', which had put him off
entering for a long time.

AMOS AND MR WILKS

Amos caught chickenpox from
Seth's son Fred, and moved into
Emmerdale to recuperate. He
was something of an
insufferable guest.

Meanwhile, Marian Wilks
came over from Italy,
determined to persuade her
father to move to the Continent
with her. Henry Wilks gave the
idea serious consideration, and
even had an old army friend,
Denyer, lined up to buy his
share of the Woolpack. In the
end, he decided to stay in the
village, among friends.

ELSEWHERE

Donald Hinton's son Clive, a
slightly dodgy entrepreneur,
visited Beckindale, and carried
out test explosions, thinking
he'd discovered valuable
fluorspar deposits. This proved
a false hope, and he left the
village. Soon afterwards he was
arrested in Athens for gun-running.

*Marion Wilks delighted
Henry with a surprise visit.*

*(right) Villagers objected to
the gypsies on the village
green.*

A group of gypsies camped out on the village green. The villagers
were almost universally hostile, with only Donald Hinton
supportive – he tried to set up a playgroup for the travellers'
children. They left after several weeks – having stolen from and
vandalised a number of properties in the village.

During gas pipeline work in the village, an old skeleton was
unearthed with a locket inscribed with 'Hannah Elizabeth 1784'.
Antony Moeketski, Amos and Hinton set about trying to discover
her history. Old editions of the *Hotten Courier* revealed that she'd
been hanged for murdering her sister. Seth, though, spotted the
most relevant fact – she'd been a Pearson. Sam was mortified to
discover that his family's past hadn't been whiter than white, as
he'd always thought.

1979

KEY EVENTS

Seth becomes the gamekeeper at Home Farm.

Dolly discovers she is pregnant.

AMOS AND WILKS

Soon after Marian Wilks returned to Italy, Amos had another cause for concern – Henry Wilks befriended widow Irene Madden, and there seemed a chance that he would abandon his partnership at the pub. In the end, the relationship didn't become a romantic one.

Horrified by the prospect of the Woolpack being redecorated, Seth and Sam offered to repaint it for nothing, as long as it ended up looking exactly the same as before. Amos was happy to oblige.

Wilks bought an antique plough and put it outside the Woolpack as a 'feature'. Amos, who never liked it, sold it to a museum when children started playing on it, risking injury.

Despite Amos being rude to the writer, the Woolpack was recommended in the new edition of the *Good Beer Guide*.

ELSEWHERE

Violent crime continued to be a problem. Wendy Hotson was raped by a stranger. For once, Amos decided that the girl's reputation came before his publishing a good story, so he didn't report it in the *Courier*. A local simpleton, Poor Ocker, was

Seth appeared regularly from this year, and continues to plague Alan Turner to this day.

Anne Gibbons took over as producer in June, and would remain in the job for six years. She decided to move away from shorter storylines and to have a more regular cast – up until now, while there had been a core group of regulars, other characters were introduced and left in the space of a few episodes, which made it difficult for the audience to care much about them. One beneficiary of this was Seth, who had only really been a semi-regular before now. She also increased the number of outdoor locations used.

suspected by the villagers. Wendy's father, Cully, beat him up, but the real culprit was a stranger who owned the same sort of coat, and who died shortly afterwards in a road accident. His identity was never established.

SUGDENS

Joe Sugden accidentally shot Phil Fletcher in the leg during an argument about game shooting. Fletcher got his son Terry to lie to the police in an attempt to get Joe charged, but the accusation refused to stick.

Sam Pearson and Henry Wilks planned to open a farm museum at the neighbouring Hathersage Farm, and the deal seemed close, but collapsed at the last minute.

Sam wrote a few entertaining articles for the *Courier* about his old friend Badger Cox. The real Badger Cox was, unknown to Sam, still alive and in the area. The villagers were highly amused that he consistently proved Sam's memory of events wrong.

Another old friend of Sam's from the First World War, Arthur Braithwaite, arrived in the village, providing plenty of companionship and entertainment.

SKILBECKS

Dolly discovered she was pregnant.

SETH

Seth's son Jimmy arrived in the village in May, with his pregnant wife Susan. He was clearly hiding something – and when Amos investigated, it emerged he had spent six months in prison. People were worried about telling Seth, but Seth already knew. Jimmy and Susan only stayed around for a couple of weeks.

HOME FARM

New estate manager Maurice Westrop had a brilliant scheme to cut poaching – he hired Seth Armstrong as the gamekeeper. This

Seth quickly established himself as the bane of Amos Brearley's life.

ended the problem at a stroke – it had been Seth doing the poaching in the first place.

Westrop's daughter Judy arrived in the village, suffering from depression and drinking problems.

KEY EVENTS

Joe's appointed assistant manager of
Home Farm – and clashes with his boss.

Jack Sugden returns to the village.

HOME FARM

Another new estate manager was appointed. Richard Anstey quickly stamped his authority on the village, clashing with locals over his plans to plant two hundred new acres of trees. Anstey also began trials of hormone injections for the beef herd.

SUGDENS

Anstey's biggest coup was to hire Joe Sugden as his assistant manager. Joe's horizons had been broadened by a trip to America, and NY Estates offered the opportunity to try out new farming methods and to invest in new technology on a scale impossible for Emmerdale Farm to match.

Sam stole Amos's slogan to win a competition to go to Ireland.

Three characters were recast in 1980 – Ruth Merrick had been played by Lynn Dalby, Pat was played by Helen Weir. Clive Hornby was cast as Jack Sugden (replacing Andrew Burt, last seen in 1976). Clive and Helen would go on to marry in real life, as well as in the series. Finally, Dolly Skilbeck returned from her bout of depression played by a new actress, Jean Rogers replacing Katharine Barker.

Perhaps the most serious continuity gaffe in Emmerdale's history concerns Pat Merrick, who was called Ruth when she was a regular character in the series in 1972. A third child of Ruth/Pat and Tom, Tommy, was also mentioned in the early years of the programme, but he'd mysteriously vanished on Pat's return, never to be mentioned again.

He and Annie hugely enjoyed their holiday.

After six years, Jack Sugden returned to live in the village. He was becoming unhappy with his writing, and was getting nowhere with his third book, a travel guide. After some soul-searching, he now felt the time was right for him to return to run the family farm. He sold his flat in Rome.

MERRICKS

By coincidence, an old flame of Jack's, Pat Harker, returned to the village just before Jack. She had been the woman he'd left behind when he'd gone to London in 1964. After Jack left, she married Tom Merrick, who'd been violent towards her. She'd returned to her roots with her son Jackie and daughter Sandie in tow. A number of villagers, including Annie, had speculated in the past that Jackie might be Jack's son, not Tom's. Tom's and Pat's marriage continued, unhappily.

Pat worked as a waitress in Hotten Market, Jackie started working as Seth's oppo on the Home Farm estate. Jackie enjoyed learning the tricks of the trade of the gamekeeper – but was still squeamish about killing rabbits.

Pat and Jack started seeing each other.

Jack returned, and was now on better terms with Matt and Joe.

SKILBECKS

Matt thought his dog Snip was worrying sheep, and was on the way to the vet's to have him put to sleep before the real culprit was found.

Eight months into her pregnancy, Dolly miscarried, and almost lost her own life. This led to the onset of depression, where she was hardly seen in the village. She attempted to pick herself up by helping to run the village playgroup.

AMOS AND WILKS

The Woolpack started selling ploughman's lunches.

Henry Wilks' cousin Alice and Amos's Aunt Emily arrived at the Woolpack at the same time, causing all sorts of headaches for the two publicans. When Amos reckoned he'd seen a UFO in nearby marshland, that was enough to scare Emily off – she was alarmed he was dabbling in the occult. The explanation for the lights was never forthcoming – although Hinton found records of them having been seen since the time of Boudicca.

Meanwhile, Amos – or at least one of his poems – found an admirer in Enid Pottle. Amos was delighted that 'the' Enid Pottle, apparently a renowned poet, liked it and met her and showed her some more of his poems. Enid sent him a detailed critique of them, which Amos couldn't understand. Enid clarified matters – she hated them. Amos's opinion of her dropped like a stone.

Mr Wilks wasn't too happy to find her pet monkey sitting on the Woolpack bar.

Amos got very jealous when Mr Wilks was asked to write for a book about the history of his old textile firm.

Mr Wilks dreaded the news that the VAT inspector wanted to check the Woolpack's books – but it turned out they were owed a rebate.

Amos bought an allotment, and proceeded to bore Wilks and his clientele with his new-found knowledge of horticulture. Amos, to his credit, grew an enormous marrow which was destined to win a prize at the Hotten Show – until Wilks

(above) Enid Pottle, eccentric local poet.

(right) Pat Merrick arrives with children Jackie and Sandie.

accidentally ran over it in his car.

The publicans of the Woolpack were indignant to discover that Ernie Shuttleworth, the landlord of the Malt Shovel, was planning to offer special Christmas entertainment and food.

ELSEWHERE

Enoch Tolly, the Bible-bashing neighbour of the Sugdens, started using illegal pesticides. This became apparent to both the Sugdens and Home Farm when they started to discover many dead pigeons on their own land. On further investigation, Jack and Seth discovered Tolly was doing a number of illegal things, like poisoning eggs and returning them to their nests. Despite any number of threats from Anstey, Enoch refused to mend his ways. Angry with him, his daughter Hannah walked out on him, followed – on his twenty-fifth wedding anniversary – by his other daughter Naomi and his wife Grace. Tolly relented.

This year saw the first appearance of Sgt MacArthur, who policed the village for many years to come.

Beckindale lost the Butterworth Ball when Robblesfield's bowls team, led by Eccky Tait, proved more than a match for them.

EPISODES 629–702 – (EPISODES 697–702 WEREN'T BROADCAST)

KEY EVENTS

Tom Merrick returns to cause problems
for Jack and Pat.

Annie is robbed.

Amos becomes addicted to the Woolpack Space Invaders machine, much to Wilks's annoyance.

MERRICKS

Tom Merrick returned to the village, intent on causing problems for Pat. When Pat told him she wanted a divorce, he hit her. The next day, Tom burned down one of NY Estates' barns, and tried to frame Jack Sugden for it. Jack was arrested, but soon released for lack of evidence.

Pat confided in Donald Hinton, saying she found it difficult to keep working in Hotten. Hinton offered her the job of housekeeper at the vicarage, which she was grateful to accept.

Romance was in the air for Pat's children. Jackie found love with local girl Jane Hardcastle. Sandie's love life was far more eventful. She started dating Andy Longthorn, Jackie's best friend, but quickly switched her affections to rich agricultural student David Blackmore, who was helping Joe at NY Estates. After that, she romanced Graham Jelks, an unemployed mechanic, and another friend of Jackie.

Tom Merrick was caught stealing Christmas trees from the Home Farm estate at the end of the year, and was given a suspended sentence.

SKILBECKS

Dolly was told that her mother was suffering from a brain haemorrhage.

SETH

Enoch Tolly died when his tractor overturned. Seth helped out his widow, Grace (he admitted he and Grace had been 'very close' before the War). He put them in touch

Jack proposed to Pat Merrick this year.

with Daniel Hawkins, who'd recently been made redundant from Home Farm, and Hawkins proved an excellent manager at the Tolly farm.

Seth was so impressed by Jackie Merrick that he appointed him his full-time assistant.

AMOS AND WILKS

Henry Wilks was elected parish councillor early in the year.

When a Space Invaders machine was mistakenly delivered to the Woolpack, Amos refused to have it in the bar – but when he set it up in the backroom, he became addicted to it. When he realised how much money he'd put in it, he had it sent back.

As a *Hotten Courier* journalist, Amos faced a challenge from his rival Frank Hencoller, whom Amos accused of writing all his articles in the pub and always mentioning his son Martin. Amos was sacked, and set up a photocopied rival to the *Courier*, the *Beckindale Bugle*. Hencoller laughed at the efforts – but stole Amos's articles, word for word. When this came to light, Amos was reinstated – but his victory was tempered by news that Hencoller would keep his job.

SUGDENS

It wasn't a good year for Emmerdale Farm. Despite the best efforts of Henry Wilks on the Sugdens' behalf, the plans for a farm museum fell through once and for all. The Sugdens

An ITV strike in November and December 1981 meant that episodes 697–702 were made but never transmitted. When the strike ended, the story picked up with episode 703 (12 January 1982) with no explanation of what had happened in the gap. One of the events the audience never got to see was Jack proposing to Pat!

Tom Merrick was recast on his return, and was now played by Edward Peel, who would return to the series in 1997 as Tony Cairns.

Joe struggled to cope with the workload as Acting Estate Manager of Home Farm.

overstretched themselves financially to buy Hathersage Farm. The cattle herd caught salmonella in April, and half the stock had to be destroyed. In response, Jack made the decision to expand his sheep flock.

Violent crime remained a problem. Once again Annie Sugden was threatened by a burglar, who escaped. Suspicion fell on Jackie Merrick, and this intensified when he reported finding some of the stolen goods in an empty cottage.

Jack and Pat decided to get married as soon as Pat's divorce came through. In a sign of the times, Annie no longer seemed to object to a premarital relationship – Jack and Pat were able to spend a romantic weekend in Scarborough without serious censure. However, when they announced their plans to marry, Sam wasn't happy that Jack planned to marry a divorcee. Sam found himself a lone voice, with even his friend Nellie defending Pat.

Pat's divorce came through at Christmas, and the way was clear for her to marry Jack.

HOME FARM

Seth was threatened with the sack when a poacher began eating into NY Estates' profits. Seth discovered his friend Sid Pickles was responsible, and handed him over, saving his job. While Joe supported Seth, Seth felt very guilty, and not all his friends approved of what he had done.

NY Estates began to get 'jumpy' about the recession, according to Joe.

Richard Anstey began an almost open affair with Virginia, the wife of his regional manager, Derek Lattimore. Anstey and Lattimore already hated each other. When he discovered the affair, Lattimore offered his wife a divorce, but when Virginia told Anstey, he made it clear their affair had been conducted simply to humiliate his boss. Joe Sugden found himself a political football in this rivalry – when he suggested developing a new pig unit at

Home Farm, both Anstey and his regional manager thought it was a bad idea, but Lattimore encouraged Joe anyway, his logic being that anything that would hurt Home Farm profits would damage Anstey. Anstey expanded on Joe's plans – wanting a thousand pigs, as opposed to Joe's fifty. Joe thought this was madness, and submitted his more modest plans behind Anstey's back.

Their superior, NY Estates manager Christopher Meadows, took a dim view of all this. He forced through the plans for Joe's smaller pig unit, and insisted that Anstey get back in line, sacking him when he refused. Joe Sugden was appointed acting manager in his place.

ELSEWHERE

House prices in the village were rising fast, and a number of young couples realised it was becoming too expensive for locals to buy a new house in Beckindale.

Sam and Amos became joint presidents of the Beckindale Horticultural Society.

Reverend Bill Jeffries briefly assisted Donald Hinton with church duties, but soon left.

1982

KEY EVENTS

Alan Turner arrives as the estate manager of Home Farm.

Jackie Merrick causes problems for Jack and Pat.

Dolly gives birth.

HOME FARM

Although Joe had hoped to be made permanent estate manager at Home Farm, in March NY Estates appointed Alan Turner in the role. Joe only found out when Turner arrived, announcing himself as the new estate manager. Turner set about trying to replace Joe, offering Matt Skilbeck the job, and the old Tolly farmhouse to live in. Matt turned down the offer.

Turner built the new pig unit, to Joe's specifications, but was keen to take the credit for himself. He also got Joe to do his dirty work – one morning getting him to drive home a woman, Denise, he'd picked up at a party. This led to rumours that it was Joe who had spent the night with her.

Joe was making no friends at his family farm, either – a helicopter spraying crops from Home Farm went astray and caused Emmerdale cattle to stampede. After a bitter argument, NY Estates agreed to pay compensation.

Nineteen-eighty-two was a bumper year for Home Farm, despite Turner's mishaps.

SUGDENS

Jack discovered he was Jackie's father. As a number of villagers – including Tom - had suspected, Pat had been pregnant when Jack had left for London, and had quickly married Tom to hide the paternity of the baby. The implications were far-reaching – for a start, Jackie was possibly now the rightful heir to Emmerdale Farm.

Jackie took the news very badly, and resented both Jack and Pat. Seth – whose mother had never been sure who his father was – did his best to calm him down.

Hinton wasn't happy with the idea of marrying a divorcee in his church. Sam was also troubled, but he did like Pat, and Annie was able to talk him round to the idea. Jack married Pat Merrick at Hotten Register Office in October.

After the marriage, Emmerdale Farm was full to the brim – Jack, Pat, Sandie, Matt, Dolly, Annie and Sam all living there. This tended to mean people were on fairly short fuses.

Members of the cast celebrate the tenth anniversary of **Emmerdale Farm.**

Emmerdale Farm celebrated its tenth anniversary in 1982 with a number of events, like a press conference in London. It was now regularly in the top ten programmes on television.

Richard Thorp had an anniversary of his own to celebrate – he joined the show, as Alan Turner, on 2 January, his fiftieth birthday. In 2002, he celebrated his twentieth year on the programme, making him the third-longest-serving member of the current cast.

MERRICK

Jackie, who celebrated his eighteenth birthday in 1982, had learned that Jack was his real father, but found it difficult to accept. Tom Merrick had disowned him, and Jackie went off the rails, developing a drinking problem and leaving Emmerdale Farm to live in a caravan.

Against Pat's wishes, he started to consider a career in the Army, and attended an interview which went favourably.

Jackie was sacked from Home Farm by Turner after problems at a shoot, and Jackie responded by setting fire to the caravan, which was owned by Home Farm. He was convicted of arson and given community service. He was no longer eligible to join the Army.

Sandie dated local vet Martin Butler.

SKILBECKS

Dolly sought help from a fertility specialist, and by the middle of the year this had paid off. Her son was born just before Christmas. Originally, she and Matt planned to call him David Samuel, but Amos and Wilks told Sam he 'must be proud he was named after you' before Dolly had a chance to tell him Samuel was the baby's *second* name. Sam was so proud that Matt and Dolly agreed they'd actually call him Samuel David.

Matt and Dolly moved into a converted barn adjacent to the Emmerdale farmhouse, easing the pressure on space. The cost of the conversion, though, meant the decoration and furniture were a little spartan at first.

SETH

Amos barred Seth from the Woolpack after he'd horrified the Bishop of Hotten (not to mention his host) by producing his pet ferret there. Seth was soon back, though.

Indeed, with both Amos and Mr Wilks attending Pat's and Jack's wedding, Seth was left in charge of the pub. Discovering him comatose on the floor when they returned, they weren't convinced by his explanation that he 'suffered blackouts'.

Alan arrived, and was keen to appear as a hands-on manager

AMOS AND MR WILKS

Wilks and Amos cheated in the Best Kept Cellar competition – repainting it between judge's visits. The judge was not amused to get wet paint on her clothes, and disqualified them.

Amos got Mr Wilks's back up by describing him as his 'assistant' to a brewery man. It was a number of weeks before Wilks forgave him for the slight.

Seth proved better at drinking pints than serving them!

EPISODES 771–842

KEY EVENTS

Joe leaves for France.

Sandie Merrick's teenage pregnancy causes heartache.

Seth Armstrong and his long-suffering (and little seen) wife Meg.

SUGDENS

Emmerdale Farm was hitting financial trouble. Annie brought Henry Wilks back in to deal with the accounts, feeling he'd not been pulling his weight in recent years. He quickly identified a number of bank errors that helped ease the situation.

Jack faced off against cattle rustlers, knocking one of them out with a thrown stone.

Joe met Barbara Peters, who was initially quite secretive. Astonished villagers reported that she had spent the night with Reverend Hinton in the vicarage. Barbara was Hinton's daughter, and she'd recently left her husband. She resisted Turner's advances, and Joe insisted to his family that 'nothing happened' when they ended up spending the night together at the Feathers hotel. But she and Joe were soon sleeping together, and within a couple of months she moved in with Joe at Demdyke. The relationship didn't last, and Barbara left when Joe proposed and she realised she wasn't ready for the commitment. Faced with that and frustrations at Home Farm, where he was being blamed for Turner's many mistakes, Joe decided he needed a change of scenery. He took an NY Estates job in Tours, breeding rare beef cattle.

Annie was rushed to hospital with peritonitis, but made a full recovery.

MERRICKS

Jackie Merrick had a busy love life, dating punky Maggie and later Angie Richards. He started to call Jack 'me dad', marking a real shift in his attitude.

Jackie found a new friend,

Rev Hinton and his daughter, Barbara.

Archie Brooks, another young lad looking for work (or, more usually, girls). They fell in with Harry Mowlem, a local dodgy dealer, who had odd jobs for them.

Sandie Merrick became pregnant, but refused to say who the father was. Dolly Skilbeck was one of the few in the village to be sympathetic – Dolly herself had been in the same situation at Sandie's age. The father was Andy Longthorn, her former school friend. Her mother, Pat, didn't want her to go through with the pregnancy. Jackie gave Andy a black eye. Andy's father promised that his son would do the honourable thing and marry Sandie. Sandie wasn't keen, and left the village to stay with her father, Tom, and her baby girl, Louise, was born there. She was later adopted. Andy left for university.

TURNER

Turner was increasingly lazy, and keen to blame Joe Sugden for any problems. He ordered a truck to be overloaded with livestock, and was caught by RSPCA inspectors. He also started losing money on the horses.

When Joe left for France, he was replaced by a new computer. Turner couldn't operate it, and chose to ignore that side of his work rather than learn. This earned him a serious censure from his bosses. He got a new secretary, Sue Lockwood, whom he secretly lusted after.

SETH

Seth's long-suffering wife Meg finally threw him out of their house on Demdyke Row, fed up that Seth spent so much time at the Woolpack and always seemed to be drunk. Reverend Ruskin managed to get them talking again, and Seth was duly allowed home.

Seth camouflaged his bike, claiming it was to hide it from poachers – in reality, it made it harder for Turner or Meg to spot that he was in the pub instead of at work.

Matt and Dolly and Samuel David – formerly David Samuel.

Smokey the dog won at the dog trials, and Seth was delighted with her.

Seth was so insulted by Amos's insinuations about the state of his garden that he dumped a huge pile of horse manure over the forecourt of the Woolpack. Unfortunately, this was just as the judges of a Best Kept Village competition were assessing Beckindale. Seth was annoyed that Amos and Wilks bagged the manure and made money selling it.

Seth was also caught out at the Skipdale Show – his prize-winning cauliflower had a supermarket price tag on it, and he was disqualified. Amos took the prize instead.

Frazer Hines, who played Joe Sugden, took a break from the part in 1983. Angie Richards, one of Jackie's girlfriends, was played by Bev Callard, who went on to play Liz McDonald in Coronation Street.

Richard Handford became the producer in October.

1984

KEY EVENTS

Jack has an affair with Karen Moore.

Pat and Sandie are reconciled.

Mrs Bates arrives to sort Turner out.

Sam Pearson, who died in 1984.

MERRICKS

Sandie Merrick and her father Tom returned to the village, with Sandie transformed from a dowdy schoolgirl into a vivacious young woman. Her mother, Pat, had never visited Sandie, or seen her granddaughter. Jack was worried by the return of Tom. He didn't have to worry about Pat's feelings for her ex-husband – although Tom became involved in petty crime, including dynamiting for fish. Significantly, Jackie didn't side with his father.

Reconciliation between Pat and Sandie came from an unlikely source – Sam Pearson, who befriended Sandie. Before long, Pat and Sandie were back on speaking terms.

SETH

Seth and Sgt MacArthur set up a road block to capture the poachers, and Seth was very upset that he'd helped to shop Tom and Jackie. Donald Hinton was also not sure that he'd done the right thing.

Later in the year, Seth's attempts to clear the cricket pitch of moles with poison gas and digging trenches made it 'look like the Somme', according to Hinton.

SUGDENS

Jack discovered that long-term love Marian had got married to Paolo Rossetti in Italy. Although Jack was now married to Pat, he was surprised how badly the news affected him. He started an affair with Hotten auctioneer Karen Moore. Pat found out after a number of months and, at a confrontation in Karen's flat, told Jack to choose between them. Given such a stark choice, Jack quickly chose to stay with his wife. Jack redeemed himself by making a real effort to salvage the marriage, and he and Pat were soon celebrating when they discovered she was pregnant.

Another old flame of Annie's, Lawrence, turned up, but soon left.

Sam Pearson died in his sleep in late November, the day after winning a prize at the village's annual show.

Joe returned to the village in time for Christmas.

HOME FARM/MRS BATES

NY Estates was making increasing demands on the Home Farm estate, which was struggling to remain viable. Mass redundancies were threatened, which Turner – now fond of the village – was

Turner's dam blocked the water supply for the rest of the village.

Karen Moore.

reluctant to initiate. The pressure was getting to him and he was gambling, drinking and womanising. This in turn affected his work as Home Farm estate manager. His boss, Christopher Meadows, gave him an ultimatum to mend his ways in three months or get the sack, and Turner promised to mend his ways.

Turner started by trying to reconcile with his wife, Jill, encouraged by Annie Sugden. Jill wanted a separation, although she did end up sleeping with Turner one night.

Jill found a new secretary for Turner. Caroline Bates arrived in the village to ease the pressure on him a little. She was separated from husband Malcolm.

Almost straight away, Jackie Merrick shot Caroline's dog Bundle when it worried sheep on Emmerdale land. Although he covered up his involvement, this was actually Turner's fault for letting him off his lead.

Turner built a dam to collect water for the new pig unit – and ended up blocking the stream into the village. This affected every other farm, as well as the houses in the village. Jack was all for blowing it up, but in the end it was Mrs Bates who did the honours.

AMOS AND MR WILKS

When all their customers upped and walked out one evening, Amos and Mr Wilks were baffled. They soon discovered that the Malt Shovel had started a happy hour, with half-price drinks. Amos was personally affronted by this 'threat to the economy', and Wilks sombrely agreed that 'this happy hour is becoming a source of general misery'.

Further problems were caused by a draymen's strike which meant the Woolpack soon ran out of Monk's beer. Ernie Shuttleworth arrived with some

The staff of the Woolpack and the Malt Shovel were in danger of letting their customers win!

Toke Townley, who played Annie's father Sam Pearson, died of a heart attack on 28 September. Sheila Mercer, Annie, appeared before that night's episode to pay tribute to him. Sam continued to appear until November, when real life caught up with recorded episodes.

Annie Hulley, who played Karen Moore (the only woman to bed both Jack and Joe Sugden!), is married to producer and director Chris Clough, who has directed for Emmerdale, *but is better known for* Brookside *and* The Bill.

This year saw the first episodes written by Bill Lyons, the longest-serving writer on the programme. Already an experienced TV writer, Bill would go on to write key early episodes of EastEnders, *and would work on* Eldorado, *but has remained a mainstay of* Emmerdale *for nearly twenty years. In 2001, he was one of the judges of the* Soapstars *television programme that picked a new family for* Emmerdale.

friends and drank the pub dry, forcing the locals to go to the Malt Shovel instead (and he'd known the strike was coming and had got plentiful supplies).

Soon afterwards, when supplies had been restored, Ernie was forced to join forces with Amos and Mr Wilks when both pubs were caught running after hours drinking sessions. They both managed to retain their licences.

KEY EVENTS

Turner wins the parish election, but runs over Jackie Merrick.

Kathy and Nick Bates arrive in the village.

Harry Mowlem causes problems.

ELSEWHERE

Harry Mowlem, owner of a local quarry, started making his presence known, and made advances on Dolly Skilbeck. He also bought 30 acres close to Emmerdale to start a pig farm.

BATES

Caroline Bates divorced her husband Malcolm when she discovered he was having an affair, ending her hopes of a reconciliation. She moved into Main Street, bringing her two children Kathy and Nick with her.

SKILBECKS

Dolly became pregnant, but once again suffered a miscarriage. She turned down the attentions of Harry Mowlem.

Matt's faithful sheepdog Nell went into retirement, and was replaced by Tess.

SETH

Seth and Alan Turner stood against each other in the parish elections, Turner winning a rather hard-fought campaign by a narrow margin.

Seth's donkey caused chaos at the annual fete.

HOME FARM

Turner may have won the election, but he and his wife Jill finally divorced this year. Their son Terence, an Oxford undergraduate, came to stay, not thinking much of the village. Terence did romance Sandie Merrick, though.

MERRICKS

A turbulent year for Turner continued when he knocked Jackie Merrick off his motorbike, sending him to hospital for five

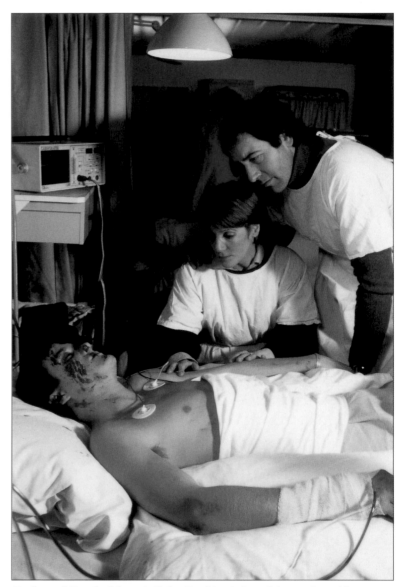

Jack and Pat hold a vigil for Jackie, injured in an horrific motorcycle accident.

months. It wasn't entirely bad news for Jackie, though – the accident put his feud with Jack in perspective, and he accepted him as his father for the first time. Jackie also fell in love with his nurse, Sita Sharma. They soon got engaged, but Jackie's haste to get married scared her away shortly afterwards. Nevertheless, the accident helped calm Jackie down, and he began to show a keen interest in Emmerdale.

Emmerdale Farm *celebrated its one thousandth episode in November, a year that saw unprecedented success and a number of changes to the programme.*

Emmerdale Farm was now shown in prime early evening slots in all the ITV regions. It saw off a significant challenger – EastEnders, which started in February, and was put on at 7 pm, the same time most areas of the country (but not London) showed Emmerdale Farm. In almost all parts of the country where the two soaps were going head-to-head, Emmerdale Farm was watched by more people. The BBC were forced to move their programme to 7.30 pm.

Actor Ian Shurrock married Pam McDonald, who worked in the promotions and publicity department of YTV. In another demonstration that the programme was now a huge mainstream success, over 4000 fans showed up on the day.

Emmerdale Farm was now seen firmly as a 'soap opera', and its success over EastEnders made ITV scrutinise it more carefully. To compete in prime time, it was felt that the programme should be faster-paced, more topical and have bigger stories.

Kevin Laffan, the creator of the series, who had continued as the most prolific writer of the series, rowed with the producer and script editor about the increase in 'sex, sin and sensationalism'. Interviews at the time suggested he was specifically worried about seeing Jack in bed with Karen Moore and the increase in violence exemplified by a fight between Jack and Tom Merrick. He also thought Jackie's road accident was a little too gory, and he was worried that the character of Annie was softening.

The Jack and Karen Moore story, though, was the one that had put the show in the top three of the television ratings charts for the first time. Sex, sin and sensationalism seemed to be what the audience wanted. Laffan was asked to change a script, but instead he chose to leave. Although Laffan is still credited as the creator of the show, and has occasionally visited the set since, he has had little input since deciding to leave the writing team in August 1985.

Sandie saw Harry Mowlem and Derek Warner steal £6000 from a security van.

AMOS AND WILKS

Doreen Shuttleworth, usually the barmaid at the rival Malt Shovel, helped out at the Woolpack while Mr Wilks visited Marian and her new husband Paolo in Italy.

Amos wrote an article for the *Courier* in which he criticised NY Estates for crop-spraying, suggesting that children had been hospitalised after coming into contact with the chemicals.

Amos started collecting antiques and curios. Henry Wilks was horrified, on his return, to discover that the Woolpack was full of this new collection. Amos promised to sell them, but hid them in the barn at Emmerdale Farm. Sandie and Phil ended up decorating Mill Cottage with some of them, and it was a while before Amos found out where his treasures had gone.

Turner's son, Terence, arrived and didn't think much of the village.

1986

KEY EVENTS

Pat Sugden gives birth to Robert – but dies soon after.

Joe becomes Turner's boss.

Matt Skilbeck is accused of murdering Harry Mowlem.

SUGDENS

Robert Jacob Sugden was born to Jack and Pat in April 1986.

Joe returned to the village again in time to attend the christening. He claimed this would be a flying visit, but had secretly applied to become regional manager of NY Estates. When he got the job, he moved into Demdyke Row, sharing the place with Jackie Merrick. For a while, it seemed that Joe and Kathy Bates were keen on each other, but the relationship didn't progress very far.

Instead, Joe started a relationship with Karen Moore, the woman his brother Jack had had an affair with a couple of years before. As she nearly wrecked Jack's marriage, the other Sugdens found it difficult to accept Karen, and she and Joe split up soon afterwards.

When Robert was only five months old, Pat died in a car accident.

HOME FARM

As regional manager of NY Estates, Joe Sugden was now Alan Turner's immediate superior. As with Anstey and Lattimore before them, Alan and Joe spent a great deal of time arguing with each other.

Joe's decision that NY Estates should buy Hotten market paid immediate dividends, and put the company in an even more commanding position.

SKILBECKS

Matt Skilbeck argued with Harry Mowlem, Matt accusing him of stealing sheep. They came to blows by the brook. The next morning, Henry Wilks found Mowlem's body there. Villagers could remember Mowlem's advances to Dolly the previous year, and an earlier incident when Matt had accused Mowlem of mistreating his dog. Matt became the prime suspect, and was arrested for manslaughter.

All seemed lost for Matt until the £6000 Mowlem and Derek Warner had stolen the previous year turned up on Mowlem's farm. Derek Warner tried to make a run for it, and held Donald Hinton hostage. Warner had murdered Mowlem, who wouldn't tell him where the money was. When the truth came out, Matt was freed.

Dolly was also busy – her illegitimate son, Graham Lodsworth, arrived in the village. He regaled the village with stories of his career in the navy – but was actually a deserter. He was located, arrested and returned to camp.

The Sugdens mourn the death of Jack's wife, Pat.

Two *future* EastEnders *appeared in* Emmerdale Farm *this year* – Craig Fairbrass played a gypsy, Ross Kemp had a more substantial role as Dolly Skilbeck's long-lost son, Graham Lodsworth.

Helen Weir left the role of Pat Sugden, after she and Clive Hornby had a baby son.

This year saw the arrival of Chris Chittell as Eric Pollard, a character who was only meant to appear in a handful of episodes but who quickly became a regular character.

Michael Russell was appointed producer in the summer.

Enter Eric Pollard – the new manager of Hotten Market and already looking out for number one.

Sandie and Phil Pearce.

SETH

Meg, Seth's wife, decided that the best way to monitor her husband's drinking was to become a barmaid at the Woolpack. It soon became clear that the arrangement didn't suit either of them.

Seth was badly beaten when he tried to stop a raid on a badger sett by badger baiters. Left for dead, it took him many months to recover from his head injuries.

MERRICKS

Jackie couldn't stay under the same roof as Joe for long, and returned to a room in Emmerdale Farm. Soon afterwards, he started a romance with Kathy Bates, who was working on the farm.

Sandie had an affair with married Phil Pearce, a builder with a young daughter. This led to a memorable fight in the Woolpack between Sandie and Phil's wife, Lesley. After that, Phil left his wife for Sandie, and after a brief spell living with Joe in Demdyke Row, the pair of them moved into the water mill Jack Sugden had sought to convert into a house in the early 1970s. Pearce's company, Phoenix (which he'd recently started up with Joe Sugden), had refurbished the building into a very desirable residence, which became known as Mill Cottage. Although Phil did divorce his wife, Annie Sugden in particular made it clear she disapproved of Sandie's behaviour.

AMOS AND WILKS

Amos managed to find himself on the receiving end of a gypsy curse when he barred a group from the pub. A number of minor accidents and breakages ensued for a short while.

POLLARD

Eric Pollard arrived as the manager of Hotten market. Whatever the truth about Pollard's army career, he quickly proved himself to be scheming and greedy. When Karen Moore left her job as a manager there, Pollard was happy to appoint Sandie Merrick in her place, imagining that she would be suitably naive.

ELSEWHERE

The Longthorn family were evicted from Lower Hall Farm when NY Estates decided to redevelop the land.

1987

KEY EVENTS

The villagers unite against plans to build a nuclear dump near the village.

Pollard begins a campaign against Sandie.

Jack reunites with Marian Wilks.

NUCLEAR DUMP

There was uproar in the village when it was discovered that the government were planning to use the old mineshafts at Pencross Fell near the village for dumping low-level nuclear waste. The village rallied, and Jack Sugden emerged as the natural leader of a vocal campaign against the scheme – he was especially angry that as a senior NY Estates manager, his brother Joe had found out shortly before it was publicly announced. The main concern was for the children in the village. Dolly Skilbeck organised a mothers' group. Local MP Harriet Ridgeley-Jones (perhaps oddly in an election year) was in favour of the scheme. At a series of heated village meetings, the villagers agreed to take turns watching the waste site and to organise demonstrations. As work started to prepare the ground, the villagers began to blockade the routes to the site. Jack Sugden found himself something of a martyr to the cause when he was jailed for seven days for contempt of court. But as he served his time in Armley Prison, Jack heard that the strength of the protest had caused a rethink in government, and the plans to use Pencross Fell were abandoned.

Kathy fell for Tony Marchant.

SUGDENS

Joe had another ill-fated love affair – this time with vet Ruth Pennington. Initially, everything went well, and they spent time horse-riding. They enjoyed sparring over

Eric Pollard came to regret crossing swords with Sandie Merrick.

Joe's old-fashioned chauvinistic attitudes.

Jack Sugden's long-time love Marian Wilks returned to the village, with her Italian husband Paolo Rossetti and new son Niccolo, to visit her father, Henry. Eric Pollard attempted to burgle them, and was chased off by Paolo, who had a gun. Paolo tripped, shooting himself, and ended up in a coma. As he remained in hospital, Jack and Marian had a brief affair, which ended when Paolo recovered and the Rossettis returned home.

KATHY

Kathy's attentions were distracted from Jackie Merrick by NY Estates trainee manager Tony Marchant. In the end, Jackie's

The people of Beckindale worried that a nuclear dump near the village would endanger their children.

attempts to win her back made Kathy realise how much she loved him.

SKILBECK
Metcalfe, a farmer who owned nearby Crossgill, died this year and unexpectedly bequeathed the farm to Matt Skilbeck.

POLLARD
Eric Pollard was appointed head auctioneer of Hotten market, beating Sandie Merrick to the job. Pollard underestimated Sandie, though, and she discovered he was arranging sales that weren't going through the books. She told Joe Sugden of her suspicions. Joe investigated and sacked Pollard. Sandie had passed her exams and was given Pollard's job. Pollard blamed Sandie personally for his sacking, and started sending hate mail. Soon afterwards, he broke into Mill Cottage and threatened her with a poker.

In his personal life, Pollard romanced Dolly Skilbeck.

HOME FARM
At the end of the year, NY Estates finally decided to cut their losses, and completely withdrew from the area. The year ended with uncertainty for the village.

MERRICKS
Jackie fell down a mineshaft while rescuing a stray sheep. The weather was freezing, but Jackie survived the night, and was rescued the next day.

Sandie's triumph at becoming head auctioneer of Hotten Market didn't last long – NY Estates' decision to pull out of the area meant she lost her job.

The nuclear dump story ran for much of the year. While previous stories had touched on 'political' issues, they had tended to be rural concerns, like hunting and agricultural policies – often rather obscure ones, like the planting of trees as a tax dodge. An 'anti-nuclear' story like this, particularly one shown in an election year, was criticised in some quarters of the press as being politically biased. Many viewers' letters to the production team worried that the programme was betraying its roots by becoming 'topical'. The story was inspired and based, in part, on a campaign in Fulbeck in Lincolnshire. That campaign also succeeded, but only after its fictional counterpart's had.

1988

KEY EVENTS

Turner and Joe buy Home Farm.

Dolly's and Matt's marriage hits trouble.

Joe and Jack are lucky in love.

HOME FARM

Early in the year, Alan Turner and Joe Sugden entered a partnership to buy the Home Farm estate. They attempted to keep things running as usual, with Mrs Bates continuing as Turner's secretary. Alan quickly found the financial burden too heavy, though, and sold his shares to businessman Dennis Rigg. Turner retained the fish and game farms (in partnership with Mrs Bates).

It was a bad year for Turner, who was banned for drink-driving. He couldn't find love either, despite joining a dating agency.

POLLARD

One side-effect of Joe's bid for Home Farm was that he had to pull out of business arrangements with Phil Pearce. Eric Pollard was keen to assist Pearce instead.

SKILBECKS

Matt hired Phil Pearce to renovate Crossgill, but carelessness on Pearce's part caused a fire that razed the house to the ground. Matt and Dolly rescued Annie from the burning building. Matt was actually a little relieved – Dolly was pressuring him into using the move to Crossgill to start showing a bit of independence, but he was happy where he was.

Dolly was getting fed up with Matt's lack of ambition and had an affair with Stephen Fuller, a forester. She managed to sneak off on holiday with him in June without Matt suspecting a thing. The relationship was never more than an occasional diversion for Dolly, but she was hit hard by the news that Fuller had died in an accident in November, and this was the beginning of the end of her marriage.

KATHY

Kathy married Jackie Merrick in February. Her wedding dress was ruined by a burst pipe the night before the ceremony. Annie Sugden lent Kathy her own wedding dress from her marriage to Jacob 40 years before, and the wedding took place on schedule in St Mary's Church, the first church wedding seen in the village for a number of years.

Kathy and Jackie honeymooned in Tunisia. They initially lived in Jackie's attic room at Emmerdale Farm, but soon moved into 3 Demdyke Row.

SUGDENS

Jack met Sarah Connolly, a mobile librarian, and the two were soon dating. Sarah was independent, and wanted nothing to do with farming. Within a matter of months, she'd moved into Emmerdale Farm with Jack, and was clashing with Annie. Jack eventually blocked off the connecting door between his and Sarah's rooms and the main farmhouse to give the two women their own territories.

Marian Wilks made a brief return to the village. Her marriage to Paolo was on the rocks, and she wanted to leave him for Jack.

Jack first met Sarah Connolly at the mobile library she ran.

Faced with a choice, Jack stuck with Sarah.

Ruth Pennington left Joe Sugden this year for horse breeder Liam. Ruth and Liam got engaged and moved to Ireland, practically before Joe realised his relationship with Ruth was over.

Joe's luck changed with the arrival of Kate Hughes and her two teenage children, Rachel and Mark. They got off to a poor start when Joe shot the family dog for worrying sheep, but after a meal at the Feathers, Kate and Joe were soon dating – to the disbelief of Kate's children, who couldn't forgive Joe for murdering their family pet.

ELSEWHERE

Nick Bates foiled a raid on the post office, but in doing so he was tempted to keep some of the cash left behind by the thieves. He hid the money with his girlfriend Claire Sutcliffe, who ran off to Leeds with it. Nick was uncomfortable with being hailed the hero of the hour.

POLLARD

Eric Pollard and Phil Pearce discovered what Nick had done and blackmailed him. But Nick didn't find it difficult to turn the tables – he knew Eric and Phil had stolen antique fireplaces from Home Farm. Pearce confessed, but Pollard kept his mouth shut – and when the police couldn't find any evidence against Pollard, Pearce was sent to prison and Eric got away scot-free.

Nick Bates kisses Claire – but she's about to take the money and run.

Kathy's and Jackie's honeymoon in Tunisia was the first time scenes from Emmerdale Farm *were filmed abroad – the furthest they'd got before that was Bridlington, the year before.*

The year 1988 was one of the turning points for the series. For the very first time, from 6 January, it was networked – the same episode was shown at exactly the same time in all ITV regions. This made it much easier to generate publicity for the programme (until now, national newspapers were reluctant to run stories about plots, as not all their readers would see them at the same time). A concerted push was made in London, with an extensive billboard campaign promising 'A Breath of Fresh Air on the Tube'. The London audience had always been the hardest one for the programme to crack – people in London got home later than the rest of the country, and the image of Emmerdale Farm *was of a sleepy show about rural issues that seemed a world away from London life.*

The new feel for the show was masterminded by Stuart Doughty, who left Brookside *to take up the challenge as producer, his first episodes appearing in March. He wanted to make the show more up to date, to increase the number of scenes per episode, and to perk up the cliffhangers to hook viewers into tuning in next time. He was well aware that one of the show's unique selling points was the rural setting, but also that its new prominence in the schedules meant it had to learn lessons from the newer soaps,* EastEnders *and* Brookside.

New characters were introduced to shake up the mix and to act as identification figures for the new viewers – both Sarah Connolly and the Hughes family were outsiders not used to country life who arrived to challenge the Sugdens' way of life and to make waves in the lives of Jack and Joe.

EPISODES 1313–1415

KEY EVENTS

Joe and Kate Hughes marry.

Rachel Hughes has a passionate affair
with Pete Whiteley.

Kathy loses her husband.

The Tates arrive in the village, after
buying Home Farm.

BATES

Nick confessed to taking the money from the post office raid, after deciding to turn over a new leaf.

MERRICKS

With Phil in prison, Sandie Merrick left Beckindale for Scotland.

POLLARD

There was now a vacancy for auctioneer, and Pollard managed to get his old job back. Nick Bates, who was working as a porter there, resigned in disgust.

SUGDENS

Mark Hughes decided to run away from home to live with his father in Germany. He only managed to get as far as Hull.

Kate Hughes, and her children Mark and Rachel.

Kate moved into the farmhouse with Joe in February. They were married in April in St Mary's Church, the first time that a divorcee had been married there (in fact, both Joe and Kate were divorcees). Kate was a regular churchgoer, and Reverend Hinton decided that as her first marriage had been in a register office, he could bend the rule. Joe and Kate settled down together.

Kate's daughter Rachel was more of a problem – she began an affair with Pete Whiteley, a married salesman, losing her virginity to him on her eighteenth birthday. Passionately in love, Rachel was devastated when Whiteley moved to Birmingham with his wife after only two months. She tearfully confessed everything to Kate, who firmly blamed Pete and supported her daughter.

Annie Sugden had been on tranquillisers since the Crossgill fire the previous year. Now Kathy became worried she was addicted to them. Annie would have none of it, but Henry Wilks was able to persuade her to throw them away. Annie flushed the pills down the toilet.

Jack's and Sarah's relationship hit trouble when an old friend, Gerry, invited her on holiday with him. She didn't intend to go, but was so annoyed by Jack's distrust of her that she ended up accepting.

Jack didn't help matters by rushing to Italy at the news that Marian had been charged by police with the murder of her husband, Paolo. Sarah believed this marked the end of their

A family photo as Joe Sugden married Kate Hughes.

Kathy didn't have much to smile about in 1989.

The Tates - Kim, Frank, Zoe and Chris are all smiles when they first arrive in the village.

relationship, but on Jack's return he insisted they should stay together.

KATHY

Setting something of a pattern, Kathy had a year full of death and disaster. She miscarried after catching the chiamydiapsittaci virus from a sheep. In August, her husband Jackie Merrick accidentally shot himself dead while hunting for a fox.

SKILBECK

Dolly finally left Matt, setting up home (with her son, Sam) in the village. Matt was unable to cope with his marriage ending, and left Beckindale to become the manager of a Norfolk sheep farm.

Dolly was kidnapped by Ted Sharp, who had become obsessed with her. She got away, unharmed.

TURNER

Alan Turner successfully defended his seat on the district council (this time against Kate Sugden).

He finally managed to get together with Caroline Bates, his secretary, whom he'd admired for many years. They became engaged, and wedding arrangements were well under way, but Caroline had to leave for Scarborough to look after her sick mother.

TATES

In November, uncertainty at Home Farm ended when it was bought, lock, stock and barrel, by fifty-something self-made millionaire Frank Tate. His family (young second wife Kim, son Chris and daughter Zoe) moved in. Frank Tate's approach combined the hard-headed business approach of NY Estates with the almost feudal belief in duty to the village of the Verneys. The Tates quickly established themselves as a powerful new force in village life.

ELSEWHERE

Dennis Rigg planned to open a large new quarry just outside Beckindale. This was a deeply unpopular move, but he succeeded in buying up a lot of property. Fate intervened when Rigg was gored by a bull while trespassing on Emmerdale Farm land. He died writing in agony on a large pile of manure.

Donald Hinton retired as the village vicar.

Nineteen eighty-nine saw Stuart Doughty's revamp of the show move up a gear. Most visibly, the programme's name changed from Emmerdale Farm to just Emmerdale on 14 November (Episode 1403), and there was a new version of the theme tune and opening credits.

One of his first behind the scenes changes was to the way the programme was written. Up until now, individual writers had been responsible for a block of up to six consecutive episodes. Now, a larger team of writers would do an episode each, co-ordinated by a storylining team. It led to longer-running stories, but also to a faster pace of storytelling – the number of scenes per episode rose from around fifteen to about twenty-five.

A number of long-running characters left the series – Phil Pearce, Sandie, Matt, Jackie, Mrs Bates and Donald Hinton. They were replaced with the Tates – Frank, Kim, Chris and Zoe. While Home Farm had often been the focus of stories over the years, the Tates would ensure that it would become a 'core' location, like Emmerdale Farm and the Woolpack, and would bring an unprecedented amount of glamour, wealth and boardroom intrigue to the show. It was a shift in emphasis that led to Les Dawson noting, approvingly, that the newly-revamped Emmerdale had become 'Dallas with dung'.

75

1990

KEY EVENTS

Kate Hughes is accused of murder.

Frank Tate is the new lord of the manor.

KATHY

Kathy's car was wrecked when Rachel Hughes left the handbrake off after a driving lesson and it rolled down a hill into a wall.

Kathy fell for Chris Tate, who wrote a song, 'Just This Side of Love', for her to sing at a village concert. Chris, who always had a keen eye for a business opportunity, secretly recorded the performance and had it made into a record. Kathy only found out when she heard it on the Woolpack jukebox.

SUGDENS

Joe was caught injecting beef cattle with steroids, which was illegal and prevented the stock from going to market.

Mark Hughes was caught shoplifting.

Sarah Connolly wrote off Kate's car by driving it into a concrete post in the Hotten driving test centre moments after Rachel had passed her driving test. She would later lose her job as a librarian after council cuts.

This was only the beginning of a year of hell for Kate. She suffered a miscarriage. Her ex-husband, David, showed up, trying to get back together with her. When she refused, he threatened Joe with a shotgun. After a tense stand-off, Kate convinced David to leave.

In August, Kate had a furious argument with Pete Whiteley in the Woolpack, after he resumed his affair with her daughter, Rachel. After drunkenly threatening Pete in front of practically the whole village, Kate drove home... and accidentally ran him over. With most of the village, including members of her family, assuming it had been a deliberate act, Kate was perhaps lucky to get two years in prison for manslaughter. Joe was left alone, bringing up two teenage children, and Kate made it clear she didn't want him to visit her in prison, a decision he found baffling.

Annie celebrated her seventieth birthday.

FELDMANN

Frank Tate evicted the Feldmanns (mother Elizabeth and teenage children Michael and Elsa) from their farm after their debts began to mount and the sale of livestock failed to make as much as they had hoped. Frank was owed £2000 in back rent, and suggested that the easiest way out of their problems would be to sell up.

Michael quickly found a new job at Emmerdale Farm. Elsa found herself pregnant by Nick Bates. Nick was keen to do the honourable thing and marry her, but Elizabeth was dead set against it. However, it became clear to Elizabeth that Nick and Elsa were in love, and she allowed Nick to move into their new house (although she insisted on separate rooms).

BATES

Nick soon found life at the Feldmanns' too restrictive. He started squatting in the cottage owned by Dolly in Demdyke Row, with his best mate Archie Brooks. Dolly found them out and let them stay as paying tenants. Elsa soon joined Nick, with her mother's approval.

TATES

Michael Feldmann was suspected of arson by Frank when a barn was burned down, but the culprit turned out to be another disgruntled ex-tenant, Jock McDonald.

Kathy sings 'Just This Side of Love', with Chris on keyboards.

A tanker accident closed Main Street and trapped Amos in the Woolpack cellar.

Frank was warming to the role of lord of the manor, and hosted the Hunt Ball. His thunder was stolen somewhat by the arrival of George Starkey, a truck driver sacked by Tate, who accused him very publicly of murdering his first wife, Jean, so he could marry Kim.

Frank shocked his family and the other villagers by admitting that he'd assisted Jean to commit suicide. She'd been suffering from terminal cancer.

The stress of the new job saw Frank (like Turner before him) start to drink heavily. He went on a binge rather than attend his daughter's graduation. His behaviour was covered up by Dolly, now the housekeeper at Home Farm.

Meanwhile, Kim told Frank she wanted a child, and Frank was persuaded to undergo an operation to reverse his vasectomy.

POLLARD

Pollard got engaged to Debbie Wilson, but when he gave her £2000 to open an antiques shop, she ran off with the money. This was only just desserts for Pollard – he'd hoped to fence items from Hotten market in the shop, keeping the profits for himself. He got into trouble, as he'd borrowed the money from crooked councillor Charlie Aindow.

AMOS AND MR WILKS

The Woolpack got a boost when a misprint in a guidebook told of the pub's 'welcoming ghost' instead of 'host'.

The rest of the year would not prove as positive. Amos was trapped in the cellar following an evacuation of Main Street after a chemical spill. He was rescued by Frank Tate. Amos would later suffer a mild stroke.

'Just This Side of Love', sung by Malandra Burrows, was released as a single, at the suggestion of producer Stuart Doughty, and ended up just this side of the Top Ten, at number 11.

1991

KEY EVENTS

Kathy marries Chris Tate.

Kate's and Joe's marriage breaks down.

Dolly has an affair and leaves the village.

The end of an era: Amos retires to Spain, and Mr Wilks dies shortly afterwards.

SUGDENS

Kate Sugden was released from prison after serving 12 months for the manslaughter of Pete Whiteley. But she had changed, and was unable to cope. Joe couldn't understand what was wrong with his wife. After a nervous breakdown she left Joe to live with her father in Sheffield.

Joe believed Kim was romantically interested in him, but this proved to be a mistake.

Sarah Connolly was kidnapped by Jim Latimer, the murderer and rapist who Jack had helped capture in 1973. Latimer was out for revenge and targeted Sarah, who resembled his victim, Sharon Crossthwaite. Sarah managed to stay unharmed, and was rescued.

SKILBECK

Dolly had an affair with councillor Charlie Aindow, not realising he was married. When she discovered this, he claimed the marriage was over, but Dolly saw this wasn't the case. After breaking off the affair, Dolly discovered she was pregnant. After some soul-searching – she had, after all, suffered miscarriages and a stillbirth in the past – she had an abortion. Soon afterwards, she left the village with her son for a new start in Norfolk.

FELDMANN

Nick Bates and Elsa Feldmann planned a Valentine's Day wedding at Hotten Register Office, but Elsa went into premature labour as she was heading there. Zoe Tate used all her veterinary skills to deliver baby Alice Bates at Mill Cottage.

The wedding was postponed, and Elsa found motherhood

Prison had changed Kate, and she told Joe she couldn't stay with him.

difficult. This led to tension between her and Nick. She finally left him on Christmas Eve, taking Alice with her.

Michael's year was a happier one – he started going out with Rachel Hughes after a night out commiserating with her on her sacking from Tate Haulage. Early on in the relationship, Michael had a one-night stand with Zoe Tate, but after that he was committed to Rachel. The pair became engaged in June. Rachel came to realise she wasn't ready for marriage – she preferred to go to university in Leeds.

AMOS AND MR WILKS, AND TURNER

Following his stroke, Amos decided it was time to retire to Spain. Alan Turner was keen to buy the pub, and duly did so. Henry Wilks stayed on to help out, but soon regretted it. Turner was keen to change the Woolpack, feeling that Amos and Mr Wilks had failed to keep up with the changing times. Mr Wilks, a committed traditionalist, saw Alan's 'progress' as the destruction of all he held dear.

Turner tried his best to move the pub upmarket, but not everything he tried was popular. When Ephraim Monk, the brewery, had supply problems, Turner switched to the rival Skipdale beer – and provoked Seth into organising a mass walkout. Alan soon reverted to Ephraim Monk.

In August, Alan was shocked when a policewoman arrived and handcuffed him. It quickly became clear this was a stripper, organised by Seth as a birthday surprise.

Alan opened a restaurant in the old taproom, and began hiring barmaids – Caroline Bates and Elizabeth Feldmann at first, then newcomer Carol Nelson.

Sadly, Henry Wilks died of a heart attack in October.

TATES

Zoe was becoming involved in animal rights issues, spurred on by her close friendship with Archie Brooks. When a march she was on ended up picketing the veterinary surgery she worked at, Bennetts, she resigned. Shortly after that, she decided to move to New Zealand to become a flying vet.

Frank hit trouble, with Tate Haulage losing money and running into debt. He considered desperate measures – insurance fraud by stealing one of his own lorries, but Kim came to the rescue by selling one of the horses from the stud farm.

Kathy and Chris marry.

Despite appearances, Turner feels at home with bikers.

Frank began to plan the opening of the holiday village. His first obstacle was crooked councillor Charlie Aindow, who wanted a bribe to allow the planning permission to go through. He and Kim outsmarted him – and all he got was a briefcase full of horse manure.

KATHY

Kathy Merrick married Chris, but only after dallying with curate Tony Charlton. Chris's and Kathy's November wedding was a register office do, but there was a lavish reception afterwards at Home Farm, laid on by Frank Tate who even arranged for them to travel back from Hotten in a helicopter. In a further act of generosity, Frank bought them Mill Cottage as a wedding present.

POLLARD

Pollard had to sell his car to pay back the £2000 he'd borrowed from Charlie Aindow.

ELSEWHERE

Pete Whiteley's widow, Lynn, gave birth to their child on the day of his funeral, 28 August. She named her son Peter after his father. Bill Whiteley, her father-in-law, had died the month before.

Ronald Magill decided to retire this year, and Amos Brearly was written out, also retiring to Spain. He would pop back to the series a few times. In August, Arthur Pentelow, who played Mr Wilks, died of a heart attack. Once again, it took a few months for the recorded programme to catch up with reality, and Mr Wilks passed away in October.

Morag Bain started a two-year stint as producer in December.

KEY EVENTS

The holiday village opens.

Pollard falls in love with Elizabeth Feldmann.

Kim has an affair.

ELSEWHERE

Elsa returned, dumping Alice with her father, Nick Bates. Elsa was finding it difficult to socialise while being a single mother. Nick proved up to the task of fatherhood, and the baby's grandmothers, Caroline Bates and Elizabeth Feldmann, pitched in, as did Archie Brooks, who moved in with Nick to become a full-time childminder.

Nick and Archie were also lucky in love, dating (respectively) Julie Bramhope and Lindsay Carmichael.

SUGDENS/HUGHES

Jack tried his best to help Lynn Whiteley, but Lynn misread this as romantic interest. Sarah wasn't worried – until Lynn engineered a more intimate evening. Sarah publicly humiliated Lynn in the Woolpack by setting her straight about what Jack thought about

Annie fell for Leonard Kempinski, and Pollard married Elizabeth Feldmann.

her. It was several months before Lynn was coaxed back into the village by Archie Brooks.

Once again, Joe Sugden left Emmerdale Farm to work at Home Farm, this time as the manager of Frank Tate's new holiday village. Joe's stepchildren refused to move with him to Dolly Skilbeck's old flat.

Joe had to fend off the advances of one of the teen visitors to the holiday village, Poppy Bruce.

Kim and Neil Kincaid.

Rachel moved new fiancé Michael Feldmann into Emmerdale Farm, but soon came to realise she'd outgrown him and broke off the engagement. Shortly afterwards she dated her friend Sangeeta's brother, Jayesh.

Mark Hughes split with his girlfriend after realising he wouldn't be going to university. Instead he became a handyman at the holiday village, where he met new love Lisa.

Annie had an admirer whom she'd met during a winter visit to Spain, but was very coy about telling the rest of her family. Towards the end of the year, she shocked them by announcing she wanted to sell her share in the farm. When her new beau, Leonard Kempinski, arrived in the village, Jack wasn't the only family member who suspected that he was after Annie's money. Leonard was upset by this, and planned to leave – and Amos revealed that he was living in Spain as a tax exile, and was very wealthy indeed. Leonard spent Christmas with the Sugdens, and proposed to Annie. They returned to Spain together at the end of the year.

POLLARD/FELDMANN

Pollard was becoming far mellower, this new kindness and generosity best seen as he wooed Elizabeth Feldmann. Turner tried to warn Elizabeth away from Eric, but she fell for his charms. However, she was a little taken aback to discover within days that Pollard was using her home as a forwarding address and storage space for his antiques business.

Michael, Elizabeth's son, was dead set against the relationship, and went as far as punching Pollard to make his point.

By the 20th anniversary, the show had a large regular cast.

Frank threw Kim out of Home Farm – literally.

Michael found it difficult to cope with being dumped by Rachel, and had a further setback when Frank Tate wouldn't let him become the new tenant at Winslow's Farm. Michael was talked into taking his revenge by joining in with a robbery on Home Farm, but this ended in violence when Joe Sugden was clubbed unconscious.

Pollard thwarted the raid by shopping the gang when they tried to offload the goods. Michael wasn't with the rest of the robbers, but the police caught up with him – ironically at the end of Pollard's and Elizabeth's wedding ceremony at St Mary's.

Emmerdale celebrated its 20th anniversary this year, with any number of commentators noting that the programme had changed over the years. New producer Morag Bain was happy to play up the idea that people's preconceived ideas about the programme were wrong. Perhaps noting the sustained success Australian soaps had at getting younger viewers to watch soaps, 1992 saw a concerted effort to attract younger viewers to Emmerdale *– the holiday village providing a new focus for teenage characters.*

This was capped with a press campaign that could only be described as 'raunchy'. Posters of the younger cast members in their underwear or, in the case of Matthew Vaughn (Michael Feldmann) no underwear at all, helped the programme shed the staid image it had.

One of the teens to pass through the programme this year was Poppy Bruce, played by Anna Friel, who went on to play Beth in Brookside, *before launching a film career. Angela Griffin and Michelle Holmes, now familiar faces from* Coronation Street *also appeared in small roles.*

TATES

The holiday village opened, marking an upturn in the fortunes of the Tates.

Kim set up a new pony-trekking venture for the holiday village. Soon afterwards, she accused young Robert Sugden of leaving a gate open, allowing one of the ponies onto the road, where it was hit by a car. This was just one of a series of disputes as holidaymakers from the village started to trample over Emmerdale Farm land.

Kim became pregnant, but lost the baby in a fall from a horse at the Hotten Show. After this, she decided she no longer wanted children.

While she was laid up with a broken leg, the Right Honourable Neil Kincaid, the local Master of Hounds, helped out at Home Farm. He helped Frank with plans to set up a working farm for the holiday village. He worked closely with Kim, running the stables – and the two quickly became lovers.

Frank suspected nothing until Christmas, when he saw Kim had bought an expensive men's watch... which after Christmas turned up on Kincaid's wrist. He threw Kim out in just the clothes she was wearing (which, unfortunately for her, was a tiny cocktail dress). After a couple of years' abstinence, this was enough to have Frank start drinking heavily again.

1993

KEY EVENTS

Frank goes off the rails.

Zoe Tate comes out as a lesbian.

Kathy has an affair.

The plane crash devastates the village.

TATES

Frank took the New Year Hunt as an opportunity to horsewhip Neil Kincaid for having an affair with his wife. As Frank's drinking problems became more pronounced, he took revenge on Kim by cutting up her dresses and starting to sell off her beloved horses. When Kim and Neil attempted to take her favourite horse, Dark Star, Frank threatened them with a shotgun. He would have shot Dark Star, but Zoe grabbed the gun. When she heard what Frank had been planning, Kathy took the horse straight round to Kim.

Frank's erratic behaviour started to have serious consequences. On a whim he sacked Joe, simply for talking to Kim in the street. He did so in front of his bank manager, who wasn't impressed by Frank's behaviour and who withdrew financial help. Chris attempted to drum up business, and was on the verge of signing another deal – until Frank drunkenly drove into the new client's car.

Frank Tate took public revenge on Neil Kincaid.

Life as an aristocrat's mistress didn't live up to Kim's expectations – he was embarrassed by her sense of taste and the fact her mother had been a hairdresser. She left Kincaid. Despite everything, Frank was hoping for a reconciliation, but Kim just wanted a divorce. She started tightening the screws on Frank, threatening to use her shareholding to demand that he step down from control of Tate Holdings. Chris saw an opportunity, and mortgaged Mill Cottage to buy her shares for a quarter of a million pounds. Chris now had control of Tate Haulage. Frank drunkenly confronted Kathy in the Woolpack over this – the first she'd heard of it – and was barred. At his new local, in Hotten, he managed to get himself arrested after a brawl.

Kim bought her own stables with the money Chris raised. Meanwhile, Chris lost control of Tate Haulage when his father outmanoeuvred him, was completely hopeless as Joe's replacement managing the holiday village and ended up starting his own haulage business, which initially just had one truck.

Frank stopped drinking when an old sweetheart, Ruth Jameson, turned up. While Frank was keen to rekindle the flame, Ruth realised that Frank really wanted to get back with Kim.

Zoe Tate and Archie Brooks had been seeing each other for a long time, but hadn't slept together. They finally did, but Zoe confessed to Archie that she had been questioning her sexuality and this had been a test. Soon afterwards, she told her father she was a lesbian. His reaction was surprising: he was completely supportive. Impressed, Zoe teamed up with Frank in the boardroom – using her shares in the company to vote down threats from Chris.

Zoe and Archie were seeing each other - but Zoe was beginning to question her sexuality.

KATHY

Kathy discovered that Kim and Neil were having an affair, and left her job at the stables. She became Chris's secretary at Tate Haulage. Chris suspected her of having an affair – but she was secretly taking lessons to get a heavy goods vehicle licence.

Kathy wasn't impressed when she learned Chris had mortgaged their house without telling her. She moved into another room and took a job at the Woolpack wine bar. Before long she was indeed having an affair, with wine merchant Josh Lewis.

TURNER

Caroline Bates returned, and Turner renewed his relationship with her – going as far as proposing. Caroline turned him down and tried to get him out a bit more, something he continued to do even after Caroline left the village again. One place he went to was a drop-in centre. One of the women working there, Shirley Foster, caught his eye. At first she found him snobbish and arrogant, but

Turner was deeply affected by the death of Tina, one of the homeless who used the centre. Shirley warmed to this new, caring Turner, and romance blossomed. It was a huge shock when he discovered that Shirley had once been a prostitute, but he came to realise that she meant a lot to him.

The drop-in centre closed due to cuts. Turner employed Shirley as a barmaid at the Woolpack.

SUGDENS

Emmerdale Farm suffered serious subsidence problems, manifested at first by minor symptoms, like finding doors sticking and small cracks in the walls, but it all came to a head when a huge hole opened up under Jack's tractor. The farmhouse had to be abandoned – Jack and Sarah eventually deciding that Hawthorn Cottage would serve as a replacement.

Annie was in Spain during this drama, and when she returned, she was horrified that the Sugdens had abandoned the

Kathy decided the best way to help Chris at the lorry yard was by earning her HGV licence

ELSEWHERE

Lorraine Nelson was causing problems. Her father Derek was violent towards her, but the police had insufficient evidence to prosecute. She took this badly, and started committing petty thefts. She got a place in art college, and left.

Dr Bernard McAllister became the villagers' new GP. His wife Angharad, and children Luke and Jessica accompanied him. Angharad became headmistress of Hotten Comprehensive.

FELDMANN

Elizabeth found a Roman bracelet at the fish farm, and got Pollard to sell it, even though legally it belonged to Frank Tate because it had been found on his land. The £15,000 paid off her debts and started a trust fund for Alice.

Michael Feldmann violated his bail conditions by following Rachel and her new boyfriend Jayesh. Luckily this meant he was in the right place at the right time to see Robert Sugden fall into the river – he dived in and saved the boy. Despite Michael's reputation, Jack rewarded him with a job at the farm. However, Michael was sentenced to four months in prison soon afterwards for his involvement in the Home Farm robbery. Rachel renewed her links with him, though, visiting him and writing to him in prison. On his release, Jayesh found him a job in Leeds.

POLLARD

When Steve Marshal was released, he swore revenge on Pollard, cutting the brakes of his car. Nick Bates pulled Pollard from the burning wreckage. Again the police had insufficient evidence to prosecute Marshal, but he was driven from town by a gang of villagers.

Elizabeth was worried when cheques disappeared from the

family home. She refused to move into the new farmhouse, instead staying with Kathy and Chris at Mill Cottage before buying Tenant House in the village itself. She was placated by Amos's suggestion that Hawthorn Cottage was be renamed Emmerdale Farm.

Annie was still seeing Leonard Kempinski, but refused his proposal of marriage. She changed her mind later in the year and began making wedding plans. In October, they married. Donald Hinton, retired vicar and guest at the wedding, stepped in to officiate when Reverend Johnson lost his voice.

Sarah became pregnant.

Joe started an affair with Lynn Whiteley, leading to family tensions – his stepdaughter Rachel had had an affair with Lynn's late husband. These tensions eventually proved too much, and Joe and Lynn split.

WINDSORS

The Windsor family arrived from Essex. Vic and Viv Windsor bought the post office and moved in with their children Scott, Kelly and Donna.

A new 'brat pack' of characters in their early twenties were brought in, or brought more to the fore. The way was led by Noah Huntley and Camilla Power as brother and sister Luke and Jessica McAllister.

In another attempt to appeal to a southern audience, the Windsor family were brought in – townies from Essex, they were outsiders coming to Emmerdale, asking the questions many of the city-dwelling viewers must have been asking. To some long-term fans of the series, it represented a dilution of the Yorkshire flavour of the programme. But there was more location shooting than ever before, and the programme was reflecting the change in the real countryside – previously it had been an insular place of agricultural work, now living in the country was increasingly becoming a lifestyle choice for the well-off.

It was clear the programme was going from strength to strength. Ironically, one of the signs of this was a return to the show's original lunchtime slot for networked repeats of the previous day's episode.

Almost unnoticed among the upheavals and sensational stories, the Sugdens moved out of Emmerdale Farm. The original farmhouse had been sold on the retirement of the farmer who'd always allowed filming on his land. A new farm was found, and the Sugdens moved in the series.

Turner and Mrs Bates.

Home Farm cheque book. At Christmas, when she discovered Pollard was responsible, she threw him out onto the street.

SETH

Seth's wife Meg became seriously ill. The villagers rallied round to help out, but she died of a stroke later in the year. Seth found it hard to cope with the loss. Pollard attempted to con Seth by buying a tin of valuable predecimal currency of Meg's for far less than it was worth, but Elizabeth persuaded him to hand over the true value.

Seth didn't want to go back to an empty cottage, but quickly realised the opportunities which playing the sympathy card would bring. He stayed with Elizabeth Feldmann, Turner and at Nick's and Archie's cottage, secretly pleased for the free board and lodging, before eventually returning home.

Seth had prostate problems, and Turner organised a fund-raising evening for him at the Woolpack.

THE PLANE CRASH

It had been an eventful year in Beckindale, but everything that had happened in 1993 was overshadowed on 30 December, when an Eastern European passenger jet exploded over the village.

Everyone on board (several hundred people) was killed instantly, and the village and the surrounding fields were showered with debris, bodies, engine parts, burning fuel and – surreally – flowers (the airliner's hold had been full of them). The impact of the larger pieces of metal ruptured power lines, phone lines and gas mains, causing further explosions and destroying the main bridge into the village.

Joe Sugden was driving Leonard Kempinski and Annie to the airport at the time. A section of wing from the plane hit their car, killing Leonard, putting Annie in a coma and seriously injuring Joe.

Mark Hughes was killed in the fire that engulfed Whiteley's Farm. He had been there simply to return a vacuum cleaner. Lynn Whitely and baby Peter barely escaped the flames.

Archie Brooks was apparently vaporised by exploding fuel. His body was never found. The hillside where he was killed was renamed Archie Rise.

Elizabeth Pollard also died that night. She had been intending to tell the police about her husband's cheque fraud, and the two had argued earlier. It's unclear exactly how she died – Pollard was found in the disaster scene, dazed, saying she was dead.

There was a huge explosion outside the Woolpack. Every window was shattered and the wine bar was destroyed, burying everyone inside under tons of rubble.

Kim's stables were hit by one of the larger sections of wreckage. Frank, there to give Kim a late Christmas present, had to hold her back from going into the inferno. Despite the efforts of Frank and Vic Windsor to fight the fire, the horses died, horrifically.

Jack and Sarah watched the devastation from their vantage point at Emmerdale Farm, scared and unable to comprehend what was happening. Jack hurried down to the disaster scene, and – with Frank – co-ordinated rescue efforts. They set up a

(top left) Frank watched his stables destroyed in the fireball. (bottom left) Archie Brooks is killed when jet fuel ignites.

(above) The Woolpack took a direct hit, and the bar was completely demolished.

temporary bridge using concrete pipes, which allowed the emergency services through.

A number of properties had been completely demolished. Demdyke Row was all but destroyed. The night was a tense wait for many – baby Alice Bates was eventually found in the rubble of Nick's house. Chris Tate wasn't so lucky – he was found alive in the ruins of the wine bar, but had been left paralysed. Villagers feared the worst for Seth, whose house had been destroyed. The body of his dog, Smokey, was found. Seth had sought refuge with an old flame, Betty Eagleton. Turner, in particular, was delighted to see him alive again.

THE PLANE CRASH

The plane crash remains one of Emmerdale's – one of British television's – best-remembered dramatic moments. Although it brought a boost in viewing figures, reports that the episodes were the highest-rated ever for the show weren't true at the time, and the ratings have certainly been higher on occasions since. That said, the plane crash gained a huge amount of press coverage and was the first, and is probably still the most successful, of British soaps' 'event' stories.

The plane crash was devised by series consultant Phil Redmond, creator of Brookside and Grange Hill, who had been brought in to attract new viewers and who worked with new producer Nicholas Prosser. It had clearly been on his mind for some time before Emmerdale hired him – in Soapbox, a 1988 book about soap opera, he'd joked that Brookside could have 'an IRA cell in one of the houses, or the Palestine Liberation Front at work, or a jumbo jet crashing in the street'.

There were concerns at the time about the insensitivity of broadcasting the episodes just days before the fifth anniversary of the Lockerbie disaster on which the plane crash story was clearly based. The production team, though, had talked to support groups such as Friends of Flight 103. An education pack, Emmerdale Rescue, was sent to schools to teach pupils about the role of the emergency services and the experiences of people in Lockerbie.

The episodes presented an unprecedented challenge for Emmerdale's regular special effects designer Ian Rowley. There are a surprising number of special effects requirements for a normal block of Emmerdale episodes – fires, explosions, car crashes, breaking glass. The plane crash episodes had a vast number of all of these, often in the same scene, and the special effects budget for the episodes came to about £1 million. Effects shots ranged from a controlled explosion on the studio Woolpack set, to the creation of rubble for the Woolpack exteriors. In another scene, a burning wing swooped down, forcing Joe Sugden's car off the road. The most spectacular effect, though, was almost certainly the fireball hitting Kim's stables, triggering a series of explosions. The crash episodes took three weeks to record, most of it shot at night in freezing temperatures.

A video Emmerdale – The Rescue, an edited compilation of the episodes, was released to the sell-through market in 1994.

Beckindale was devastated by the plane crash – but the real-life location Esholt survived unscathed.

1994

KEY EVENTS

The village comes to terms with the plane crash.

Beckindale is renamed Emmerdale.

Joe Sugden leaves the village for good.

New arrivals include the infamous Dingle clan.

THE PLANE CRASH - AFTERMATH

Clearly the events of the end of 1993 would dominate the village for some time. Village life struggled to get back to normal as clearing up, and a string of funeral services, continued.

To mark the new start, the villagers agreed that Beckindale should be renamed Emmerdale – a mark of respect for the Sugdens and all they had done for the village.

WHITELEY

Less happily, Lynn Whiteley sold her story to tabloid journalist Gavin Watson. They also embarked on what Gavin would undoubtedly have called a 'steamy affair'. Watson was only interested in the story – as soon as tabloid interest died down he left the village, and Lynn, behind.

Lynn opened a country club in Emmerdale, which had a memorable opening night – including male strippers, the Nobbies. Lynn wasn't to stay for long – she left for Australia with sheep-shearer Sven Olsen.

Pollard helps Frank unveil a memorial to the dead - but is happy to rob the memorial fund.

BATES

Nick Bates spent time in hospital, temporarily blinded, and traumatised by seeing Archie die. Elsa reclaimed custody of Alice and attempted to make this permanent, spreading the rumour that Nick and Archie had been gay lovers and exaggerating incidents where Alice was endangered. The court didn't agree, and custody was reawarded to Nick.

TATES

Kim and Frank were able to put their problems into perspective. Frank had saved Kim's life, and the two got back together early in the New Year. Kim took over the running of the game farm, and helped Frank set up the model farm.

Frank suffered a heart attack while driving, an experience that nearly killed him.

Kim and Frank decided to remarry, and had a huge ceremony at Ripon Cathedral, followed by a lavish party for the whole village. They then left for a honeymoon in Hawaii.

Seth considers a career change as the country club hires male strippers for its opening night.

The McAllisters.

Kim and Frank remarry.

KATHY

Kathy had planned to leave Chris for Josh Lewis, but became racked with guilt at seeing him in a wheelchair. She stuck with her husband.

On their third wedding anniversary, she saw Chris and Rachel kissing. Rachel had become a shoulder for Chris to cry on.

Kathy became obsessed with Bernard McAllister, but he was having none of it – he was faithful to his wife.

SUGDENS

Emmerdale Farm suffered in the aftermath of the plane crash – most of the livestock had been killed, and the fields had been polluted with fuel and other poisonous waste. Toxins got deep into the soil – even after an expensive clean-up it would be many years before the land would recover. It ended Jack's plans to switch to more lucrative – and just as importantly for Jack, more ethical – organic farming.

Joe had lost a stepson, Mark, and his new stepfather Leonard. His mother Annie remained in a coma for months. Joe became depressed. When Donna was injured by a tractor, and Viv threatened to sue, Joe found himself in a barn, pointing a shotgun at himself. Vic Windsor talked him out of suicide, but enough was enough for Joe – he left for Spain shortly afterwards.

Annie recovered consciousness just in time to see her new granddaughter, Victoria, the daughter of Jack and Sarah. The pair married in May, and Annie was able to attend.

Victoria was soon rushed to hospital, and was found to have a heart defect. Relations between Jack and Sarah were strained – she was becoming just a farmer's wife, something she'd dreaded. Sarah left Emmerdale with Victoria, but Jack tracked her down to York, and persuaded her to return – and Sarah convinced him to treat her a little better.

GLOVERS

Ned and Jan Glover and their children Dave, Linda and Roy Glover arrived in the village.

TURNER

Shirley Foster helped Turner to cope with the disaster and to refurbish the Woolpack, which had been heavily damaged. They married in February, leaving the register office in a pony and trap. Shirley noticeably mellowed Turner.

But it was not to last long. Shirley was shot dead after a raid on the post office. Viv's ex-husband Reg Dawson arrived in the village with a gang of masked robbers. They made their getaway with Viv and Shirley – who was passing – as hostages. Turner was

Turner marries Shirley Foster, having come to terms with her past – again, happiness would be short-lived.

injured by a stray bullet. Barricading themselves in at Home Farm, the raiders became scared. Reg accidentally shot one of his accomplices. When he was about to kill Viv, Shirley stepped in, and died in her place. Police marksmen stormed the house, shooting Reg dead.

Turner couldn't cope, and hit the bottle. The Woolpack suffered without Turner (and Shirley) there, and Pollard attempted to capitalise on this by manipulating Turner into signing the pub over to him.

Six months after the plane crash, the post office raid was another 'explosive storyline' concocted by Nicholas Prosser and Phil Redmond. Both it and the plane crash earned censure from the ITC, the standards watchdog, this year.

Frazer Hines left the programme, leaving Sheila Mercer (Annie) as the only remaining original member of cast. Madeline Howard left, but Sarah Sugden was recast, and when Jack tracked Sarah down in York he found she now looked like actress Alyson Spiro.

While there were departures, the cast continued to expand, with the introduction of the Glovers, Biff Fowler and Betty Eagleton.

Eagle-eyed viewers now would spot Melanie Brown, Mel B of the Spice Girls, as an extra in one episode. Mel was born in Leeds, and her younger sister would appear as a regular in the show in 1998.

Claire King, who played Kim, and Peter Amory, who played her stepson Chris, married in real life in July this year.

The Swedish group The Cardigans released their debut album this year – and it was called Emmerdale. *The series has been popular in Scandinavia since the mid-1970s.*

Nicholas Prosser left the programme, and was replaced as producer by Mervyn Watson.

POLLARD

Michael Feldmann became suspicious when Pollard insisted on a quick cremation for Elizabeth. Without any evidence, Michael accused Pollard of murdering his mother. He attacked Pollard, apparently killing him. Terrified, he took Pollard's car, which was later found at the airport. Pollard was merely unconscious, and had seen off one threat to his position. Another was soon to emerge.

Pollard's first wife, Eileen, arrived and started to blackmail Pollard – his marriage to Elizabeth had been bigamous, and if that news got out, he could lose out on the insurance money on his second wife's death.

That wasn't the only way Pollard gained from the plane crash – he sold a painting donated to the disaster fund for £175,000, but only paid the fund £15,000.

Pollard also executed a textbook robbery of Briardale Hall, stealing a king's ransom's worth of goods while using Turner as an alibi. He'd invited Turner for a meal, then drugged the food, causing him to fall asleep. When the police asked, Turner told them Pollard had been with him the whole time.

Pollard also tried to make money on a land deal, when Councillor Hawkins proposed building an open prison on Betty Eagleton's land. Pollard tried to get Betty to sell up, and when she declined, he spun a yarn about how much money she

Seth and Betty didn't get married – but a forties theme party was near enough.

could make if a rave were held on the land. In the event, the rave was a disaster

SETH

Seth and Betty quickly established themselves as a couple. They planned to marry in December, but called it off – they felt the formality was unnecessary. Instead they had a 1940s-themed party. The two had been sweethearts during the war and had almost married in 1944 – although Betty had left him for Wally Eagleton.

DINGLES

At the rave, Ben Dingle, member of a family of local yobs, and

Luke and Ben Dingle fight.

his friends started a fight with Luke, Biff and the other bikers, resulting in Ben's death.

Luke was arrested for murder, but was lucky to get off the hook when it transpired that Ben had been suffering from a fatal condition, and it had been that which had killed him.

The Dingles swore revenge on the McAllisters, and this culminated in a huge fight outside the Woolpack that seemed to involve every young person in the village.

For Bernard McAllister, this was the last straw, and he made plans to leave the village.

The feud between the Dingles and the rest of the village ended with farm worker Ned Glover and Dingle patriarch Zak in a bare-knuckle fight. Ned won a hard-fought and bitter contest, and the Dingles retreated.

BIFF

Jessica fell for Biff Fowler, a biker mate of her brother's. Biff had slept with Jessica's friend Dolores, who was now seeing Luke.

Biff became a handyman at Home Farm, but was warned to steer clear of Jessica's anti-hunt activities. Jessica was almost trampled by a horse at one demonstration.

1995

KEY EVENTS

Tina Dingle jilts Luke at the altar.

Joe Sugden dies in a Spanish car crash.

Kathy and Dave Glover become lovers.

KATHY

Chris and Rachel moved into Mill Cottage. Kathy returned to the house from Scarborough and discovered Chris proposing to Rachel, who was pregnant. Kathy made it clear to Chris that she would fight for a large divorce settlement, and that she wouldn't leave the cottage until she got it.

Dave made a move on Kathy, but she didn't want to jeopardise her divorce settlement, or embark on a new relationship so soon after leaving Chris. In May, Kathy accepted £120,000 from Chris, and decided to invest it in buying the Old School House, which she converted into tearooms. Her first employees were Betty Eagleton and Dolores Sharp.

With her divorce finalised, Kathy and Dave became lovers, and quickly got engaged. However, she was unaware that Dave had started an affair with Kim while he'd been waiting for the divorce to come through, and that he was continuing it now. When Kathy discovered the truth, she called off their engagement.

SUGDENS

Rachel collapsed and went into labour at the news that her stepfather Joe had been killed in a Spanish car crash. Only Kathy was around, and she comforted Rachel, who was giving birth six weeks prematurely. It became a bonding experience for the two women, who became best friends – but kept that fact secret from Chris. The baby, Joseph Mark Hughes, was born healthy.

Annie returned from Spain with Joe's body for the funeral. Joe's share of the farm went to Annie, who passed it on to baby Joseph in trust until his eighteenth birthday. Soon afterwards, Annie proposed to Amos, and the two married in Spain that November.

Sarah started working for Professor Andrew McKinnon, helping him with research for a book. Jack suspected them of having an affair, and followed her. On one occasion, he left Robert alone in the car while he tried to catch them together – and Robert wandered off.

The Sugdens received a phone call saying if they wanted to see Robert again, they'd have to pay a £5000 ransom. The police traced the call to Sam Dingle – who didn't really have Robert. It had just been a crude attempt to make money. He was given a suspended sentence. Robert turned up safe – he was with a hermit, Derek Simpson, who was looking after him.

TATES

Chris and Rachel settled down together with their new son. Frank proved to be an attentive grandfather – a little too attentive, and when he arranged for the infant to be enrolled in a private school without her knowledge, Rachel argued with him. Chris and Rachel married in December, their service a marked contrast to Chris's and Kathy's – another register office do, this was only attended by Joseph, Jack and Sarah.

Zoe began exploring her new sexuality, quickly falling for interior designer Emma Nightingale. The two moved into Smithy Cottage together.

Now openly 'out', Zoe was attacked by one of her clients, Ken Adlington, who was convinced she just needed a good man. Zoe escaped, but the police wouldn't press charges. Frank and Ned Glover made it clear to Adlington that he wouldn't be welcome in the village in the future.

Rachel Hughes and Chris Tate moved in to Mill Cottage.

Producer Mervyn Watson felt that the show lacked comedy, and reintroduced Zak and Butch Dingle and expanded the clan to fulfil that function. Nellie Dingle, Zak's wife, was played by Sandra Gough, who'd previously appeared in the series as Malt Shovel barmaid Doreen Shuttleworth.

Ian Botham appeared as himself to reopen the Woolpack, as did Hunter, from the ITV programme Gladiators.

Billy Hartman, who plays Terry, joined the programme this year. He had previously appeared as Duncan MacLeod's uncle in the cult fantasy film Highlander.

Frank hired Dave Glover as assistant farm manager.

Kim seduced Dave, and their affair was conducted just out of sight of Frank – in the stables, in a Leeds hotel, at Home Farm when Frank was out. Oblivious to what was going on, Frank did notice that Dave was spending a lot of time on the estate – and gave him a bonus!

Frank was delighted when it became clear Kim was pregnant, but overheard Dave and Biff discussing who the father was. Frank hit the bottle once more, and this led to liver failure and hospitalisation. Returning home, he caught Kim and Dave together – which led to him collapsing and being rushed back to hospital.

Battle was joined for control of the Tate empire – Kim won comprehensively, and got Chris disinherited.

Annie returned to bury Joe in Emmerdale

The village was coming to accept Zoe and Emma's relationship.

Dave Glover spent much of the year in a state of undress

Tina Dingle gets ready to walk up the aisle with Luke McAllister – but she's got no intention of marrying him.

GLOVERS

Linda Glover took up a job as the receptionist at Zoe's surgery. She was soon invited to Amsterdam for a naughty weekend by one of the clients, Danny Weir – who, it turned out, was the son of local bigwig Lady Weir. The romance continued for some time – until Linda read in the paper that Danny was engaged to Libby Foster-Cuthbert.

Linda was pregnant by this time. She attempted to abort the

The McAllister Dingle feud was resolved, in the worst possible way.

baby using drugs from the vet's surgery, which left her seriously ill in hospital. Ned Glover, her father, confronted Danny at home, pushing him into the swimming pool, then jumping in to finish him off. Dave Glover arrived in time to intervene and save the young man.

Linda was soon back on her feet, and fell for Biff Fowler.

McALLISTER

Bernard and Angharad left Emmerdale, fed up with the feud with the Dingles. Things came to a head when it became clear Angharad would have to teach Tina Dingle. Meanwhile, Kathy's interest in Bernard had practically become stalking.

Jessica didn't accept the decision to leave, and ran off with Biff. She lost her virginity to him, but soon returned to her family, and left the village with them.

Luke stayed behind, and with the rest of his family gone he had the family home to himself. Without family pressure, he was able to have a relationship with Tina Dingle, and the two conducted a secret affair.

Jessica visited in April, and was shocked by this development. She phoned the Dingles to tell them. It was too late – Tina was pregnant. Luke suddenly began to realise that his life had changed: this was underlined when he missed an A-level exam because Tina had stomach pains. Tina also sold a valuable grandfather clock belonging to his father to raise money.

Tina and Luke still planned to get married and set a date for July. Tina turned up in a tiny (leather!) wedding dress, and ditched him at the altar. She'd never intended to marry him, she'd never been pregnant – she was just out for revenge for the death of her brother.

A few weeks later, Luke bundled Tina into his car, driving off, intending to have it out with her. The car crashed, and Luke was killed. Tina survived, and was grief-stricken. The McAllister–Dingle feud was resolved, in the worst possible way.

DINGLES

This year saw the first appearances of Mandy Dingle, Zak's niece. She first arrived at Luke's and Tina's wedding – chatting Luke up

The Dingles aren't worried about fitting in with the rest of the village.

the two became lovers. She left him soon afterwards, when she realised how he was using Turner's grief to milk the Woolpack accounts for money. Frank Tate found a novel way to punish Pollard, crushing his car in front of the pub.

WOOLPACK

Turner asked Emma Nightingale to revamp the Woolpack. This would be a costly process, so Turner asked the Ephraim Monk brewery to help cover the costs. A little wary of Turner, given his record, they requested that Turner employed a bar manager to cope with the day-to-day running of the pub. Turner agreed, hiring Terry and Britt Woods, a married couple who'd run a bar in Benidorm.

Ian Botham reopened the pub in February. Nellie Dingle won a competition for a 'free meal for all the family' – and the next night brought twelve Dingles to claim her prize. Turner reluctantly fed them – and the Dingles have been customers in the Woolpack ever since.

Terry sold Seth's and Vic's moonshine in the pub. Turner threatened to sack him when he found out. Britt intervened, and Turner accepted her plan for her to become sole bar manager, with Terry becoming just a barman. This, in turn, put a strain on their marriage.

Things became even more strained when Britt's father, Ronnie, turned up. Britt had told Terry her father was dead – what had really happened was that Ronnie had abused her, and she'd run away. Terry felt betrayed: he could have helped her if he'd known the truth.

Britt was looking for a new start – she was offered the management of a flagship pub in York. Terry refused to go, and was surprised when Britt went without him. Terry became manager of the Woolpack again, and – after the briefest of liaisons with Tina Dingle – found romance with _Hotten Courier_ journalist Helen Ackroyd.

ELSEWHERE

Terry Woods and Vic Windsor were quickly becoming good friends, and came up with a plan to hire strippers for a sportsmen's dinner at the village hall. Their wives found out – and gave them the fright of their lives by changing places with the strippers, coming out onto the stage, then literally pouring cold water over their husbands.

once it became clear the wedding was off.

Her next visit was in October. Frank Tate had attempted to evict the Dingles, promising the Holdgates' Farm (of which the Dingle barn was an outbuilding) to the Glovers. He was surprised when the villagers – pretty well all of whom had had run-ins with the clan in the past – rallied round. Even Chris supported the Dingles as the bailiffs moved in. Mandy helped man the barricades.

Frank let the Dingles stay on, but started charging them rent.

A month later, Nellie returned to Ireland to look after her sick father. Tina was left as the woman of the household, much to her annoyance.

POLLARD

Pollard capitalised on Caroline Bates's return to the village, and

EPISODES 2040–2146

KEY EVENTS

Kim's and Dave's affair ends in tragedy.

Terry and Viv have an affair.

Lisa brings new love into Zak Dingle's life.

TATES

Chris began demonstrating greed and ruthlessness on a scale that scared his wife Rachel. She walked out on him, returning to Emmerdale Farm, although she soon went back to Chris.

Another test for the marriage came with the arrival of Steve Marchant, a friend of Rachel from university who was now an investment banker. He had moved into the village with girlfriend Faye Clarke, but quickly moved her to a job in New York so he could concentrate his attentions on Rachel. He asked Rachel to help run his business. Rachel decided on a change of image and discovered a campaigning streak. Unfortunately she usually ended up demonstrating against Frank – she manned the barricades at the Dingle eviction, and was active in trying to prevent the quarry expansion. Chris threw her out.

Zoe and Emma decided to make their relationship more formal. This plan for a 'gay wedding' raised the hackles of a number of villagers, including Turner. But the plan came off the rails when Emma's ex-lover Susie turned up. At first Zoe was jealous – then she fell for Susie, and left Emma on the day of the ceremony. Emma left the village – and Susie followed soon afterwards, after cheating on Zoe.

Kim called in all the loans Frank had given Chris over the years.

Frank, though, was outdoing both of them. He knew about Kim's affair with Dave, and that Dave might be the father of her child. He let a cottage out to Dave, but planted hidden cameras in it, connected to his computer. Frank walked in on Dave and Kim while they were in bed together. He fired Dave and threw him out of the house, and tried to loosen Kim's grip on his company. Kim, though, simply moved Dave into Home Farm. Dave quickly got fed up of the rows between Kim and Frank, and moved to Annie's cottage. Kim moved in with him, but the age and social difference – and the comedown for Kim after living in Home Farm – strained the relationship.

Frank came up with a new offer – he'd give Kim a million

Emma and Zoe have their relationship blessed but – as the picture suggests – Susie's about to come between them.

pounds if his name went on the birth certificate and she left Dave to spend the baby's first year at Home Farm. Kim accepted, told Dave that the baby was Frank's and moved back to Home Farm. Frank hired a full-time nurse for Kim, who quickly grew to feel confined.

Zoe found out about the deal, and this led to a flaming row between her and Kim – one that ended with Kim slapping her stepdaughter.

Kim gave birth in September to a son, James Francis, but seemed more concerned about one of her favourite horses, Valentine, who had fallen ill at the same time. She left her baby in hospital to check on the horse – but it had been put down.

Kim soon got the hang of motherhood, and realised she loved baby James.

Somewhat unexpectedly, Emmerdale *found itself at the cutting edge this year, when there was a brief craze for linedancing, coinciding with a story in the show about Terry, Vic, Zak and Lisa (Billy Hartman, Alun Lewis, Steve Halliwell and Jane Cox) forming a country rock group. The Woolpackers, as they became known, released a single, 'Hillbilly Rock, Hillbilly Roll', that got to number five in the charts. There was a hit album,* Emmerdance *(which got as high as number 26, at Christmas), and an instructional linedancing video with the same title.*

DINGLES

The Emmerdale Dingles were led into serious crime by their Uncle Albert, who got them to help him rob criminal boss Kenny Dillon. Dillon tracked the Dingles back to the village and kidnapped Tina, taking her to his mansion. Tina was freed in return for Albert – she was extremely reluctant to leave the luxury of the mansion. Dillon and Albert were both caught by the police.

Zak learned that Nellie wasn't coming back and the new woman in his life, Marilyn, turned out to be there to steal his money. She stole their van, which was later recovered. However, before the year was out, Zak had found love with Lisa Clegg.

Mandy returned to the village, this time permanently. She and Tina worked as escorts for Pollard. After that, Mandy opened the Munch Box, a caravan converted into a roadside hamburger stall. She quickly fell foul of a public health inspection, unsurprising

Nick's confrontation with a poacher ends in disaster.

Kim wants nothing to do with her new baby – at first.

Mandy goes into business – and Butch and Zak seem happy enough.

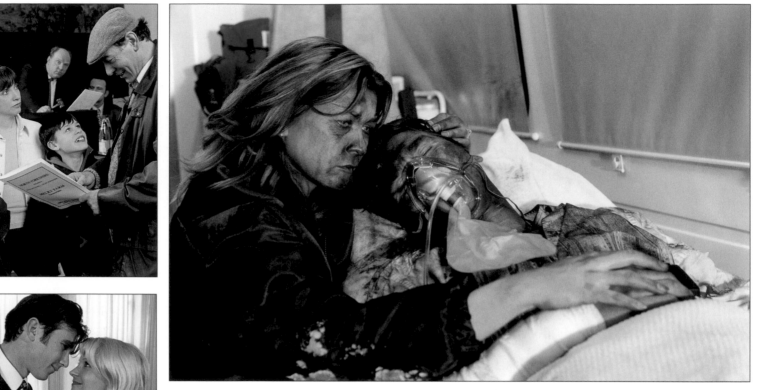

Andy's delighted Jack and Sarah will look after him.

Kathy marries Dave ...

...but he's having an affair with Kim and dies saving her baby from a fire.

given that the main source of meat was one of Jack Sugden's cows that Zak and Butch had found dead at the side of the road after it had been hit by a car.

Sean Rossi, the chef at the tearooms, set Mandy up on a blind date with Dave Glover, but Dave wasn't interested and ended up picking up another woman on their night out. Mandy was heartbroken.

Tina became housekeeper at Home Farm, much to the annoyance of Kim. Frank was much more receptive – even taking Tina on holiday to the Caribbean. Frank made Tina his personal assistant, but Tina rejected his romantic advances. Shortly afterwards she left the village.

Sam was arrested after stealing a plate. He jumped bail and fled for Ireland.

Marlon Dingle, one of Albert's sons, came to live in Emmerdale, and proved a little smarter than the average Dingle when he opened a Santa's grotto.

SUGDENS

Jack and Sarah started looking after Andy Hopwood, a troubled lad whose grandmother was finding it difficult to cope with him. He almost died when he fell into the quarry, but was rescued by Jack and Biff. In August, when his granny died, Andy moved in with the Sugdens while foster-parents were sought, and late in the year the Sugdens applied to foster him.

Frank intended to extend the quarry site, and wanted to use land Emmerdale leased from him for the project. The Sugdens' problems were compounded when Annie arrived from Spain, intent on liquidating her share in the farm. She sold to Steve Marchant, an investment broker, and Jack assumed this would put a stop to Frank's plans for a quarry – but Steve meant simply to sell the land on to Tate after marking up the price. Frank, never one to be outdone, refused to pay Steve's asking price and, knowing Steve had borrowed heavily, expecting a quick sale, waited until mounting interest payments forced Steve to sell up. This also ended Steve's brief relationship with Tina Dingle, whom he accused of leaking business information to Frank.

BATES

Nick was attacked by poachers, who left him tied up. He and Seth caught them the next month, but the confrontation escalated, and Nick ended up firing a shotgun at them as the poachers made their escape. Unfortunately he hit one of the gang, Jed Connell, and killed him. He was arrested and put on remand.

BIFF

Biff and Linda became lovers, moving into her cottage together – but agreeing not to have sex before marriage. Biff proposed in August, and they married on Christmas Eve. Dave was best man, but left the wedding reception to meet Kim up at Home Farm…

KATHY

After Nick was jailed, Kathy agreed to looked after his daughter Alice.

Kathy also began a partnership with Eric Pollard, who set up a wine bar at one end of the tearooms, to be used in the evenings.

Unable to get near Kim and the baby, thanks to Frank, Dave returned to Kathy. When Kathy realised Dave was disgusted with Kim, she proposed. The couple were married in secret in late November.

But the marriage didn't last long. Kim approached Dave and told him she was planning to leave, and take James with her. She invited him to join her. It took Dave a couple of weeks to decide, but he finally chose Kim, and hurried up to Home Farm to run off with her.

Frank appeared on the scene, and confronted Dave and Kim. But disaster struck – a fire had started in the nursery. Dave rushed

Vic and the rest of the family discover Viv's having an affair with Terry.

to save baby James, and passed him down to safety. But he had suffered burns and smoke inhalation – he died in hospital on Boxing Day.

WOOLPACK

Terry discovered he had a son by an ex-girlfriend, Elaine. Meanwhile, when he met up with Britt he discovered she had a new boyfriend, Gerald, and was expecting a child. Terry tried, and failed, to get back with Tina Dingle.

WINDSORS

Terry invited Viv to join him for dancing lessons at the village hall. Vic was jealous – and wasn't helped when a photo in the *Courier* identified Terry and Viv as 'Mr and Mrs Windsor'. Kelly just assumed the two were having an affair, and managed to convince Vic. Vic punched Terry – and shortly afterwards Terry and Viv did indeed start an affair. When Vic found out that Viv was sleeping with Terry, he threw her out, and she moved into the Woolpack.

Scott left to join the Army.

GLOVERS

The Glovers didn't have a happy time of it. Jan was attacked by a gang as she tried to sell fruit and veg on her stall. She was also having money problems, and was sacked from the Woolpack by Turner, who caught her stealing from the till.

Biff Fowler marries Linda Glover.

EPISODES 2147–2304

KEY EVENTS

Kim dies... and comes back from the dead.

Lord Oakwell is responsible for Linda Fowler's death.

Underage Kelly has an affair with her teacher.

TATES

Kim surprised many by attending Dave's funeral in full widow's dress, and by throwing a red rose onto the coffin before Kathy, his actual widow, could. Kim explained that they had been planning to run away together, leading to a cat-fight at the funeral between the two women.

Kim was genuinely in mourning, and was devastated when blood tests revealed that baby James was Frank's child, not Dave's.

Frank was investigated by the Inland Revenue over a tax fraud. He suspected that Kim had tipped them off, and confronted her. She walked out, not even taking her baby with her, and vanished. The police were eventually called in to find her – and discovered the wreck of Kim's car at the bottom of a quarry, with her body inside.

Frank was immediately arrested for murder, and remanded.

Steve Marchant was put in charge of Home Farm by Zoe. Steve was romancing Chris's estranged wife, Rachel. Predictably this led to all sorts of complications – the most serious being that Steve knew Chris was heavily in debt (to the tune of £400,000), which seriously affected Rachel's divorce settlement.

Chris made advances to Linda Glover – a move that saw Ned Glover attack him, pulling him out of his wheelchair.

In May, Frank was released after being attacked in prison, but he faced life imprisonment. He began putting things in order – buying Mill Cottage and giving it to Rachel as settlement for her divorce from Chris.

And then, out of the blue, Kim walked into Home Farm. She had faked her death and framed Frank, knowing that at his age he'd never live to see his release. Realising that he may as well be hanged for a sheep as a lamb, Frank moved to strangle Kim... but suffered another heart attack. Choosing to touch up her lipstick rather then get his heart pills, Kim watched him die, then slipped away. She had her revenge for Dave's death. Zoe discovered her father's body the next morning.

Kim reappeared at the funeral, and now had almost complete control of the Tate business. She hired Jan Glover as housekeeper (paying for her son Roy's driving lessons), and bedded Steve Marchant, an ally

Kim was determined to upstage Kathy at Dave's funeral

Frank looks like he's seen a ghost.

in the Tate boardroom. She also made a move on Lord Alex Oakwell, another wealthy potential investor. Kim invested in his stud farm, and Oakwell continued to show an interest in Kim even after he married his fiancée, Tara Cockburn.

Steve proposed to Kim, and offered his shares in Tate Holdings once they were married. Kim accepted.

Chris and Tara went into business together by setting up an outdoor activity centre in the village. It was run by Tony Cairns, a retired army major.

James disappeared, and Kim feared he'd been kidnapped. He had been taken by Jan Glover, who was found at St Mary's Hospital in Hotten, mumbling to the baby, thinking he was her dead son Dave. A judge ordered that Jan get medical treatment.

Zoe began a relationship with Sophie, James's nanny. It was Sophie's first lesbian experience.

... and the next morning, Zoe discovers her father's body.

POLLARD

Pollard returned from a holiday in the Philippines, having met young Dee de la Cruz. They were secretly engaged and got married in May. Sam Dingle, on the run from the police, turned up for the ceremony.

DINGLES

Paddy Kirk started working at the vet's surgery, covering for Zoe, who found herself increasingly drawn into business matters at Home Farm. He lodged with Betty and Seth and quickly became close to Mandy. He nearly lost his job when he treated Jed Outhwaite's animals without charge.

THE DINGLES DOWN UNDER

Vic, Terry, Lisa and Zak were invited to Australia to play in their band. While there, Zak and Butch tracked down their Australian relative, Crocodile Dingle.

KATHY

Nick was finally tried for the murder at the fish farm the previous year – and there was shock when he was sentenced to ten years in prison.

Kathy became the legal guardian of Alice – although there was a rival claim from Nick's American girlfriend, Karen Johnson, who wanted to take Alice to Boston before the extent of Nick's sentence was known.

Betty didn't approve of Eric marrying Dee – what did she see in him?

Lisa Dingle is pleased to see Zak, Butch and Mandy safely back from Australia

Oakwell drove Linda home after Kim and Steve's engagement party. The car crashed, killing Linda. Kim helped Oakwell cover up the incident and escape the country.

SUGDENS

The Sugdens had to move out of the old Hawthorn Cottage, as it was being demolished to make way for an access road to Demdyke Quarry. After thinking about moving into Woodside Farm, Jack decided too much work was needed and sold it (at a tidy profit) to the Cairns family. The Sugdens moved into the old Melby farmhouse instead.

Jack and Sarah had to cope with rowdy behaviour from Andy, who hit both Donna Windsor and a teacher. Billy Hopwood, Andy's father, was released from prison, and Andy went to live

WOOLPACK

Alan employed Mandy Dingle as a barmaid, and sacked Terry after he let Donna drink unsupervised in the Woolpack bar. Terry worked in Pollard's Bar, and lodged with Seth and Betty. He got his job back when Turner broke his leg and needed help. Terry was re-employed as bar manager, but only came back when Turner offered him a share in the profits.

CAIRNS

When Linda Fowler found a newborn baby outside the vet's surgery one morning, the search was on for the mother. Two days later, thirteen-year-old Emma Cairns was admitted to hospital with haemorrhaging. She was the mother – and the father was her sister Charlie's boyfriend, Greg Cox. Charlie left the village at the news.

FOWLER

Little Geri Cairns made Linda broody, but Biff had a secret – his father had just died of Huntington's disease. When Linda announced she was pregnant, Biff was horrified – in case the baby had inherited the condition. Biff almost committed suicide over the guilt – but was later to be tested negative. Sadly, Linda miscarried.

Worse tragedy followed when a drunk and drugged-up Alex

Emma Cairns becomes a mother - at thirteen

Alex Oakwell's drunk driving leads to the death of his passenger, Linda Glover.

Emmerdale's *twenty-fifth anniversary year saw the programme gain a third weekly episode – the show now went out on Tuesdays, Wednesdays and Thursdays. In a bad year for ITV ratings,* Emmerdale *was one of the few programmes to see audiences rise. There were also hour-long episodes to mark the beginning or end of big storylines – Kim's return from the dead being an early one – and the occasional five-nightly weeks. Hour-long episodes clashed with* EastEnders *on BBC1 – and, once again, far more often than not, when the two shows went head to head,* Emmerdale *won the battle of the soaps.*

Behind the scenes, the beginning of the year saw production move from Farsley to a new purpose-built studio and production centre in Leeds. The studio was opened by then Prime Minister John Major. Even more ambitious than that, the new village set was constructed in 18 weeks, although it wasn't seen on screen until the following year.

The Dingles Down Under was the first specially made Emmerdale *video, and sold very well.*

Kelly has an affair with her teacher – but it would all end in tears.

with him in a caravan after Billy got a labouring job. But Billy was intent on committing crimes – and, as before, neglected Andy.

WINDSORS

Kelly Windsor lost her virginity to her teacher, Tom Bainbridge. Their affair continued for some time, and when Vic found out he was understandably furious and got Tom transferred to Wales. Kelly ran away to follow him – and found him in bed with another pupil.

Terry's and Viv's affair came to an end – Terry had begun seeing Helen Ackroyd again.

Kelly started work at the holiday village, having a number of run-ins with a co-worker, Lyn Hutchinson, whom she already knew from school. Chris was forced to intervene when Biff proved unable to control the situation – and was quite taken with Kelly. He appointed her his personal assistant, to much derision.

Kelly was seeing Roy Glover, but also dated Will Cairns. She got him in to fix one of the Home Farm computers – and pocketed £200 by fiddling an invoice. She spent the money on a party.

Keeping busy, Kelly had a one-night stand with Biff Fowler (Roy's brother-in-law, whose wife had only just died).

EPISODES 2305–2466

KEY EVENTS

Lady Tara's personal and business decisions cause chaos in the village.

Kelly seduces Chris Tate – and loses her father.

Tricia's arrival causes mayhem at the Woolpack.

SUGDENS

Jack and Sarah rowed about Andy returning to Billy. Jack's method of relieving some of the tension was to start an affair with Rachel Hughes – his brother's stepdaughter. Sarah discovered the affair and threw Jack out – but allowed him back so they could provide a home for Andy when his father had left him once more.

Rachel began working as a secretary at Hotten Comprehensive and met Graham Clark, a teacher there. Graham seemed a little reluctant to commit at first – he had been widowed a couple of years before – but love blossomed after they left the other competitors standing in a close-fought Emmerdale Fun Run.

Billy Hopwood, Andy's natural father, reappeared. He was on the run, and encouraged Andy to believe they should live together as a family.

WINDSORS

Kelly paid a price for her one-night stand with Biff – she found out she was pregnant. Quickly, she seduced Chris, assuming he'd pay for an abortion. But Chris was desperate for a second child, and – to her immense displeasure – told Kelly he'd do the decent thing and look after her and the baby. The whole village was shocked when Kelly moved in with Chris, who was old enough to be her father.

Kelly made herself at home – and when Kim found her trying on one of her dresses, they tussled, and Kelly fell down the stairs, miscarrying. Chris was devastated, and Kelly found herself realising she had wanted the baby after all.

Kelly moved back home, taking a job as Zoe's receptionist.

Scott returned to the village, quickly gaining a reputation as a womaniser, having one-night stands with Marlon's girlfriend Lyn and with Paulette Lewis, who worked at the holiday village. It transpired he'd been thrown out of the army for sleeping with an officer's wife.

Vic was killed on Christmas Day. Billy Hopwood thought the post office would be deserted, with the Windsors having Christmas dinner in the Woolpack. But Vic popped back, and interrupted Billy breaking into the safe. Billy clubbed him with the butt of his shotgun, and Vic died a slow death. Over the road at the Woolpack, Viv was oblivious to her husband's fate, and grew increasingly annoyed at his absence.

TATES/HOME FARM

Kim started receiving blackmail threats – Jimmy Daniels had helped Kim to frame Frank for her 'murder' and now wanted £500,000 to keep quiet. Steve paid him £10,000, and kept the tape for himself.

Chris was delighted to see Kim's and Steve's business ventures collapse. Steve was losing friends fast – he'd persuaded some of the more affluent villagers like Turner and Rachel to make a series of poor investments. Kim and Steve kept each other in the dark about their financial problems – both hoping that, once married, they'd be able to use the other's money to resolve the situation. They discovered the truth after marrying in May. Practically bankrupt, they ended up living in Steve's small cottage. Kim and Steve were forced to sell their shares to Lady Tara, who now had a majority share of Tate Holdings, much to the shock of Chris and Zoe.

Sarah discovers Jack and Rachel are having an affair when she catches them together in the barn.

Zoe discovers Kelly at the bottom of the steps - did she fall or was she pushed?

Steve will stop at nothing to prevent his and Kim's secret from getting out – he's even prepared to murder Kathy.

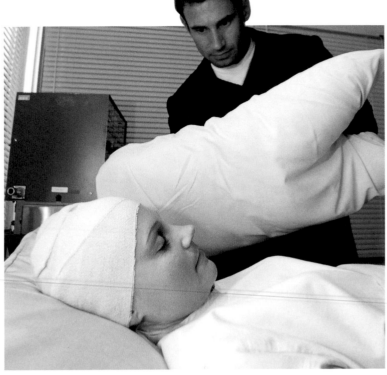

Tara's father had just died, and she was faced with enormous debts and death duties. To preserve her own assets, she began a ruthless series of evictions and other sell-offs of Tate Holdings property, bringing in lawyer Laura Johnstone to take charge of the process. She also accepted a proposal from Lord Thornfield, an old, rich aristocrat, whose money would help solve her problems. It would be a marriage of convenience only – and Tara began a torrid affair with her chauffeur, Biff.

Steve and Kim concocted an elaborate scheme to steal one of Kim's racehorses, sell it on, then wait for the insurance money to come through, before fleeing the village. They'd have Zoe as an alibi, using the baby monitor to trick her into believing Steve was working upstairs while he conducted the robbery.

The robbery itself went smoothly, but disaster struck when Kathy saw Steve driving the getaway car – and Steve ran her over, putting her in a coma. It was unclear for several weeks if Kathy would live – and Kim and Steve found themselves trapped in the village, facing a possible murder charge. DI Spalding of Hotten CID quickly made Kim his prime suspect, but couldn't pin the crime on her. Eventually, Chris's dogged determination to find Kim guilty paid off, and the two were arrested at the end of the year.

Chris was also busy setting up a new Tate Haulage in Hotten, investing the money he was making from his share of the sell-off of Home Farm.

The culmination of Lady Tara's changes came when Laura arranged the auction of Home Farm itself. The house was bought by lottery winner Stella Jones.

KATHY

Pollard persuaded Kathy to swap the flat above the tearooms for Victoria Cottage – with Alice present, and the wine bar open in the evenings, the flat was no longer suitable.

Kathy was romanced by Doug Hamilton, and even continued the relationship when he confessed to being married. However, when it turned out he was actually gay, and in a long-term relationship with someone called Richard, that proved to be the last straw.

POLLARD

Eric and Dee moved into the flat. Will Cairns, who was working as a waiter in the wine bar, developed a crush on Dee. Dee was flattered, but didn't cheat on her husband.

However, it became clear that Pollard had been withholding letters from the Philippines. Dee's mother was sick, and Pollard didn't want Dee to leave… but she discovered the truth when her mother died. Dee stormed out on him.

Pollard's problems mounted – he was raided by the police after the wine bar had become a regular haunt for underage drinkers. Kathy bought his share in the business – at a knockdown price, as it was worthless to him – and closed the wine bar. Pollard had

The new purpose-built village set first appeared on screen in February.

Emmerdale *was doing well in the ratings, and settling into its new three-times-weekly slot. There were changes within the ITV network, which was consolidating into essentially two large blocs as Carlton and Granada bought up the smaller companies. Granada (the makers of Coronation Street) bought YTV, the makers of* Emmerdale.

Kieran Roberts was brought in as producer in the spring, and decided to concentrate on longer, more dramatic stories, feeling that the holiday village and Dingle scam stories that had become a mainstay of the show were a little lightweight. One key change was to the Woolpack – it was felt that the combination of Terry and Turner was just too 'safe' compared with the turbulent goings-on at the Rovers Return or the Queen Vic. The characters of Tricia and Bernice were introduced to shake up (indeed, in Tricia's case, blow up) things at the pub.

Another big change was necessitated by the decision of Claire King, who played Kim, to leave the show. Again, it was felt that too many of the Tate stories were a little abstract – arguments about sums of money and shares in the ownership of businesses. Kim's departure represented a perfect excuse to dismantle the Tate empire.

Turner falls for biker Jo, but won't leave Emmerdale for her

him to go to America with her, but he didn't want to leave Emmerdale behind. Terry and new barmaid Heather Hutchinson also had a relationship.

In September, Turner's long-lost granddaughter, Tricia Stokes, turned up out of the blue. Turner was delighted to see her – so much so, he was blind to her many faults. He employed her as a barmaid on the spot. Terry was smitten, and fancied his chances. Ever-impulsive and eager to please, Tricia slept with Terry. She instantly regretted it – but in October, when Turner was away for the night, she persuaded Terry to have an illegal lock-in. After that was over, Terry tried it on again, and Tricia found herself letting him into her room. Unfortunately, in his haste to get upstairs, Terry hadn't extinguished a candle on the bar… and Tricia had failed to put away a box of fireworks she'd bought.

Turner returned to discover the entire Woolpack bar had been gutted by the fireworks exploding. When he learnt about the lock-in from Pollard (who'd been very, very slightly injured in the explosion, and was threatening to sue), he sacked Terry, refusing to believe that Tricia could have done anything wrong.

Ashley arranged for the village hall to be used as a temporary Woolpack. The brewery sent an agency barmaid, Bernice

Tricia comforts Alan as he surveys the damage to the Woolpack.

discovered how lucrative the teenage market could be, so Kathy set about converting the tearooms into an American-style diner to appeal to them. Pollard continued to live in the flat above the property – but without Dee or his business, he grew increasingly bitter. He even planned suicide – burning the diner down, with him in it, but Marlon talked him out of it.

Reverend Ashley Thomas, who looked after the village hall, got fed up of the building being used as a place to store Pollard's antiques, and began selling them off at £5 a time. Pollard bought Farrers Barn, adjacent to the tearooms, and used it as a base to store and sell the antiques, falling back on his old trade. He let out the upper floor to Mandy Dingle, who used it to sell second-hand clothes.

WOOLPACK

Mandy moved into the Woolpack. Turner and Terry weren't happy – and contrived to leave the place a mess until she left in disgust.

Alan found love, briefly, with biker Jo Steadman. She wanted

Blackstock, to help out. The opening was a huge success, with Bernice being almost supernaturally efficient. Bernice was obsessed with the idea of finding a man in the week she had in the village. Ashley was keen, but Bernice was put off when she discovered he was a vicar, and set her sights on Biff instead – but was horrified to attract the attentions of Roy.

SUGDENS

Biff Fowler and Marlon Dingle, who'd been thrown out by their respective families, started squatting in Tenant House, Annie's old house. Sarah discovered them, and wanted them ejected – but Kathy persuaded the Sugdens to rent it out to them instead. Jed Outhwaite soon joined them when he was evicted from his farm. When Jed left, Will Cairns joined them.

CAIRNS

Becky Cairns took over as Zoe's receptionist following Linda's death. She was unhappy in her marriage – and made a move on Zoe. Her son saw them kissing, and when Tony found out, he walked out, leaving for a new job in Düsseldorf. It became clear that Zoe wasn't interested in Becky – she left the village to follow her husband. Will followed later in the year.

GLOVERS

After being released from hospital, Jan left Ned to go and live with her sister in Skipton.

EMMERDALE: REVENGE

Roy learned that Lord Oakwell, who had killed his sister Linda, had resurfaced in London. He volunteered to join Pollard at a collectors' fair in the capital. Along with Kathy, Marlon and an undercover policeman, he discovered that Oakwell had fallen in with a London drugs gang. Oakwell died falling off a roof after a chase.

DINGLES

Mandy was delighted when Paddy returned full time to the vet's surgery. Early in the year, he and Mandy moved into the outhouse conversion at the Dingle home.

Zak and Lisa married.

The Dingles were becoming almost respectable entrepreneurs. Lisa set up a car-repair business in an abandoned garage tucked away in the middle of the village. Marlon became Pollard's chef at the wine bar. Mandy opened a second-hand clothes shop on the top floor of Pollard's barn. Butch was now a paid labourer at Home Farm. Zak maintained the family traditions with a series of minor robberies and scams.

Bernice arrived looking for a man - but they were all more interested in motorbike magazines!

Butch became obsessed with Sophie Wright, the nanny at Home Farm. Although she was in a relationship with Zoe, it was fair to say that Sophie sent Butch mixed signals – sleeping with him a couple of times. Butch became obsessed: he took photos of her secretly, followed her around. He confronted Sophie at home in a rage, but Sophie realised he was essentially harmless when he broke down in tears. Zak promised to keep his son away from her.

Tara's string of evictions reached the Dingles – they were offered the chance to buy the barn for just £6000. The Dingles didn't have anything like that kind of money. However, Paddy did. Mandy assumed he would use the money to save the family – but instead he bought into the vet's surgery. He did it to assure his and Mandy's future – but she promptly left him for betraying the Dingles. The Dingles were evicted – Zak and Butch accepted a half-hearted invitation from Rachel to live at Mill Cottage, Mandy and Lisa stayed with Seth and Betty. Salvation came from an unusual source – Paddy's mother. Mrs Kirk hated the thought of her son marrying Mandy. Not knowing they had split up, she offered Mandy the money to buy the barn – if she married someone else. Mandy attempted to find a suitable partner, but the best she could do was Butch. They married at Hotten Register Office, and got the money. Butch assumed that now they were married Mandy would come to love him – but he was wrong. The Dingles moved back into their home, with Zak becoming the first Dingle ever to own his own home.

Lisa and Zak had a surprise on Christmas Day, when Lisa unexpectedly gave birth to a baby girl – she hadn't even known she was pregnant. Paddy got back into the clan's good books by helping to deliver the baby, who was named Tinkerbell, or Belle for short.

EPISODES 2467–2631

KEY EVENTS

Bernice becomes the first landlady of the Woolpack.

The Reynolds family arrive in the village.

Graham murders Rachel.

Kim fled the village, but she had everything she wanted.

TATES

Kim stitched up Steve, framing him as the sole perpetrator of the horse robbery. It was a ruthless ploy – and it failed. It became obvious there was evidence against Kim and that she was heading for prison. She was out on remand, and the day before the verdict was read, she decided to make a break for it with the money she'd made from selling Orsino. But Chris had found the money (she'd buried it in Frank's grave!). Kim confronted him at Home Farm, found the money and smashed his skull with a paperweight, leaving him for dead while making her escape with baby James in a helicopter.

Steve was sent to prison for ten years after being found guilty of attempted murder.

As Chris recovered, he romanced Laura Johnstone. But Laura was smart – she realised that Chris was trying to get back together with Kathy. Although she loved Chris, she realised she was better off without him.

Zoe fell for one of Tate Haulage's truckers, the lesbian Frankie Smith. Ridiculed by Chris, particularly as Frankie had a partner, Zoe persevered, and was just getting somewhere when Frankie was arrested and sent to prison in Germany for drink-driving.

Equally dramatically, Chris disappeared in November, and Zoe started receiving ransom demands. The kidnapper was Liam, Frank's illegitimate eldest son. Frank had walked out on Liam's mother, who had become mentally ill. Liam spent his life in and out of institutions; he'd watched his mother die in poverty. All the time, he'd seen Frank and his family prosper. He

wanted that life for himself. Despite the best efforts of DI Spalding, who managed to suspect Sean, Laura and Terry of the crime, Chris wasn't found for months. Finally Zoe located Liam and Chris – and shot Liam with his own gun. Chris and Zoe destroyed all the evidence that Liam was related to them, leaving the police baffled as to Liam's motive. Zoe wasn't charged with Liam's death, and the matter was dropped.

Zoe spent much of the year in a futile attempt to woo Frankie Smith – although Zoe did eventually get to kiss her

WINDSORS

Following Vic's death, Scott and Kelly Windsor became closer, until they slept together. While not technically incest (they were the children of Vic's and Viv's respective previous marriages), they managed to break even their own moral code with the act.

Guilty, Kelly launched into a lightning-fast relationship with Roy Glover, who'd always idolised her. Against the advice of her friends, who couldn't know why she was so keen, they were married in May.

Scott, meanwhile, set up a computer repair company with his school friend Richie.

However, Kelly gave into temptation again, and within weeks of marriage slept with Scott. She became pregnant, and was unsure who the father was.

RACHEL

Graham moved into Mill Cottage with Rachel, and he seemed to

Liam resented the life of luxury that Chris had led, and made sure Chris knew it.

KATHY

Kathy recovered from her coma, but suffered from mood swings and erratic behaviour for a little while afterwards.

Biff and Kathy became engaged, but Kathy was worried that he was on the rebound from Tara, and Biff was convinced that Kathy was interested in Graham. Kathy and Graham had become close friends after Rachel's death, and Graham actively encouraged Biff to think there was something going on between him and Kathy.

On the wedding day, Biff decided he couldn't go through with it, and instead rode off into the sunset on his motorbike.

WOOLPACK

Tricia and Mandy battled it out for the job of bar manager of the newly refurbished Woolpack, each trying to impress Turner. The rivalry between the two of them ended in a cat-fight in the Woolpack car park. Watching this, Turner decided to get Bernice Blackstock back to do the job.

Bernice arrived, and duly began organising the pub, rubbing Tricia and Mandy up the wrong way. Tricia, in particular, grew to believe that Bernice was mad. Bernice was joined by her fiancé, Gavin. She was utterly devoted to him, and unable to see he was, at best, indifferent to her – Gavin had slept with Tricia within days of arriving. He was very attracted to the thought of being a kept man in a country village, so stuck around.

After Turner had a health scare and decided to sell up, Bernice

be the ideal man as he redecorated, cooked and even alphabetised Rachel's entire CD collection for her. Rachel's friends, like Kathy, were a little worried he was taking too much control over her life. Graham got Rachel to dress differently and dye her hair auburn – and Rachel was shocked to discover a photo of Graham's first wife, Rebecca, looking remarkably like the 'new' her.

On a walk on Burview Crag, Rachel realised the truth – Graham had an overwhelming need to control, to change the women he went out with. It had been this that had driven Rebecca to suicide. Rachel tried to escape, but Graham caught her up and threw her over a cliff.

Pollard became suspicious of Graham, who claimed that Rachel had just accepted his proposal of marriage before she died. Pollard had talked to Rachel the day before, and knew she was thinking of ending the relationship. He tried to find incriminating evidence, but – for the moment at least – none was forthcoming.

Roy looks like the cat who got the cream as he marries Kelly – but it's about to go sour.

Graham made Rachel change her image – then killed her when he discovered her secret.

Turner is disgusted to find Tricia and Mandy in a mudfight – the punters don't seem to mind.

and Tricia both launched into campaigns to buy the pub. Tricia's was typically disorganised and relied mostly on mindless optimism. Bernice's, equally typically, was brutally organised but she was let down by other people – her ex-husband's debts gave her a bad credit rating.

Gavin, realising Bernice wasn't going to be able to support him in the style to which he'd become accustomed, started an affair with Stella Jones, the lottery winner who'd bought Home Farm.

Ashley Thomas, the local vicar, had fallen for Bernice, but knew she was engaged, and wasn't sure whether his distrust of Gavin was based on jealousy.

When Stella left, ironically she gave Gavin a good reason to stay – she paid the deposit on the Woolpack, allowing Bernice to buy the pub. Bernice began planning her wedding to Gavin. However, when Paddy's cousin Jason turned up in the village, Tricia thought she was in with a chance. She and Bernice found out he was gay, though… when they caught him kissing Gavin. Bernice threw him out.

SUGDENS

Jack and Sarah adopted Andy, but were facing mounting financial problems. This led to tensions in the family.

Sarah befriended Angie Reynolds.

GLOVER

In 1999, Ned was given a golden opportunity to put his past behind him. Meeting an old flame, Dawn Wilkinson, by chance in a supermarket car park, he discovered she'd recently been widowed, had received a large insurance payout, and was planning to go to Ibiza to open a bar. She invited Ned along, but he couldn't imagine a life outside Emmerdale, and wasn't comfortable with the idea of a woman supporting him financially. This changed when Eric Pollard discovered a Steiff teddy bear among Linda's belongings. Pollard, grudgingly, paid Ned £10 for it, knowing it was worth £20,000. Ned discovered the deception just in time to see the bear auctioned, take the money and hurry to the airport to meet up with Dawn.

Stella has the money to make Bernice's dreams come true.

Mandy and Paddy get married

DINGLES

Zak settled down to the life of a house-husband, while Lisa worked at her garage. He was a loving father, if not always a responsible one – he managed to leave Belle behind at a Hotten bookmakers and get all the way home without realising it. He also took her with him when he went out to steal from a building site – she cried when she saw a security guard, tipping Zak off and saving him from being caught.

Lisa went legit, and won the contract to service the Tate Haulage trucks.

When Ezra Dingle arrived for Belle's christening, he was disgusted – Zak had gone soft. He now owned his home and had a wife who was VAT-registered. Zak joined him in stealing lead from the church roof during the christening.

Zoe intervened to get Paddy and Mandy back together.

Butch and Emily met and fell in love, notwithstanding the disapproval of Emily's stern father.

Paddy and Mandy finally married – despite Mandy getting in trouble with the law. On the day of the wedding, Butch's brilliant diversionary tactic of putting on one of Mandy's dresses so that the police ran off in the wrong direction saved the day.

Paddy and Mandy honeymooned in Venice, with the other Dingles not far behind.

REYNOLDS

The Dingles were also wrong-footed by the arrival of new next-door neighbours, the Reynolds. Angie Reynolds, the mother of the house, was also a police sergeant, and was well aware of the Dingles' reputation. As the Dingles had already robbed the delivery van and the house, plus Zak had connected his house to next door's electricity supply to get free electricity, before he even knew who his new neighbours were, it quickly became clear they would have to mend their ways.

Sean Reynolds had first appeared as a disgruntled rival of Chris's new haulage firm. The two companies had engaged in dirty tricks campaigns against each other, until Angie had suggested they merge. Now Tate Haulage thrived – although conflict between Chris and Sean was never far away.

Kim's departure is thought to mark the highest ratings an episode of Emmerdale *has ever had, with over sixteen million people tuning in. The hour-long episode in which Graham murdered Rachel was also a success – screened later in the evening, partly because of the violence of her demise.* Emmerdale *went head-to-head with* Brookside *for the first time – and* Brookside *got its worst ever ratings, with less than a million viewers tuning in (about a quarter as many people as normal).*

The hour-long episode 2500, broadcast in March, featured a take on the Cinderella story, with Mandy as Cinders, getting to the Vets' Ball with the help of 'fairy godmother' Zoe Tate. The making of this fondly remembered episode was shown in Access All Areas, *a video presented by Chris Chittell, released later in the year.*

Don't Look Now: The Dingles In Venice became the third annual Emmerdale *drama video. By now, every soap had followed the lead of* Coronation Street *and* Emmerdale. *This year saw six soap tie-in videos released within a week of each other!*

The Reynoldses arrive in the village

2000

KEY EVENTS

The bus crash – Butch marries Emily on his deathbed.

Sarah Sugden has an affair with Richie
– and dies in an arson attack.

Ashley and Bernice get married at Christmas.

SUGDENS

Sarah was becoming increasingly irritated by Jack's penny-pinching. Not only was she having a miserable time, the children were missing out on school trips because they didn't have the money to send them. The last straw was Jack selling her car without telling her first. She was becoming more and more friendly with Richie Carter, whom they'd taken in as a lodger. Richie was young, ambitious, and had a lot of disposable income. They began an affair.

The Sugdens were split by the news. Andy and Robert stayed with Jack, Victoria moved in with Sarah and Richie in a cottage in the village.

The farm was now in a perilous financial state. Andy learned that the paper value of the farm was still enormous. He realised that the insurance value of just one barn would be enough to pay their debts. He set fire to one of the barns – not realising that Sarah and Richie were in there. Sarah died in the fire, and Richie was badly injured.

The police suspected Jack, and he was arrested and put on remand. Richie had seen someone deliberately start the fire, but not their face – he was convinced, though, that he'd seen Jack.

Diane and Jack began secretly seeing each other.

Sarah is killed – but who by?

GRAHAM

Graham Clark and Kathy became lovers, and planned to marry. But Pollard discovered that he'd killed his wife, and

Graham threatens to kill Kathy.

persuaded Marlon of the fact. Graham plotted to leave Emmerdale with Kathy, telling her, on a weekend away and at the top of another cliff, that it was because of Pollard's suspicions. Kathy tried to get away, but they ended up trapped in their car over the edge of the cliff. Pollard and Marlon arrived in time to see Kathy clamber to safety. Graham died as the car plummeted to the base of the cliff.

POLLARD

In the aftermath, Pollard was very annoyed not to be hailed the hero, and sold his story to the papers.

THE BUS CRASH

The twentieth of March saw a terrible accident, when the brakes failed on one of Tate Haulage's trucks and it crashed into a bus parked outside the post office. Pete Collins, the driver of the truck was killed instantly, as were two other villagers. Others trapped included Sarah and Victoria, Kathy, and Butch Dingle, who died shortly afterwards from his injuries. Butch married Emily on his deathbed, and they spent his last few moments together.

DINGLES

The villagers blamed Tate Haulage, thinking it was clear that the trucks hadn't been adequately serviced. But that was the job of Lisa Dingle. The Dingle family were torn apart as this became clear – Zak blamed Lisa for the death of his son.

Cain and Charity Dingle arrived for Butch's funeral, and both decided to stay in Emmerdale for a while. Cain quickly

Butch and Emily marry on his deathbed

became involved in petty crime. Charity began a 'business arrangement', sleeping with Chris for money.

Mandy was spending increasing amounts of time in Southampton, apparently nursing her father, Caleb. But when Paddy went down to Southampton, he was shocked to discover she'd been having an affair with Neil, her father's care assistant. Mandy followed him back to Emmerdale, but it was clear their marriage was over. Mandy returned to Southampton.

Paddy hit the bottle, unable to imagine life without Mandy.

TATES

Chris and Zoe closed ranks to limit the damage to Tate Haulage. The official crash investigation report cleared them – but many in the village remained angry with the company. It was enough to split Frankie and Zoe, and Frankie left the village.

WINDSORS

Pregnant and depressed, Kelly attempted suicide. She was found by Scott, who got her to hospital – and was careful to destroy the note that blamed their affair for her wanting to kill herself.

When she recovered, Roy and Kelly planned to leave for Ibiza together for a fresh start. Roy discovered she'd slept with Scott, and left on his own.

Annoyed by Viv's affair with Bob, Kelly tried to seduce her stepmother's new man – but ended up humiliating herself. She fled the village.

Donna slept with Marc.

SETH

Seth was mugged in Hotten after winning money on the horses. When he returned home, he'd become agoraphobic, but Betty and the other villagers nursed him out of it.

Emmerdale won the BAFTA for best continuing drama series, surprising many commentators. While this rewarded the achievements of the programme for the whole year, the specific episode put before the judges featured the heart-rending deathbed marriage of Butch and Emily, written by Karin Young.

After a couple of years testing the water with occasional five-episode weeks, Emmerdale started broadcasting every weekday, the first major British soap to do so.

Mandy's view on her departure was charted in the novel Mandy's Secret Diary. In the 1970s, Lee MacKenzie had written a long series of novelisations of TV episodes, but this was the first original novel.

December this year saw episode 2807 – the point at which there had been more episodes with the 'new title' of Emmerdale than there had been of Emmerdale Farm.

WOOLPACK

Bernice got Tricia and Marlon together, and the two quickly proved to be soulmates.

Tricia agreed to marry Joe Fisher, so that he could stay in the country, for £5000. This would be the start-up capital needed for Marlon to open his restaurant, Chez Marlon.

As part of the preparations for his wedding to Bernice, Ashley got in touch with Bernice's father, Rodney.

Bernice's parents arrive, and continue their feud.

KEY EVENTS

Jack is found not guilty of Sarah's murder.

Charity marries Chris Tate... after an affair with his sister.

Kathy leaves the village.

SUGDENS

Kathy tried her best to look after Robert, Andy and Victoria while Jack was on remand, but found it very hard going.

Jack faced hardship in prison, and feared the worst for the trial. But when the case came to trial, Richie realised that he wasn't sure he had seen Jack, and changed his testimony. Jack was found not guilty, and returned to freedom – and a farm that was facing almost certain financial ruin. Tensions in the Sugden family were high, and made worse when Robert discovered the truth about Sarah's death. It marked the end of Andy and Robert's friendship.

Richie left the village.

Jack discovered a way to solve his problems – siting a mobile phone mast on his land. But Viv and Edna teamed up to provide strong opposition to the proposal, and the phone company got cold feet. That was Jack's last hope – and he was forced to put the farm up for sale.

Zoe finds a lover – her brother's fiancée, Charity.

TATES

Zoe sacked Adam after he gave the wrong injection to a client's horse.

Charity Dingle continued her relationship with Chris, but began an affair. Chris suspected any number of men in the village – Rodney, Sean, Terry – but the truth was closer to home: Charity had been sleeping with Zoe. When Charity chose Chris over her, Zoe tried to blackmail Charity, but Charity called her bluff and confessed to Chris. Chris sided with his mistress, not his sister and the two married in November.

DINGLES

Zak told Cain that he was his real father. Cain was extremely angry at first, but quickly calmed down and accepted the news.

Zak discovered a lump on one of his testicles. Too scared to go to a doctor, he lashed out at his family instead, particularly Lisa. In the end, Sam convinced him to see a doctor, and he had an emergency operation that saved his life. He began rebuilding

Andy and Robert Sugden come to blows.

his relationship with Lisa.

Paddy and Emily became an item, and quickly moved in together. Both Dingle in-laws, they worried about the other Dingles accepting them, but Zak was delighted. Mandy returned, looking to resume her relationship with her husband. Paddy slept with her, but soon realised he'd rather be with Emily.

WINDSORS/HOPES

Carol bought the B & B, gazumping a furious Viv. But shortly afterwards, Carol left the village, with Turner taking over the running of the B & B.

Viv married Bob in February, but Bob couldn't afford to take them on honeymoon because (unknown

Zak and Lisa's marriage is strengthened after his health scare.

Viv and Bob marry.

to Viv) he had to pay child maintenance to his ex-wife. Bob got sacked from Naughty Nylons when Viv won a competition to model for them, hiding the fact she was related to an employee.

Scott and Chloe became a couple, and Chloe soon moved into Pear Tree Cottage.

POLLARD

Pollard opened his 'tat factory', selling wooden objets d'art which cost next to nothing to make because of the people he employed to make them.

He employed Gloria Weaver to help him run the factory, and she headed off a number of strikes as the workers realised that Pollard was taking them for a ride.

But Gloria was depressed and lonely, and tried to commit suicide. Pollard did his best to look after her, but she left the village when it became clear he was a little embarrassed by her.

115

The Calder-Weston's arrival makes news on and off screen.

DAGGERTS

Cynthia Daggert came to the village to work in the tat factory, bringing her son Danny. They were joined by her daughter Latisha who, with the help of Jason Kirk, gave birth to a son on the journey to Emmerdale. She named the baby Kirk.

WOOLPACK

Bernice tracked down her sister, Nicola. Initially she was upset to discover that Nicola had always known she had a half-sister, but had done nothing to find her. But they were soon firm friends – which in turn put Diane and Tricia's noses out of joint.

Bernice became pregnant, but miscarried. Tricia blamed herself for this (she'd argued with Bernice just before), and left the village. It also damaged Bernice's marriage to Ashley. Bernice found comfort with new chef Carlos, and quickly became pregnant again. Unsure of the paternity of the baby, Bernice spent much of the year torn between the two men in her life. Things were further complicated because Carlos was engaged to her sister, Nicola, who was also pregnant. On Carlos's and Nicola's wedding day, the truth came out – Nicola had faked her pregnancy to keep Carlos… and Bernice's secret affair also came out into the open. Bernice chose Carlos, and the two became pariahs in the village. Tricia returned and stuck with Bernice.

Louise arrived to work as a barmaid, and quickly fell for Rodney, who was old enough to be her father. Neither Bernice nor Diane were impressed.

REYNOLDS

Tara started to give Marc driving lessons. Marc hoped she was doing it through romantic interest, but it was really just to annoy his father, Sean, who resented Tara's privileged lifestyle.

When Marc dumped Donna, she accused him of sleeping with Bev, their teacher. She nearly got the innocent woman sacked.

Sean discovered that Cain had been having an affair with Angie, and had slept with Ollie. He beat up Cain, who had him arrested. It was enough to get Angie suspended from work. Sean moved to divorce Angie and began an affair with Tara, and the two decided to leave the village together.

Sean's father, Len, arrived just in time to see the family torn apart.

Nicola discovers the truth about her fiancé and her sister.

Sean and Tara run off together.

HIT AND RUN

On 10 September, the teenagers of the village went for a night out in Hotten. Missing the last bus home, they stole a car... and hit someone on the road. They were horrified to discover it was their headmistress, Ms Strickland. They vowed to keep quiet, but the tensions within the group built over the weeks – eventually Marc, the driver of the vehicle, was arrested.

KATHY

When Alice visited the village, Kathy realised how much she missed her. She decided to leave the village and return to Australia with her niece.

ELSEWHERE

Ray Mullan arrived in the village, and began buying up property, including the Emmerdale farmhouse.

HOLIDAY VILLAGE

Chris and Rodney entered a partnership to buy the holiday village, and Rodney hired Maggie Calder to run the site – not realising she would bring her children, her new partner Phil and his daughter. Stuck in a small chalet, the Calder-Westons tried to stick together, as Maggie struggled to get the holiday village open in time. She and Rodney's daughter Nicola quickly fell out.

The village's teenagers are all implicated in a terrible accident.

Steve Frost became the producer; his first episodes were broadcast in April.

Emmerdale: Their Finest Hour *was published, a novel depicting the lives of Betty, Seth, Annie and the other inhabitants of Beckindale during the Second World War.*

The Calder-Westons were selected in the reality show Soapstars, *after huge filmed open auditions. The five who made it to the end were Dee Whitehead (Maggie), Mark Jardine (Phil), Jason Hain (Craig), Ruth Abram (Jess) and Elspeth Brodie (Lucy). The process was controversial, and earned the programme the wrath of Equity – which was rapidly withdrawn when it became clear that all five were trained actors and Equity members. The Soapstars story was charted in a book and a video, which also included a 30-minute prequel story featuring the new characters which was filmed in Blackpool.*

2002

KEY EVENTS

Zoe is diagnosed as schizophrenic.

Jack becomes the estate manager of Home Farm.

Bernice leaves Ashley holding the baby.

DINGLES

Peg Dingle, Zak's mother, was dumped on him by his cousins Elvis and Marilyn, and made a nuisance of herself, refusing to leave. Zak attempted to pass her on to Home Farm, but eventually accepted money from Chris to keep her away.

Zak broke Sam's arm in an attempt to win damages from the Council, but Peg told an investigator that's what he'd done, and the Dingles won nothing for their troubles.

Zak discovered that his father was still alive – he'd thought he was dead (and even suspected Peg of doing the deed). Instead, his father was a drunken drifter. Zak had always idolised his father, and so those of his family in the know had kept the truth from him.

Eventually, Zak and Peg grew so fed up with each other, they agreed on a plan to con Elvis and Marilyn to take her back. They had to resort to Peg faking her death to do so.

Sam joined a dating agency.

Peg Dingle arrived, much to Zak's annoyance.

SUGDENS

After thirty years, it was the end of an era: the financial pressures had built to the point where the Sugdens were forced to sell Emmerdale Farm. The family moved into Annie's cottage in the village – a cramped space after the farmhouse, and one that took some getting used to. The farmhouse was sold to Ray Mullan, the pick of the land to Chris Tate. Jack was persuaded to try for the job of Estate Manager of Home Farm – Chris couldn't see it working, but Charity convinced him that Jack was the best man for the job.

Andy started seeing schoolmate Katie Addyman, who soon moved to the village with her father, Brian, (who had taken up a job at Home Farm). Katie was forbidden from seeing Andy, but the two were soon sleeping together. Caught together by Brian, they quickly became annoyed that they were being treated as children – and resolved to have a baby, to prove they were adults. The truth came out in the most public way possible, at the Jubilee parade, where Katie was Queen of the Jubilee. Their fathers placed

Andy and Katie

a huge amount of pressure on them, and Katie briefly left the village – but Brian became reconciled with Andy over Katie's first scan. Andy, meanwhile, had left school. He struggled to get a job – and began to feel left out when Robert and Katie started back at school. Katie and Andy vowed to elope – but things didn't go smoothly.

Meanwhile, Robert, jealous of Andy, was keen to lose his virginity. He had his sights on Lucy Calder, so was surprised when Nicola Blackstock propositioned him.

PADDY

Paddy's mum died, and Jason inherited the house, leaving Emmerdale. Paddy and Emily had reconciled, and got engaged. Emily was completely unable to pass her driving test, and soon found it difficult even to find an instructor who would give her lessons.

Emily and Paddy started thinking about fostering a child – but soon found themselves with an unwelcome visitor. Nicola Blackstock moved in to the house, claiming the boiler in her house was broken. Paddy was unhappy from the word go, although Emily was more tolerant. But when she discovered that Nicola was bringing teenager Robert Sugden round to have sex with her, that was the last straw for Emily, and Nicola was thrown out.

HOLIDAY VILLAGE

Maggie Calder found herself at constant loggerheads with Nicola over the running of the Holiday Village. Because Nicola's dad Rodney was one of the bosses, Maggie found it difficult to get her side of the story across – except it soon became clear to Rodney just how vindictive his daughter could be. Eventually, he backed Maggie and sacked Nicola.

The strains were too much for the Calders and Westons – Ruth returned to her real mother, Phil followed a few months later. Maggie sought solace with Rodney – but

Paddy and Emily get engaged.

became unnerved that Rodney saw their relationship as something that could become more serious. Nicola had just as much reason to be horrified – she'd been hidden under the bed when Rodney and Maggie consummated their relationship. When Lucy discovered that Robert was sleeping with Nicola, the family decided to make a clean break, and Maggie accepted a job elsewhere.

HOPES

Viv opened Café Hope, much to Bob's chagrin. It proved a popular meeting place for the village's teenagers, particularly for its Internet access.

TATES

Charity began using her initiative to help run Home Farm – some of the people around Chris began wondering if his new wife was now calling the shots. It was Charity who was the driving force behind the setting up of Tate Trash – a refuse collection company that quickly won a couple of lucrative contracts from Hotten Council.

Charity discovered that Ray was up to no good. She realised that one of his 'business interests' was running prostitutes. Charity had her own experiences of violent pimps – and when she confronted Ray, he proved just how violent he could be.

The stresses of the last few years finally proved too much for Zoe, who suffered a breakdown. At first her friends suspected it might be an alcohol problem. Ashley was a good friend to her – but he was shocked when she offered to sleep

Bernice couldn't cope with the stresses of motherhood.

with him. Zoe ended up bedding Scott Windsor.

Terry and Ashley had come to realise that Zoe was in trouble and, in fact, Zoe's problem was far more serious than people knew – she had developed schizophrenia. Chris refused to accept the diagnosis, but it became clear that Zoe was no longer always in control of her actions. She began hearing voices – including Frank's. She was sectioned after burning down the village church.

WOOLPACK

Bernice couldn't cope with her new baby crying. Her estranged husband Ashley looked after baby Gabby, and it seemed to bring the two together again. But Bernice eventually decided there was no future for her in Emmerdale, and left the village. Diane was left in charge of the Woolpack.

Louise Appleton, the barmaid, fell for the rogue Ray Mullan, turning a blind eye to his faults – including his threatening Charity. Using Ray's money, Louise bought Bernice's share of the Woolpack.

Tricia helped to organise the Emmerdale Village in Bloom competition.

Tricia and Marlon moved into Kathy's old cottage, renting it from Turner, but Tricia had her sights set on a bigger house. When Rhona, a woman Marlon had once had a fling with, appeared in the village, Tricia began to worry she would lose him. Tricia left, with Marlon and Turner going straight after her. Marlon proposed – and Tricia's mother arrived in the village in time for the engagement party.

REYNOLDS

Marc was sent to prison for the hit and run incident the previous year, but released with an electronic tag. He seemed to attract criminal activity wearing it – working with Scott at the garage, he realised he was doing work on

stolen cars. Finally, he saw the fire at the church and broke his curfew to get down there to save people – luckily, his sentence had elapsed shortly before, so he wasn't punished.

SETH

Seth accidentally created an Internet cult site when he left his webcam on, broadcasting pictures of his front room. People visited his site to watch live pictures of Betty going about her business, and soon the 'BettyCam' was one of the main attractions at Café Hope. Betty was not best pleased when she found out, but soon forgave Seth.

This year, it all got too much for Zoe Tate

Ray and Louise

POLLARD

When Pollard discovered that the local mayor was standing down, he decided he would get the job, by fair means or foul. He enlisted the help of Gloria Weaver, who had returned to the village, and began clawing his way to the top. He became mayor by blackmailing and bribing his fellow councillors. Gloria and Pollard brought out the worst in each other, and were soon inseparable in public and private.

Pollard and Gloria got engaged – but Gloria's ambitions didn't end there. When she met the local MP, Harry Partridge, she was convinced that Pollard could do a better job. Whereas most people are put off politics by the idea of 'Westminster sleaze', Pollard saw an opportunity, and set his sights on becoming an MP.

ELSEWHERE

Edna Birch's beloved dog, Batley, died this year. Edna drew more laughs than sympathy from her fellow villagers when she set up a gravestone in her front garden.

THE GOLDEN JUBILEE

The village celebrated the Golden Jubilee in June, along with much of the rest of the country. Pollard and Gloria were at the forefront, keen to emphasise the Mayor's role in events. Viv Hope was also keen to get Donna into a modelling career, starting with her being crowned Queen of the Jubilee pageant, but Katie won the honour.

The Dingles revealed themselves to be staunch republicans, and conned visitors to the village by charging them for parking, while planning their own street party to celebrate Jesse James' birthday, which fell on the same day as the Jubilee.

As part of the show's anniversary and the Queen's Golden Jubilee Tour, her Majesty Queen Elizabeth II visited the Emmerdale Village set in July 2002, where she toured the set and met many members of the cast and crew.

Batley's death won the Best Exit award at the British Soap Awards, beating a couple of very high-profile deaths on EastEnders *and* Coronation Street. *The clip visibly moved the presenter of the ceremony, Graham Norton!*

Pollard and Gloria are ruthless in their hunt for power.

TIM FEE

Tim Fee is the Line Producer of Emmerdale, *the man who's job it is to solve the logistical problems of making* Emmerdale, *and to manage the studio and village site. He's also a keen ambassador for the programme, whose enthusiasm for* Emmerdale *is infectious.*

I started on *Emmerdale Farm* in 1973, as a trainee floor manager, so I was very much at the bottom of the ladder, but I loved every minute of it. I always loved working on *Emmerdale*, it offered so much in terms of studio work and location work. Back then, with location filming, the problem wasn't what you had to shoot, it was parking all the vehicles, then unpacking all the cables, then unloading the cameras.

I certainly didn't think I'd be on *Emmerdale* 30 years on, or that the programme would be as huge and successful as it is now. There was a completely different perception of the show, it was an afternoon serial drama. We all loved it and we had a good quality of actors in the cast, but it was never top of the ratings – we never talked about ratings in those days. It was pleasant television in the afternoon. Soap didn't really exist, except for *Coronation Street*.

It was gentle, gentile rural drama, about blue skies, harvesting and the corn waving in the breeze – all the things some people say they want to see more of now, but they'd turn over in droves if we did that. The cast were so good, but if we dragged those first episodes out today... it isn't what viewers expect now.

When I started, I did more studio work. Location work was done by the big boys, like Mr Bridgeson, the boss. I did some filming at Arncliffe, but it had shifted to Esholt by the time I was doing much on location. Esholt is a lovely village, but we couldn't always shoot it as it looked, because not everyone who lived there wanted to be shot. As *Emmerdale Farm* gained more and more popularity, the tourist industry latched on to it. We were sworn to secrecy, but the local council started advertising 'Emmerdale Tours'. Even without that, there was a lot of disruption for the residents – we always tried to look after them,

but we were there every week. Location filming has to be carefully planned and takes a lot of setting up, but there could be two or three hundred tourists there, all asking for autographs or taking photographs. We timed it, and found we were spending more time managing the tourists than shooting the programme. So there was disruption all round.

I moved on to shows like *Main Chance* with John Stride, and *Hadleigh*, then on to co-productions like *Orient Express* with Cheryl Ladd, and *The Attic*, about Anne Frank.

I rejoined *Emmerdale Farm* in 1988, when it was planned to relaunch the show as *Emmerdale*, and I spent three months watching how the programme was made, and trying to work out how I could re-establish it. Nothing about how it was made had changed from the 1970s! We were getting our evening spot, so the first thing we did was move to a new studio in Farsley. Everyone who worked there has fond memories of Farsley, being there really established us all as a team, and gave us an identity.

We move with the times behind the scenes, too. The biggest change is the technology: the cameras now are half the size they were, and the cables are only slightly thicker than the ones people have at home. You used to need three people to lug the machinery around, now you just take the cameras out the box, screw on the legs and shoot the scene. And all the editing can be done straight on a computer, which really saves time.

What I love is the producer coming along and saying, 'We've had an idea, do you think we could do it?' The challenge of that. We do have a well-oiled machine, but we've got to have excitement and originality to push us. Not sensational stuff, not all the time, but we like those big moments, the plane crash, the bus crash, a car going over a cliff. The actors, writers, directors, we all like to be kept on our toes.

We craft the scripts carefully to make sure everything's planned and scheduled, and there aren't 'quiet' blocks of episodes. Give us enough notice, and we can do anything, on time and on budget. We don't mess around – if we're doing a stunt, we'll make sure we book the stunt people from a Bond movie, and give them plenty of time to plan. If you think of it this week and shoot it next week, it would cost a fortune, but if you plan things carefully, you can do it.

I love the challenge. I've been here since 1988, I could easily come in at nine and go at five, but I'm here at seven-thirty, reading scripts. That's part of my job, and the baseline is the script. If we had boring scripts, I'd be bored out of my mind and would have retired by now. It's the new ideas and situations that make the job worth doing. And

The burning barn where Sarah Sugden met her death.

most of the wacky ones get filtered out before they get anywhere near me. There's no point doing stuff for the sake of it, it's got to be right for the artists and characters, right for the story.

Every so often a producer comes in and... well, I remember when [former producer] Kieran Roberts came into my office, only a couple of months after we'd moved into the new village, he hadn't been with us very long, and he said, 'You're going to hate me, but we want to blow the Woolpack up.' I couldn't believe it. I reminded him we'd only just built the thing... But we did it, and we had glass blowing out and Eric Pollard diving out of the way of a firework, and it looked terrific. And the next day, like all those special effects, you wouldn't have known we'd done it.

Sometimes, I'm the one who comes up with an idea. For example, they'll say, 'Do you mind if we do this?' And I'll say, 'It's a bit naff and we can really beef it up'. Their job is to go for it and we'll only trim it back if we have to. Give me the notice, and we'll do most things.

We've got fervent fans. In 1989 we were approached by a lady, Jane Godfrey, who wrote to Keith Richardson, asking if she could set up an *Emmerdale* fan club. We weren't sure it would last a year, but didn't think it would hurt anyone to give it a go. And now it's got 1500 members, which is not a vast number compared to the viewing figures, but that's great for a fan club. We put on special weekends for the fan club – we've just had this year's and next year's is already booked up. People spend the whole weekend with us from Friday to Sunday, and they get to see the studio, and they meet the actors and we auction off scripts and props and things like that for charity.

And we have the website – it's a new area of interest, and it attracts younger viewers, and it helps them appreciate the show

more. The website also has message boards, so the fans can talk to us and about us. It's a really active fanbase.

For years we've taken the programme out into the country, far more than any other programme does. We go out playing cricket, golfing and football, marathons, ten kilometre runs. This year we're going to Aberdeen, Ireland, London, and of course we do a lot in Yorkshire.

In May, we went up to Aberdeen with 25 members of the cast, that's phenomenal – 25 cast members committed to spend their weekend with the fans. We played a golf tournament, then other cast members went on a ten-kilometre run, others were in town signing autographs. There was a cricket match where people could meet everyone. The police had to close one village off, so many people turned up. Finally, there was a big charity dinner, where we raised £35,000. We met thousands of people in the north of Scotland, who never usually meet anyone from the telly.

And we're big in Scandinavia, especially Finland. At the moment, I'm reading a *Survival Guide to Finland*, because I've been invited to go on cruises there, and address the Finnish Emmerdale Fan Club, of which I am the honorary president.

Last Christmas, Chris Chittell and Ben Freeman went on a charity trip to take children to Lapland, and they stopped off in Finland and were met with a barrage of press and the fan club. It's staggering really. There are couple of hundred members, and they're coming over this year.

For the anniversary, we're planning a number of big events. I'd like to think we can have one celebrating the history of Emmerdale. We want Kevin Laffan to be here, because without him we wouldn't be here, he created the characters. Running alongside that, we want an event for the current cast and crew to celebrate the hard work and commitment we have today. We've also been granted a Queen's visit, and she'll be visiting the village in her Golden Jubilee year, and our thirtieth.

Nowadays, we're a rock in the schedule. ITV love us, the advertisers love us, the viewers love us. Sometimes the critics take us for granted – although we got the BAFTA, and we'll get another. We're a great British soap, and part of Great British life.

Emmerdale

WHO'S WHO

CHAPTER THREE

The current population of Emmerdale is a mix of
old and new – but all of them have an interesting
family history.

THE SUGDENS

Sugdens have worked the land in the Emmerdale area for centuries – possibly since before the Domesday Book. They've been at Emmerdale Farm since at least the mid-nineteenth century. The villagers of Beckindale recognised the central role the Sugdens have played in local life in 1994, when they voted to rename the village Emmerdale, after the Sugdens' farm.

Jack does some farming

JOHN JACOB SUGDEN (Jack) (played by Clive Hornby, originally played by Andrew Burt [1972-1976])
Born: 28 November 1947
First Appearance: 16 October 1972 (played by Clive Hornby: 19 February 1980)

The central character of *Emmerdale*, until recently the owner of Emmerdale Farm. Over the course of 30 years he has gone from the black sheep to the bedrock of the Sugden family. Jack is the eldest son of Annie and Jacob, the father of Jackie, Robert, Victoria and the adoptive father of Andy. Jack has been married twice, and has had a number of other relationships, casual and serious. He has seen his son, brother and two wives die. Above all, he is a man of principle, someone who has come, over the years, to accept the duties he has to the land, to his family and so to his community. On the surface, he can often appear stubborn and taciturn, even inexpressive. But this simply isn't the case – he's capable of going to ridiculous, even whimsical, lengths to prove a point. He has a deep love for his family. His mother's assessment of him, that he 'likes to kick against things whenever he feels penned in' remains as true now as it did 30 years ago.

Jack left Beckindale (and his teenage sweetheart, Pat Harker) in 1964, having argued with his father Jacob about plans to introduce intensive farming methods. Jack was committed to a more romantic, almost old-fashioned model of country life – and while his family struggled to keep the farm running, he made a fortune down in London by writing a novel set in the idyllic rural Yorkshire that was already becoming an anachronism. His father's death saw Jack return to the village and inherit the farm. His younger brother Joe had expected the farm to pass to him, and his nose was put out of joint. Conflict between Jack's values and Joe's commercial instincts would dominate their relationship for the next 20 years. Jack's abiding interest is to see the land carefully farmed, not overrun with tourists or turned into a factory.

As such, he had many run-ins with Home Farm over the years, mainly because they share a border with Emmerdale, and anything done on the Home Farm estate tended to affect the Sugdens. There was traditional conflict between the Sugdens and the Verneys, and this continued when NY Estates took over, and pledged to run their land along precisely the short-term, commercial lines Jack so despised. Joe Sugden crossed the lines to run Home Farm in the 1980s, and the

Jack used to be a writer.

two brothers were constant rivals.

When Frank Tate took over at Home Farm, the situation became worse, if anything. A townie, and one with firm ideas about how the countryside should be run – essentially as a playground and museum for tourists – the two clashed constantly. Frank had money and power, and Jack could only ever win small victories. A symbolic moment was when Frank forced Jack to sell the Emmerdale Farm building to make way for an access road to Demdyke Quarry.

His family is equally important to Jack, and he has dedicated his life to looking after them, particularly his children.

In the 1970s, Jack was a little ill at ease with his new role as patriarch of the family. He was a ladies' man, dating – amongst others – Marian Wilks. He intended to convert Mill Cottage into his writer's retreat, but this came to nothing. In the end, he left for Italy to write, as well as to see Marian, who had moved there. It's unclear quite what Jack and Marian's relationship was in the six years he was in Italy. Both Jack and

Marian would return to the village from time to time, but never together, and they were always coy about each other. Marian married an Italian, Paolo Rossetti, in the early 1980s, but had an affair with Jack on one return visit to the village. Marian was last seen in 1988, now a widow, but Jack made the firm decision to stay with Sarah.

Leaving Rome and returning to Beckindale in 1980, Jack was now committed to making Emmerdale Farm work. He rekindled his affair with Pat, who had just left her husband, Tom. He also discovered that he had a son – Pat had been pregnant when he left for London, and her son Jackie was his. Jack and Pat married in 1982, but within a year, he began an affair with Hotten Market manager Karen Moore. Pat discovered him, and forced Jack to decide between them – he chose Pat and they rebuilt their marriage.

Pat and Jack had a son, Robert, in April 1986, and were truly happy

Jack and his son Jackie

together. This was cut short when Pat was killed in a car crash in September of the same year.

Jack was left bringing up a child on his own, and for the next few years, he had a couple of brief flings, one with Marian, one with a schoolteacher called Barbara.

He met Sarah Connolly in 1988, and after a slow start she moved in with him in 1990. Sarah wanted to avoid becoming a farmer's wife, and they didn't marry until a couple of months after the birth of their child Victoria in 1994. Again, Jack had a short affair – in 1998, this time with his brother's stepdaughter, Rachel. This damaged the marriage, and Rachel's death a couple of years later brought up old feelings and resentments, and affected Jack badly – he'd found Rachel's body. Money was tight, and Sarah was getting fed up – when Jack sold her car without telling her, she walked out on him. When Sarah was injured in the bus crash, there was a brief moment where it looked like they could be reconciled – but it wasn't to be. What Jack didn't know was that Sarah was having an affair with their lodger, Richie.

Jack found comfort with Diane Blackstock, who snapped him out of his depression and stayed over on a couple of occasions. But 2000 was a terrible year – the farm missed the deadline to apply for subsidies, Sarah was making divorce demands that might mean the selling of the farm. And, in November, Sarah was burned to death in an arson attack on a barn she was in. The next year would be even worse.

Even before Jack inherited Emmerdale, family farms like it were

in decline. There have been good times in the last 30 years, but these have been overshadowed by cash-flow problems, debt problems and the inability to invest in the latest machinery. In the 1970s, the one thing Joe and Jack could agree on was the need to market quality products, milk and meat that could fetch premium prices. In the early

THE SUGDEN FAMILY TREE

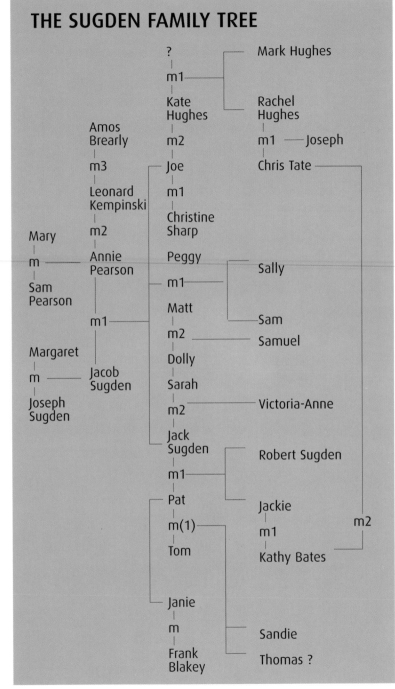

FIELD OF TARES

Thirty years on, it's hard to imagine Jack Sugden was once a novelist. Field of Tares, his debut novel, was a commercial and critical success. In the late 1970s, Jack moved to Rome to work on a film version of the book, although it's unclear whether the film was ever made. Field of Tares did seem particularly popular in Italy – in 1974 he won an Italian literary prize for it, and Sam and Annie flew over to attend the ceremony. A tare, for those who don't know, is a type of wild bean that grows in a cornfield.

The original book, the film rights and the advance for the second novel must have made him a relatively large amount of money – he was able to spend six years living in 'a posh flat' in Rome without any other apparent source of income. Exact details of the plot of the book were never made clear, but there have been hints – it was apparently a steamy novel about Dales life. When Jack's passionate romance with Marian Wilks foundered because he refused to make a commitment to her, a number of villagers who'd read the book commented that life was imitating art.

Jack struggled to write his second novel. Despite many years trying, he just couldn't find the inspiration. Sam Pearson joined him in Italy for a time, when Jack decided that the second novel should be based on his life. This bore fruit in 1978, when One Man in Time *was published. Sam didn't like the book, but other villagers were keen on it. Very little was said about the commercial success or otherwise of this second novel, but its publication marked the end of Jack's literary ambitions, and less than two years later he had returned to Beckindale to dedicate his life to running the family farm, abandoning plans to write a travel book. His last piece of creative writing to date was a competition slogan in 1983 – 'Shepherd's seeds supersede other seeds', which won.*

1990s, Jack was committed to turning the farm organic. But the plane crash put an end to that – his fields were dowsed with aeroplane fuel and other toxic substances. Even after an expensive clean-up, it will be many years before the Soil Association will approve the land as organic.

In 2001, this all came to a head. Jack spent months on remand for the murder of Sarah. He was acquitted, but the farm had suffered. A serious TB outbreak meant the herd was destroyed. The national rural crisis was, as for many farmers, the last straw for the Sugdens. Jack was forced to sell up in early 2002 – the farmhouse going to Ray Mullan, the land to Home Farm. Jack continues to work the same land, though – with both of them fully appreciating the irony, Chris Tate has appointed him the estate manager of Home Farm.

ANDREW SUGDEN
(originally HOPWOOD), 'Andy'
(played by Kelvin Fletcher)
Born: 28 January 1986
First Appearance: 4 July 1996

Andy was an inner city kid, the son of career criminal Billy Hopwood. A teenage tearaway, living with (and later being adopted by) the Sugdens calmed him down, and gave him a sense of belonging and duty, but he's still tempted to take part in petty

Andy breaks down at Sarah's funeral – he did kill her, after all.

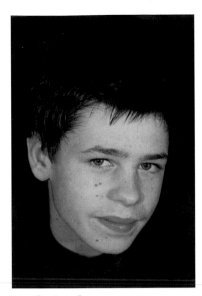

Andy Sugden.

crimes, and he's still is quick to anger.

In 1996, he came to stay with the Sugdens as part of a schools programme, and got trapped in Demdyke Quarry. He returned some months later, saying he'd run away from home. Jack took him back to Leeds, and was shocked to see he lived with his alcoholic grandmother. When she died, shortly afterwards, Andy came to live with the Sugdens while a foster family was found. He ran away from this foster family to live with the Sugdens, hiding in the barn. Jack and Sarah agreed to try to foster him themselves.

Andy suffered from asthma when young, having a serious attack soon after moving into the new Emmerdale Farm building. He started causing trouble – skiving and encouraging other kids to do the same. He quickly got a reputation as a bad influence, and was suspended from school twice for vandalism.

When his father was released from prison, Andy found the idea of

living with him appealing – his father wasn't so strict. He left the Sugdens to live in Billy Hopwood's caravan, but his father stole from the Sugdens and abandoned him.

Andy's first crush was on Emma Cairns, and he wrote her a truly appalling love poem. While he'd bullied in the past, he now found himself the victim of bullying, but got into trouble when he stood up for himself.

Billy Hopwood returned to the village again. This time, Andy was more reluctant to go with him. He was scared to see his dad had a shotgun, and inadvertently tipped him off that the post office would be empty on Christmas Day. Billy robbed the post office, but Vic Windsor was there, and Billy accidentally killed him, following a struggle. Andy told Jack about his dad, and Billy was arrested.

Andy was bullied when kids at school discovered his dad was a murderer, and he ran away, back to Leeds. He was found by Kelly and Donna, who persuaded him to come home. A social worker was assigned to him, and recommended he stay with the Sugdens rather than going into care.

Andy really enjoyed working on the farm, and looked forward to leaving school to do the job full time – a marked contrast to Robert, who was beginning to doubt there was a future in it. Andy also developed a big crush on Ollie Reynolds, who wasn't remotely interested. The year 2000 saw Jack's and Sarah's marriage hit the rocks, and Andy worrying that he was about to lose another family. The adoption process hadn't been completed and,

Andy burns down the Sugden's barn.

of course, if Jack and Sarah got divorced it would stop it dead. Jack and Sarah played happy families, and the adoption went through.

When Jack and Sarah split up, Andy tried to keep the rest of the family together and to run the farm while Jack suffered bouts of depression. Andy became aware that the farm was worth more on paper than as a business, and came up with the solution – burning down a barn for the insurance money. He didn't realise Sarah and Richie were in the barn at the time – Sarah died in the

fire, Richie was injured.

Jack realised what had happened, but even when he was charged with Sarah's murder, he didn't tell the police it was Andy who'd started the fire. Andy was racked with guilt. He broke into Richie's house and threatened him – but during the exchange, Richie realised it was Andy who had started the fire. Richie didn't tell the court and he retracted the statement that he had seen Jack do it. The case against Jack collapsed.

Bullied at school once again,

Robert Sugden.

Andy skived off and met up with Cain Dingle, who quickly led him astray, stealing a car and burgling a house. Recently, Katie Addyman, his first girlfriend, has helped as a calming influence. But they risk the wrath of their fathers – Katie is pregnant.

> **ROBERT SUGDEN**
> (played by Karl Davies, originally by Christopher Smith)
> Born: 22 April 1986
> First Appearance: Christopher Smith, 22 April 1986 ; Karl Davies, 28 December 1989)

The son of Jack and Pat Sugden, the oldest surviving Sugden heir. Robert's mother died when he was six months old, making him initially rather shy and sensitive. Since Andy has come into the family, Robert has gone from close friendship to seeing Andy as a serious threat to his inheritance and birthright.

Robert was quite accident-prone as a youngster: drinking sheep dip, falling off his horse and falling into the river.

He was aware from a very young age that Sarah, Jack's partner (and later wife) after Pat died, wasn't his natural mother, but always treated her as such.

Robert befriended Andy Hopwood, and started learning some of Andy's bad habits – bunking off school and getting drunk on alcopops with Donna. As Jack and Sarah began making it their business to look after Andy, Robert began to grow jealous and picked more than one fight with him. Andy, though, was always the tougher of the two, and started bullying him.

When he learned that Jack and Rachel were having an affair, he took the news badly, refusing to talk to his father. He and Andy put up graffiti around the school about Rachel.

Like Andy, his first crush was on Emma Cairns, to whom he sent flowers, but he also teased Andy for fancying her.

Robert was bullied at school by a group of girls, including Donna and her friend Chelsea. He asked Ned Glover, who was staying with the Sugdens, to give him some tips. Ned, not realising that it was girls causing the trouble, taught Robert to throw a punch – and Robert duly punched Donna Windsor in the face.

Robert could see that the farm was a lot of work for little reward, and began wondering if his future was as a farmer. Resentment towards the farm grew when he was kept out of school by Jack to help on the land. Andy was far more open to the idea.

Robert blamed himself when Jack and Sarah split up, and worried Jack was having a breakdown. He was, naturally enough, devastated by Sarah's death, firmly blaming Richie but never being entirely sure of Jack's innocence. When Jack was acquitted, he was desperate to know who had really killed Sarah.

When he discovered it was Andy, it was the end of their friendship. By then, Andy was his adopted brother, and calling himself Andy Sugden. Robert was sick of Emmerdale, and left for Spain to spend time with Annie.

On his return, he started a concerted campaign against Andy, trying to split him up from Katie.

> **KATIE ADDYMAN**
> (played by Sammy Winwood)
> Born: September 1987
> First Appearance: 19 July 2001

Katie is Andy Sugden's girlfriend. She's popular at school, and – in marked contrast to Jack – her father is able to make sure she has the right clothes and the latest gadgets. She's not a spoilt brat, though. Katie's her daddy's treasure, but she respects him. She is in the year below Andy at school, but has dated older boys in the past, much to her father's disapproval.

She met Andy in detention (her mobile had rung in class). They quickly became friends, but Katie had to take the initiative, as Andy was very shy. Andy's brother Robert exploits this to hurt him – he often flirts with Katie.

Katie was in the car which ran over Miss Strickland. She found the guilt increasingly hard to deal with and wanted to tell her father. When the truth was revealed, her dad told her never to see Andy or the others again. This proved impossible to enforce when Brian got a job at Home Farm and they moved into the village. Andy and Katie started sleeping together – and Katie became pregnant.

> **BRIAN ADDYMAN**
> (played by Martin Reeve)
> First Appearance:
> 6 November 2001

The father of Katie. He was the owner and manager of the Greendale Garden Centre in Hotten. He disapproved of Andy Hopwood, Katie's boyfriend, mainly because of Andy's involvement in the hit-and-run incident that killed Miss Strickland. He applied for the estate manager's job at Home Farm, and was angry that Jack Sugden – a late applicant – got the job. Jack offered him another job, and the Addymans moved into Emmerdale.

Katie Addyman

THE TATES

The millionaire owners of Home Farm, the main landowners and businessmen of Emmerdale. Their boardroom (and bedroom) dealings have an impact on everyone else in the village. They take their duties seriously, but all are ruthless and manipulative in their own way – it must be something in the blood.

CHRISTOPHER TATE
(played by Peter Amory)
Born: 11 December 1963
First Appearance:
16 November 1989

The wheelchair-bound head of the Tate business empire, son of the late Frank Tate. Chris has emerged from the shadow of his father to prove himself at least as manipulative and selfish. He loves his immediate family, especially his son Joseph – but is often infuriated by his sister Zoe. Married three times, Chris can be eminently charming, but has far more enemies than friends.

On arrival in the village, Chris quickly set his sights on the recently widowed Kathy Merrick, going as far as sacking George Starkey, a driver whom she showed an interest in. Within a year, he and Kathy were living together at Home Farm. She was disconcerted by him showering her with gifts, but did enjoy singing the love song 'Just This Side of Love' he wrote for her.

Chris idolised Frank, and spent his life trying, and failing, to impress him. Even early on, Chris was prone to hit the bottle when Frank was particularly dismissive of him. Frank loved Chris, but didn't rate him – Frank had pulled himself up from the gutter, Chris was the pampered son of a millionaire. Frank continued to prop up his son, buying back a motorbike he lost in a poker game to Turner. Throwing himself into the business to prove himself almost cost Chris his relationship with Kathy, who walked out on him. Used to getting his own way, he attempted to rape her, and she had to be rescued by Nick.

Chris tried to mend his ways. Frank put him in sole charge of the haulage business, and he and Kathy moved into Mill Cottage (where Chris proved hopeless at DIY). When he hit money troubles, though, he accepted Frank's offer to buy the cottage for him. It was becoming clear – and a worry to him – that he had inherited Frank's temper and bullying way with people. He was increasingly angry with Kim, who he knew was having an affair and supported Frank's decision to divorce her (but not what he saw as the generosity of the settlement). As Frank hit the bottle and started behaving erratically in the aftermath of his break-up with Kim, Chris made moves to take more control of the business, secretly mortgaging the cottage to buy Kim's share for £150,000. Frank, though, sold the company from under him.

His personal life was no better – Kathy was no longer sleeping with him (she was having an affair with

TATE FAMILY TREE

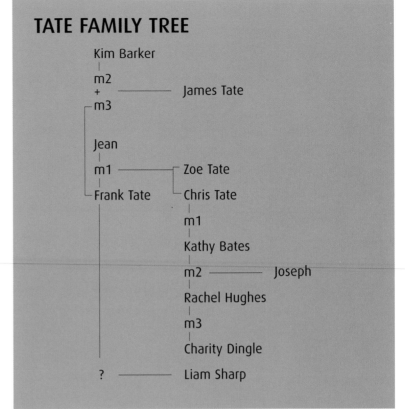

```
Kim Barker
  |
  m2
  +  ———————— James Tate
  |
  m3
  |
Jean
  |
  m1 ——————┌ Zoe Tate
  |        |
Frank Tate └ Chris Tate
  |            |
  |           m1
  |            |
  |         Kathy Bates
  |            |
  |           m2 ———————— Joseph
  |            |
  |        Rachel Hughes
  |            |
  |           m3
  |            |
  |        Charity Dingle
  |            |
  ? ———————— Liam Sharp
```

The Tates on their arrival in the village.

Chris. his second wife Rachel and their son Joseph.

wine merchant Josh Lewis) and on top of this Chris, who'd always been close to Zoe, found it difficult to cope with his sister coming out as a lesbian.

Everything changed after the plane crash. Chris was buried under the remains of the wine bar. He survived, but a spinal injury rendered him paraplegic.

Kathy stayed with him out of a sense of duty. Chris became bitter, then depressed. He refused to sell Mill Cottage to move into a specially equipped bungalow, and insisted he wouldn't use an electric wheelchair, wanting to retain at least some independence. Rachel Hughes helped him cope, and they went swimming together. This developed into an affair. When Rachel became pregnant, Kathy moved to divorce Chris. Once again, Frank bailed him out, giving Kathy the money she wanted. But Chris was angry with Frank for remarrying Kim, and ended up supporting the Dingles when Frank tried to evict them. He and Rachel married, and Frank wasn't invited. Chris was becoming

obsessed with ruining Kim, and gained leverage when he discovered her affair with Dave Glover.

Frank's hiring of Tina Dingle as his PA annoyed Chris. Rachel left Chris, but he tried to win her back. He went to the US for fertility treatment, wanting more children, but Rachel was secretly on the pill.

When Dave Glover died, leaving Kim distraught, Chris was delighted, and missed no opportunity to taunt her. Kim swindled him out of £350,000, but disappeared soon afterwards. Chris wondered if Frank had killed her.

Frank died of a heart attack, and Chris, for all his differences, was grief-stricken – almost suicidal. Kim returned and inherited everything of Frank's. Once again, Chris was venting his frustrations – accusing Rachel of having an affair, trying to force himself on Linda Glover. He and Rachel parted, and she got Mill Cottage in the divorce settlement. He began an affair with Kelly Windsor, and was shocked when she announced she was pregnant. He helped her arrange an abortion, but

later decided that he wanted her to keep the baby. He moved Kelly into the nursery flat at Home Farm, and was devastated when Kelly had an accident and lost the baby.

As Kim's financial problems mounted, she was forced to sell Tate Holdings to Lady Tara, who proceeded to break up the family empire. Chris continued to hound Kim, and his persistence was one of the factors that got the police to arrest her and her husband Steve Marchant for the horse robbery and attempted murder of Kathy at Home Farm in 1998. When Kim put on a brave performance in court, and Chris realised there was a chance she would get off, he made an outburst in court that got him thrown out. He found the money Kim had hidden,

and took it. Kim tracked it down, and nearly killed Chris as she made her escape with it.

With Kim gone, Chris was in charge of Tate holdings. He had a new vim and vigour, and started a new Tate Haulage firm, rapidly coming into conflict with rival Sean Reynolds. He supported Kathy as she recovered from being run over by Steve, and they became close again. Meanwhile, Chris was in a relationship with Laura Johnstone, the lawyer assigned to run Home Farm for Tara. His attempt to have both meant he lost both. He was upset by Rachel's death, and took it upon himself to make sure Rachel's son Joseph would be all right. He was also keen to see Kelly was happy, paying for an expensive

Chris and Joseph Tate.

Chris and Charity.

honeymoon in Paris for her and Roy Glover. He also took great pleasure in buying Steve's old cottage for a knock-down price.

Rivalry with Sean briefly turned to violence until Angie Reynolds and Zoe talked them into merging their business.

Before long, someone else was gunning for Chris – Frank's grave was vandalised, lorries were damaged, Chris's car had its tyres slashed. The culprit was his half-brother, Liam, who felt he ought to have had what he saw as Chris's great life. Liam kidnapped Chris and Chris remaind Liam's hostage for nearly four months. As time passed, the two came to realise that Liam was far more like Frank than Chris and that Chris's life had hardly been a bed of roses. Sympathetic to Liam, Chris was genuinely upset when Zoe found them, and shot and killed Liam.

Understandably a little paranoid, Chris hired Terry Woods as a bodyguard... although he ended up as a dogsbody. Chris didn't help matters when he bedded Claudia, the nanny Terry had been lusting after,

The production team have the following document that they use to keep track of Chris's (often rather complicated) business interests.

Chris Tate – Business history

1991 – Chris resigned from Tate Haulage when Frank decided to come back to work.

He was put in sole charge of the haulage company later that year.

1993 – Chris was frustrated when Frank's drinking affected the business, and remortgaged Mill Cottage to buy Kim's 20 per cent share in the haulage business behind Kathy's back. He paid Kim £150,000 for her shares which she used to buy new stables. Meanwhile, Chris aimed to become Chairman of Tate Holdings, but ended up having the haulage company sold from under him by Frank. He started to work at the holiday village instead, although Frank later helped him buy his own lorry.

1994 – After being paralysed at the end of 1993 he began to cope better when he started doing a bit of desktop publishing.

1996 – He was written out of Frank's will.

1997 – Chris paid Kim £350,000 for her livery business and stables and was delighted when she disappeared, but later found out that she had swindled him out and he was not the owner of the livery business.

He couldn't believe it when Kim inherited everything, and then got engaged to Steve, who was also a shareholder.

1998 – Chris hoped that Steve's and Kim's current financial misfortunes would see them out of Home Farm for good, although his position there was also threatened now that Lady Tara's lawyer, Laura Johnstone, had been placed in charge of Home Farm.

1999 – Invested in the haulage business again. Experienced some trouble with a rival haulier, Sean Reynolds, but eventually decided to merge companies – an uneasy alliance.

Was upset when Rachel died, as he now had to cope with his son as well as his troubled business. Luckily, Zoe stepped in and invested half a million pounds to keep them afloat.

2000 – Chris struck a deal with Richie over DaleTech. Chris wanted Scott left out of the deal and the new company was named Tate Technology.

When Tara returned to the village Chris was after her money. When her divorce settlement finally came through Tara had money to invest and set up a stud farm with Zoe and Chris. The Department of Transport investigation report on the crash absolved Tate Haulage of any blame.

Marlon pitched his business plan about reinventing the diner as a posh restaurant to Chris. Initially Chris wanted nothing to do with it but came round when Marlon pitched the idea to him a second time. Kathy sold half the diner to Marlon, but Chris wanted the fact that he was Marlon's backer kept secret.

2001 – Went into business partnership with Rodney Blackstock when they bought Dale Park Holiday Village for £900,000.

Bought Home Farm from Zoe for £2.5 million.

2002 – Set up Tate Trash, a refuse collection company, run by new wife, Charity.

but wasn't that interested in continuing the relationship.

Chris invested in DaleTech, Richie Carter's computer firm, which became Tate Technology. He also set up a stud farm with Tara and Zoe.

A closed bridge meant that Tate lorries were driving through the village at all hours of the day and night, alienating the villagers. Chris also insisted that the lorries run even if they hadn't been serviced. One of the lorries hit a bus, killing four people, including Pete, the truck driver, and injuring many more.

Chris initially thought Joseph was in the bus, and that Kathy had been killed... but when he realised both were safe, he showed no remorse. He was far more interested in covering his tracks and keeping the business solvent. The DoT crash investigation duly absolved Chris of any blame.

Chris arranged to pay for sex with Charity, a deal they found mutually agreeable. He bought her dresses and jewellery – and eventually moved her into his cottage in the village.

Chris added another string to his bow when, together with Rodney Blackstock, he bought back the holiday village.

But personally, life was a little complicated as Chris suspected Charity of having an affair. Zoe attempted to reassure him, at first... then announced she was the one sleeping with Charity. He was mortified and torn between who to believe, his sister or his lover who denied the affair. He chose Charity, and proposed to her. Zoe wanted nothing more to do with him, and sold Chris Home Farm, so she could move out.

ZOE TATE
(played by Leah Bracknell)
Born: 27 April 1968
First Appearance: 12 December 1989

Chris Tate's sister. Zoe Tate is one of Emmerdale's local vets, and is 'out' as a lesbian. Thanks to her inheriting Tate business interests and the sale of Home Farm, she is the richest person in Emmerdale, and must be worth at least four or five million pounds. While she is charitable and reasonable compared with the other Tates – and has a romantic streak – Zoe also has a dark side. She can be moody, and can get angry. She's had bouts of depression and periods of mild dependency on alcohol, and she once shot a man in cold blood.

Zoe graduated from veterinary school in July 1990. She got a job with a vet in Hotten, but resigned when she found out that he supplied animals for experiments at a local animal laboratory. In June 1991, she left her home to take up a job as a flying vet in New Zealand. She returned to the village after 18 months. She was then offered a job in Edinburgh, but for personal reasons (Frank had hit the bottle again and she was confused about her relationship with Archie Brooks) she decided not to take it. She worked for a vet in Hotten for a while, but then started her own practice at the Heritage Farm. She currently runs her own surgery in the village of Emmerdale in partnership with Paddy Kirk.

Zoe sticks up for what she believes in. She's committed to animal rights and animal welfare, and has campaigned against vivisection and hare-coursing.

In her personal life, Zoe was jealous of Rachel Hughes's friendship with Michael Feldmann, and had a one-night stand with him to prove she could get any man she wanted. On her return from New Zealand, she showed off her new boyfriend Patrick, who was almost the same age as her father. Her main relationship, though, seemed to be with Archie Brooks. They were good friends, but Zoe was never comfortable taking it further. They

Zoe Tate.

did sleep together, but in June 1993, Zoe confessed that she was questioning her sexuality. Archie was shocked, but encouraged her to meet and seek advice from lesbian groups. She joined a poetry group, and was friendly with the woman that ran it, Jude Clayton.

Frank Tate was surprisingly supportive, which Zoe was immensely grateful for. She and Frank were close – while he always seemed faintly disappointed with Chris, he loved Zoe unconditionally. In return, Zoe helped him in the boardroom, and covered for his alcoholism, his breakdown when Kim left him and his heart problems.

But there was intolerance from much of the rest of the village when Zoe came out – Ned Glover banned Linda from working as Zoe's receptionist, and others were equally prejudiced.

Zoe's 'marriage' to Emma was over by the reception.

By January 1995, when Zoe met Emma Nightingale, an interior designer, she finally seemed to be at ease with her sexuality. They moved into Smithy Cottage together, facing another round of abuse. She was almost raped by Ken Adlington, a local farmer convinced she just needed a man to set her straight. Frank recruited Ned to show Adlington the error of his ways. The village soon grew used to the arrangement, though.

Emma's ex-girlfriend, Susie, arrived in the village in May 1996 as Emma and Zoe planned to have their relationship blessed – the nearest to a 'gay marriage' that was allowed. Susie flirted with Zoe, and Zoe began to wonder if she was ready to settle down with Emma. The blessing went ahead, but that evening Zoe confessed she'd rather be with Susie. Emma moved out, and Susie moved in. Susie and Zoe lasted six months together.

Zoe's relationship with Kim was always awkward, and usually openly hostile. It reached a low in September 1996 while Kim was in hospital, giving birth to James. Zoe had to put Kim's favourite horse to sleep, and Kim was convinced this had been done out of revenge, and threatened to sue. Nevertheless, Zoe became James's godmother.

In 1997, Zoe and the Tates' nanny Sophie became lovers. In October, Zoe started getting broody. Sophie didn't want a baby, but didn't want to lose Zoe. After much soul-searching, she left the village.

Zoe was the last person to see Frank alive (or so she thought) and the first to discover his body. She always suspected Kim of the death –

but was shocked to discover that Frank had, in turn, plotted to kill Kim.

Despite their differences, Zoe didn't believe Kim and Steve had stolen Orsino from Home Farm and run over Kathy. As Kim escaped, almost killing Chris, she realised she'd been used, and felt utterly betrayed.

Zoe made a conscious effort to change her life, to stop living in the shadow of others. Deciding to enjoy life, she went to a Hotten lesbian bar, and spent the night with Denise, a woman she picked up. However, she found Denise trying to sneak out early the next morning and discovered she'd only been looking for a one-night stand. Zoe, like Frank and Chris before her, hit the bottle.

This led to disaster at the vet's surgery – Zoe missed appointments and got some terrible publicity when her secretary, Lyn Hutchinson, trying to cover for her, killed one of Jack's sheep by botching an injection.

Zoe picked herself up, and soon afterwards met Frankie Smith, a female driver for her brother's haulage firm. Zoe took a sudden interest in Tate Haulage, buying a 30 per cent stake, and was undeterred at news that Frankie had a steady partner, Maggie. Zoe decided to play hard to get, which intrigued Frankie. They ended up getting matching tattoos (a Celtic design on their left shoulders).

However, Zoe's machinations backfired – she sent Frankie away on a haulage trip to Germany for three weeks, thinking that would drive a wedge between her and Maggie. Instead, Frankie was arrested for

Zoe has a dark side – here she kills Liam in cold blood.

drink-driving. When it became clear that Frankie really only saw Zoe as a pot of cash, Zoe refused to pay her bail.

More dramatically, Zoe was forced to take control of the Tate empire when Chris vanished. She bought Home Farm back for the family and took care of Joseph. Zoe attended an emotional press conference appealing for information, and shortly afterwards started receiving ransom demands. She befriended one of the truckers, Liam,

but eventually became suspicious of him. Checking his CV, she discovered he had lied about his past. Frustrated by the lack of police action, she took matters into her own hands, and enlisted Terry to break into Liam's house. Liam discovered them, knocked out Terry and took Zoe to the isolated farmhouse where he'd been keeping Chris.

Liam was Frank's illegitimate son. Chris had developed some sympathy for Liam, who had led a

Chris clearly doesn't want to get involved as the women in his life argue.

Joseph Tate.

terrible life. But Zoe was having none of it and, grabbing Liam's gun, she shot him dead.

Chris and Zoe destroyed all evidence linking Liam to the Tates, baffling the police, who just couldn't establish Liam's motive. Chris ensured that Liam was buried in St Mary's churchyard, next to Frank.

Zoe lied at the coroner's court hearing, and Liam's death was ruled lawful killing.

Frankie had returned to the village, and Zoe rekindled their relationship. But this was strained by the bus crash, with Frankie accusing Zoe of being more interested in the business than the people that died. The relationship ended when Zoe suspected Frankie of stealing a couple of expensive watches. The final straw, though, was the revelation that Frankie had married

an American man to get herself a green card.

Zoe increased her stake in the haulage business when Laura sold her her 10 per cent stake.

Zoe was throwing herself into family life, and was angry that Chris's relationship with Charity (in which he paid for sex) was a bad example to Joseph. She threatened to tell the Dingles about the relationship – Zak held Chris responsible for Butch's death. Charity responded by kissing Zoe. Upset at first, Zoe came to realise that she was attracted to Charity. They began an affair, Charity's first lesbian experience, but Charity soon chose Chris over his sister.

Zoe has a number of firm friends in the village – she's the friend and landlord of Paddy Kirk, and helped him and Mandy get back together

after the eviction crisis. Her best friend is Ashley, who's always been fairly coy about his feelings about her homosexuality, but who has been a confidant to her. In turn, she was his best man when he married Bernice.

JOSEPH MARK TATE
(played by Oliver Young)
Born and First Appearance:
8 June 1995

The son of Chris Tate and his late second wife Rachel.

He was born on the same day that Joe Sugden died, and was named after him. His middle name is that of Rachel's brother, who died in the plane crash.

Chris's and Rachel's marriage didn't last long, and Rachel looked after Joseph until her death in 1999.

Joseph then went to live with Chris, who soon found it difficult juggling his business and his responsibilities to his son.

While there could conceivably one day be a rival claim from James Tate, Frank's and Kim's son, Joseph is the heir to Chris Tate's fortune. He is also the major named beneficiary in Zoe's will.

CHARITY TATE (née DINGLE)
(Played by Emma Atkins)
Born: 1978
First Appearance:
30 March 2000

Charity is Chris Tate's third wife and a member of the Dingle clan. Charity knows how to flatter people, but can also be brutally blunt. She has the ability to move in different social circles – a skill learnt through a promiscuous, dangerous life. She's a Dingle, but she's mainly looking out for number one.

Charity was first seen at Butch's funeral, where she stole Pollard's wallet. She's the daughter of one of Zak's brothers, but her father's name

Charity Tate.

hasn't been established – we do know she's not the sister of any of the other young Dingles. She quickly settled in Emmerdale, but it soon became clear she was on the run from her pimp in Leeds.

Charity quickly identified Chris Tate as a potential client, and Chris – perhaps unsurprisingly, given his record – was happy to pay for an uncomplicated sexual relationship. Terry Woods, Chris's minder, was rather less comfortable with the arrangement. Charity soon realised that Zoe was a threat, and contrived to gain the upper hand – making sure Chris snubbed Zoe on her birthday, for example.

Chris Tate, though, was the man that the rest of the Dingles blamed for Butch's death. Cain attacked Charity when he discovered her involvement with Chris, but Charity was quite happy to have Chris call the police and drag Cain away.

Zoe offered Charity £5000 to leave the village. Charity found this tempting – but realised Chris was worth far more to her, and got herself moved into his cottage in the village. She also became Chris's PA, moving ever closer to power and influence.

The tension between Charity and Zoe mounted – and Charity shocked Zoe by kissing her. Charity's flirting began to worry Chris, who was clearly becoming emotionally involved with her. He suspected her of having an affair and ordered Terry to monitor her.

Although Terry never discovered it, the affair was with Zoe. Charity claimed this was her first lesbian experience, and Zoe seemed to enjoy both Charity's company and withholding such a powerful secret

from her brother. It soon became clear, though, that Charity would choose Chris over her. Zoe decided to reveal the affair to Chris.

Chris didn't believe Zoe, who found herself alienated from her brother as he grew ever closer to Charity. Zoe moved out, and Chris soon proposed to Charity.

Zoe moved to prevent the wedding, taping Charity confessing to their affair and blackmailing her. Charity called Zoe's bluff, admitting to Chris that she'd slept with his sister, and revealing the blackmail attempt. Charity thought that Chris would throw her out but, far from it, Chris sided with Charity, not Zoe.

Chris and Charity married on 27 November 2001, with Charity calling the shots – and arranging a funfair at Home Farm estate during the reception.

Since the wedding, Charity has become a key player in the Tate empire, gaining a great deal of influence over Chris's business. It was her idea to set up Tate Trash and bid for the lucrative waste disposal contracts in the area.

Zoe and Charity.

THE DINGLES

Compiling a Dingle family tree is difficult. There are a lot of Dingles, and they are prone to lie, exaggerate, intermarry and use nicknames and aliases. The Dingles are an extended family of rogues and petty criminals. There are Dingles all over the world – including Italy and Australia – but most live in Britain. For generations, a contingent has lived in the village.

ZACARIAH DINGLE ('Zak')
(played by Steve Halliwell)
Born: 19 January 1952
First Appearance: 20 October 1994

Zak is the patriarch of the Emmerdale Dingles. Ostensibly a scrap dealer and pig farmer, Zak spends most of his time either doing nothing at all, or dreaming up scams and schemes.

Although not seen until relatively recently, Zak has always lived locally – he was born in the family farm. He has claimed to be one of seven sons, he's apparently one of the oldest, after Mandy's father, Caleb. His father Jeb walked out on the family when Zak was eight. Zak thought he'd died (even suspecting his mother had killed him), but discovered in 2002 that he's still alive, travelling between hostels and slowly drinking himself to death. He married Nellie and had four children – Ben, Butch, Tina and Sam. In early 1974, he had a fling with his sister-in-law, Faith, and – although he didn't know it for many years – fathered Cain. He once said his mother's name was Molly, but

An early Dingle family shot.

when she turned up in 2002, she was called Peg – both, though, are diminutive forms of the name Elizabeth.

Ben Dingle, his oldest son, died after a fight in the village with Luke McAllister, and this started a long feud with Luke's family and much of the rest of the village.

Zak Dingle.

At times a violent man, Zak is also prone to jealousy. He got angry with Nellie for spending time with Eric Pollard and even for kissing Ian Botham, who was reopening the Woolpack. In 1995, he accompanied Nellie to Ireland, where her sick father lived, and returned without her. In 1996, Nellie wrote to tell him she wasn't coming back, and he rushed to Ireland to talk her round – returning a few weeks later with a blonde called Marilyn, who would quickly con him out of some money and leave.

Failed ventures around this time included the Dingle Rat Catching Corporation and sheep-rustling. His younger brother Albert conned Butch and Sam into a more serious

robbery, and forced him to give himself up to the police.

When Tina jilted Luke at the altar, Zak was surprisingly upset, as

he had initially hated Luke who was a McAllister. However, he was happy to sell off the wedding presents.

He soon met Lisa Clegg, admitting he admired 'a woman that can weld'. As their friendship blossomed, they joined a band started by Vic and Terry (Zak playing the drums). This happiness was marred when Sam was forced to go on the run to Ireland.

Zak's first proper job was as a security guard at the quarry, but he grew restless when his nephew Marlon arrived in the village and set up a Santa's grotto scam. Then, when Albert returned to the village, and Lisa left Zak in protest – Zak won her back with presents and poetry. He blotted his copy book again when he showed an interest in getting involved with Lisa's estranged husband Barry's plan to build an amateur rocket.

By now, Zak was becoming more of a part of village life, and was immersing himself in scams. So much so that he failed to notice Lisa

had had a makeover. She left him, and became engaged to his brother, Albert. He persuaded her to leave Albert on their wedding day, and Zak and Lisa have been mostly happy, ever since. They married in January 1998.

Zak still enforced discipline on the family living under his roof – he beat Butch for stalking Sophie, and threw Marlon out for allowing Sam to get injured. He still needed his family to conduct scams – poaching, horse-napping and stealing clothes from the lines at the holiday village, as well as more imaginative schemes, like pretending to see an osprey on his land to attract birdwatchers and their money.

Perennially threatened with eviction, the Dingles were finally thrown off their farm in autumn 1998. The day was saved when Mandy was paid off by Paddy Kirk's mother, who was desperate to stop her marrying her son. However the deal did mean she had to marry her cousin Butch. Zak bought the Dingle

The Woolpackers - Terry, Zak, Lisa and Vic

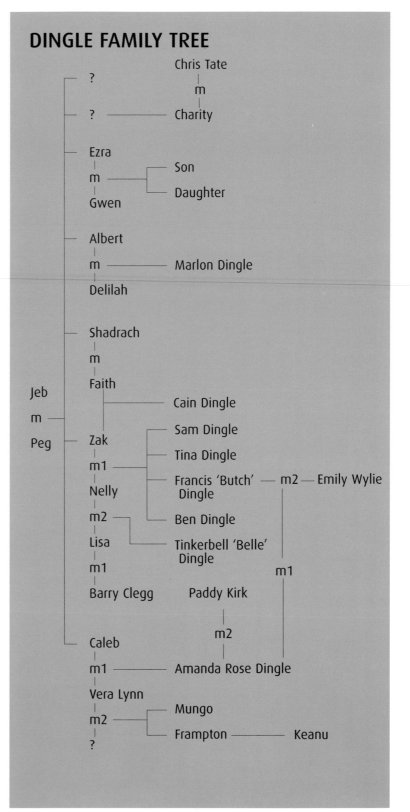

Zak and Cain come to blows.

farm, becoming the first ever Dingle homeowner.

Zak reconciled with Marlon on Christmas Day 1998, after Marlon helped them fight eviction. Marlon was invited to lunch – which ended unexpectedly, when Lisa gave birth to Belle.

Zak declared he would become a house husband, and nobly offered to sit around the house all day while Lisa worked in her garage. It wasn't the easy life Zak was expecting, though – he left Belle in the bookie's at one point. When his brother Ezra turned up, he accused Zak of 'going all middle class' – an impression reinforced when Lisa announced the garage business was going legit, and she'd be paying tax. Zak was also kept on his toes when the Reynolds moved in next door – Angie Reynolds, the mother of the house, was a policewoman, and was well aware of Zak's reputation.

Zak is increasingly aware that he's not as young as he was, and he has new responsibilities. This was

underlined by the death of Butch in the bus crash. Zak became increasingly protective of Sam, his only surviving son, who was allowed out of prison for the funeral. Also attending the funeral were other members of the clan, Charity and Cain, who came to stay. He threw Charity out when she started a relationship with Chris Tate (owner of the truck that killed Butch), and was shocked to learn that Cain was actually his son. Soon, though, he realised that this was another chance for him to be a good father.

Late in 2001, Zak was diagnosed with testicular cancer. Zak had always thought he was invincible, and found it very difficult to admit he had a problem or to seek treatment for it. Sam convinced him to, and the revelation of his condition helped reconcile him with the rest of his family.

In 2002, Peg Dingle was dumped in Emmerdale by cousins Marilyn and Elvis, who were fed up with her. She annoyed Zak and abused his hospitality for several months before he tricked Marilyn and Elvis into taking her back.

Lisa Dingle.

LISA DINGLE
(played by Jane Cox)
Born: 1956
First Appearance:
13 August 1996

Zak and Lisa met at a singles night in the wine bar, and they instantly hit it off. She was initially reluctant to move in with him as she had her own farm to look after. There was also the complication that both Zak and Lisa were still married, although both were estranged.

She played in a band with Zak, Terry and Vic (Lisa playing the fiddle), and eventually chose Zak over her estranged husband Barry and Zak's brother Albert. They married in January 1998. That year, she decided to set up as a car mechanic, and Zak found her an abandoned property in the village. She was increasingly concerned about Zak's thieving and the way he lived his life. She gave birth to her first child, Belle, completely unexpectedly, on Christmas Day – she'd assumed she'd hit the menopause. When Laura Johnstone

offered her the contract to service Tate Haulage vehicles, on the condition she registered for tax, Lisa jumped at the chance, much to Zak's disgust. Things came to a head at Belle's christening – a church do, against Zak's wishes. Lisa served the Dingle clan a quiche, leaving many of Zak's extended family bemused.

In early 2000, Nellie Dingle returned, causing tension between Zak and Lisa. Preoccupied, she fell behind with her work on the Tate trucks. When one of them crashed, killing Butch, she blamed herself for not checking the brakes. Nellie exploited Lisa's guilt, and got Zak to throw her out. Lisa went to live with Paddy and Mandy… at just the time when their marriage was starting to break up. Lisa left, moving in with Seth and Betty. Zak came to realise how upset Lisa was, and kicked Nellie out. But Nellie's parting shot – revealing that she and Zak had slept together – damaged the marriage.

Lisa lost a lot of custom after the bus crash, and the owner of the garage caught up with her and demanded back rent. It forced her to close down. Only a few weeks later,

Butch's funeral saw many Dingles gather in Emmerdale.

Zak, Lisa and Belle.

Sam Dingle.

she was completely exonerated by the crash report.

She started a decorating business with Jason Kirk, decorating the interior of Chez Marlon and Pollard's tat factory. Cain proved a major source of conflict – he stole keys from Lisa to rob a place she was decorating and the revelation that Zak was Cain's real father shook Lisa.

Lisa started working at the tat factory to earn a regular wage. Her relationship with Zak was tested again when he was diagnosed with cancer, but they emerged stronger from it.

> SAMUEL JONAH DINGLE
> (played by James Hooton)
> Born: 16 August 1977
> First Appearance: 14 February 1995

Zak's youngest son, Sam is extremely loyal but simple-minded, and is perpetually in trouble.

When Robert Sugden disappeared, Sam demanded ransom money – he didn't have Robert, and it was simple to track Sam down. He was arrested and put on remand. On his release, he ended up doing odd jobs for Eric Pollard, who found it easy to con Sam out of his wages. In the meantime, Zak had him doing the legwork for many of the Dingle scams. Both Zak and Pollard often had to cope with Sam messing up the simplest of orders – he once got trapped in a field by some sheep, explaining, 'Them sheep tricked me.'

He was arrested again for stealing a plate from a shop. Lisa helped get him to Ireland to escape prison. He returned the following year for Pollard's wedding, where he was the best man. He returned to Ireland. Later in the year he came back to Emmerdale, gave himself up and was fined.

Sam was illiterate. He got reading lessons from Kathy, and developed a crush on her. When Kathy's date, Jez, said something nasty about Kathy, he hit him – and once again was arrested. At his trial, he said he was glad he did it, and bail was refused.

Sam didn't resurface until 2000, feeling he wouldn't be welcome. Pollard found him, and told him about Butch's death. Sam returned for the funeral, and stayed. He became a delivery boy for Viv's shop, and continued to do jobs for Pollard.

When both Viv and Pollard stood for council elections, he saw no problem with canvassing for both of them.

More seriously, he and Cain took revenge on Tate Haulage for Butch's death by breaking in and tying up Sean. Sam got nervous following this, and soon afterwards said he was returning to Ireland. Sam returned, but became the subject of Cain's bullying, and went into hiding in the holiday village. Zak learned where he was, and welcomed him back into the family. Sam began working at the tat factory.

Sam's Criminal Record:

30/3/95 – arrested

13/7/95 – given community service

26/9/96 – arrested for theft

1/10/96 – released on bail

13/11/97 – arrested for failing to answer bail and theft

18/11/97 – appeared in court and was fined

16/4/98 – arrested for hitting Jez, the fireman

21/4/98 – in court: bail refused; has to remain in custody awaiting trial at Crown Court

Marlon Dingle.

Cook, thief ...

...and lover. Marlon Dingle.

MARLON DINGLE
(played by Mark Charnock)
Born: 23 March 1974
First Appearance:
17 October 1996

Marlon is smarter than the average Dingle, and works as hard as the rest of the clan put together, but is still prone to schemes and scams that never quite come off.

Marlon is the son of Zak's younger brother Albert. We don't know his mother's name. He appears to be an only child. He turned up out of the blue in a flashy car – he had hitched a ride. He quickly brought his business mind to the Dingles' scams, setting up a Santa's grotto in the village hall which proved to be a moneyspinner.

Albert came to the village and involved the Dingles in a number of serious crimes – burglary, stealing cars and building supplies. When it became clear to Marlon that his dad was prepared to shop him to stay out

of trouble himself, Marlon decided to go for an honest job, and ended up working in the kitchens of Pollard's wine bar. He enjoyed this work, and had an aptitude for it, and became involved with Lyn Hutchinson. However, when Sam got injured in a scam Marlon had set up, the Dingles threw him out. Marlon ended up squatting in Annie's Cottage with Biff.

Marlon was becoming ever more involved with running the wine bar, and began to picture himself in charge himself one day. He struck up a good working relationship with Pollard – but was pragmatic enough to side with Kathy when it became clear Eric was going to lose his licence. When Pollard decided to burn down the wine bar rather than lose it, it was Marlon who talked him out of it. When Kathy refurbished the tearooms into a diner, Marlon became a full-time, proper chef. By the end of 1998, he was in a steady relationship with Lyn, the Dingles had forgiven him

and he had his dream job.

It couldn't last. Lyn dumped him for not paying enough attention to her – he said he'd do anything to get her back. Lyn responded by saying he'd have to do something impossible, like dye Pollard's moustache pink. Marlon duly managed it, but dumped Lyn at his twenty-fifth birthday party when he discovered she'd recently slept with Scott.

Fond of Kathy, and a good friend of Biff, Marlon made sure the two got together. Kathy really trusted Marlon now. When Biff left her at the altar and Kathy needed some time alone, she left Marlon in charge. Marlon saw this as a chance to put his mark on the diner... but when Kathy returned, she was horrified by the changes and sacked him.

Bernice took him on as a gourmet chef at the Woolpack, and this proved to be a huge success. Here, he developed a huge crush on Tricia Stokes, who was going out with Adam Forrester at the time.

When Tricia dumped Adam for two-timing her, it was Bernice's turn to play Cupid, and Marlon and Tricia got together, quickly rushing off for a holiday in Spain together.

They returned with grand plans – they were going to open their own restaurant. For a while it looked like they'd get to run the Woolpack, but this fell through. But Marlon's 'Chez Marlon' gourmet nights were a huge success, and gave him the confidence to approach Chris Tate and Kathy to convert the diner into a quality restaurant.

Marlon's relationship with Tricia suffered when she agreed to marry Joe Fisher, a gay Australian who wanted to stay in the country. The money she got from that helped fund the restaurant, though. Another source of tension was new waitress Chloe, whom Marlon hired and clearly fancied.

Business at the restaurant was always slow, despite good reviews. Pollard was also on the prowl, continually sabotaging the running of the place.

Tricia disappeared from the village suddenly, thinking she'd caused Bernice to miscarry. Marlon was devastated, losing all interest in the restaurant.

He had a fling with locum vet Rhona, but she soon left the village. Marlon continued to struggle to pick up the pieces in Tricia's absence. He was back on his feet when Tricia returned, saying she still loved him. He first wanted nothing to do with her, but soon realised he loved her.

When Kathy left the village, Tricia and Marlon moved into her house while it was on the market. Marlon was shocked to discover

Tricia was sabotaging the sale by putting prospective buyers off. In the end, Tricia convinced her granddad, Alan Turner, to buy the house and rent it to them.

CAIN DINGLE
(played by Jeff Hordley)
Born: 30 November 1974
First Appearance:
30 March 2000

Cain, like Charity, represents a new generation of Dingles – ones who are smarter and more ruthless than Zak's children, and who don't feel as bound by the Dingle code of honour.

Cain Dingle.

A thief, a hard man and a womaniser, Cain can be genuinely dangerous.

Cain first appeared at Butch's funeral, arguing with Sam about who got to lead the funeral procession. He's the son (or so he grew up thinking) of Zak's brother Shadrach and his wife Faith. The day he arrived, he started a fight with Sean Reynolds, and at a village meeting about the bus crash a couple of weeks later he punched Chris Tate and was arrested. He was the prime suspect when Tate Haulage lorries were vandalised.

Cain broke ranks to blame Lisa for Butch's death as she should have serviced the trucks. He eventually got over this, and volunteered to help her with her decorating business – the perfect way into properties to steal stuff.

Cain is fascinated with the Reynolds. It's often hard to see whether this is genuine interest, or just a way of hurting them. He horrified Angie by starting to pursue Ollie, who was attracted to him, but smart enough to be wary.

When Charity started her relationship with Chris, she was well aware that Cain would be the Dingle most likely to turn his anger into violence. Several months down the line, that was exactly what happened. He hit Charity, then broke into Home Farm to threaten Chris.

Cain and Sam were arrested on suspicion of armed robbery, although they were released without charge. Cain assumed Angie was responsible for setting them up. He began to unnerve her by flirting. When she was called on to search him, Angie became very uncomfortable, and it was obvious she found the forbidden fruit attractive. Cain played up on this – sending Angie a Valentine's card, telling her he'd be keen if she were single.

When Cain discovered that Zak was his father, he took the news badly, taking a long time to calm down. Zak eventually smoothed the waters by giving Cain his guitar. Tensions between Cain and Sam continued – Cain had no time for Sam's stupidity, and bullied him. Cain stole money from Jack Sugden and Charity, and didn't contribute to the Dingle pot of money.

Cain started to lead Andy Sugden astray – they stole a car and burgled a house together. Andy told Cain that he was responsible for the death of Sarah.

Angie gave in to temptation, starting an affair with Cain, always managing to avoid discovery. But she became increasingly guilty, and Cain sensed she was trying to break up with him during a romantic getaway. Cain began to pursue Ollie again, and Angie was devastated to realise Cain was after

Angie takes down Cain's particulars.

Cain sees to Len Reynolds.

her daughter. Cain offered a simple choice – if Angie didn't sleep with him, he'd take Ollie's virginity. Thinking he really loved her, Ollie slept with Cain. Len Reynolds caught them in bed together and tussled with Cain – ending up unconscious at the bottom of the stairs. He then blackmailed Angie into forcing Len not to press charges.

Angie and Ollie vowed to keep what had happened from Sean and to pull together. It was simple enough for Cain to derail this plan – revealing his affair to Sean. When Sean attacked Cain, Cain refused to be drawn into a fight – and successfully pressed charges for assault. When he told the police about his affair with Angie, and it became clear that she had abused her power to cover up her family's problems, she was suspended. The Reynolds family suffered a blow from which it wouldn't recover.

Cain became involved in a counterfeit money scam run by newcomer to the village, Ray Mullan. He also began sleeping with Latisha Daggert.

EMILY DINGLE (née WYLIE)
(played by Kate McGregor)
Born: 1968
First Appearance: 5 May 1999

Emily's mother died when she was two, and her father, John, who was strictly religious, brought her up living a sheltered life on the family hill farm. Emily went to school (presumably in Hotten), but was quiet with few friends, and didn't take part in after-school activities. She is hard-working, almost incapable of lying and teetotal. She is adept at mental arithmetic and is a very fast study – she once memorised the rules of cricket overnight, and was able to correct an experienced umpire on a point of detai, although she's a terrible driver.

In May 1999, John Wylie's hill farm was in serious financial trouble. Against his better judgement, he agreed that Emily should apply for a job as the assistant in the village shop in Emmerdale. Viv welcomed a hard-working, honest and cheap employee, although was occasionally exasperated by some of Emily's eccentricities, such as rearranging the shop's shelves in colour order.

Emily Dingle

Mandy Dingle is surprised when Paddy chooses Emily over her.

Emily had been sheltered from the outside world – she'd never stepped inside a pub until Viv took her for lunch one day. She'd never had any interest in boys. But on her way to her interview, she'd met Butch, who had helped steady her nerves, and she felt strongly attracted to him. Betty Eagleton could see that it was mutual, and acted as a matchmaker. She invited Emily and Butch for tea, and they got on like a house on fire, laughing at old photographs and talking about their pets – Butch's pigs and Emily's sheepdog, Patch. Viv was a little annoyed at Butch coming into the shop all the time, especially when he brought in a piglet he had named after Emily.

When Emily's father found out, he forbade her from seeing Butch, and even threatened him with a shotgun. Emily defied her father, and eventually moved out and into Mandy's old room at the Dingles. By now her relationship with Butch had progressed to the occasional kiss and holding of hands.

In March 2000, Butch plucked up the courage to confront John Wylie, and to ask for his approval to marry Emily. And then tragedy struck – the bus he was on was hit by a Tate Haulage truck. Butch was fatally injured. He survived just long enough to marry Emily from his hospital bed. Emily campaigned to see Tate Haulage take some responsibility for the accident, and organised a collection to pay for a memorial bench.

Emily soon met Ed, a young labourer at Home Farm. They became good friends. Emily moved out of the Dingle farm, eventually ending up with Nicola Blackstock in Dale View. Emily supported Nicola as her plans to marry Carlos collapsed. Emily's relationship with Ed faltered, though, as she and Paddy realised they had feelings for each other.

Emily and Paddy slept together, and Emily was soon living with him at Smithy Cottage. The Dingles approved of the relationship – Paddy was family after all. When Paddy's estranged wife, Mandy, returned to the village wanting to make amends, Paddy and Mandy ended up in bed together. But her return only proved to Paddy how much he loved Emily. Emily forgave him, and the two are now a solid couple.

THE WINDSORS

It seems ironic now that the Windsors came to Beckindale from Essex looking for a quiet, crime-free life. Before they arrived, their family history was already fairly convoluted. Vic and Viv Windsor had each been married before, and each had a child. Once in Yorkshire, though, they were faced with the plane crash within months of arriving, and after that the Windsors were involved in affairs and crimes aplenty, and even a spot of almost-incest.

There's a little confusion about dates – Reg was released in May 1994, after serving exactly ten years in prison. Viv has said she divorced him two years after he went to prison – which ought to be mid-1986. But Vic and Viv married in June 1984. Vic never met Reg until he turned up in Emmerdale, as he was in prison, but it would seem Viv was still technically married to Reg when she and Vic started their relationship. Vic was definitely married – his first wife, Anne, died running out into the street after finding Vic with Viv. Donna was born in wedlock in 1986.

The Windsors arrive in the village.

VIVIENNE HOPE (VIV) formerly Dawson, previously Windsor, Maiden name unknown (played by Deena Payne)
Born: 19 May 1956
First Appearance: 30 March 2000

Viv is a sharp-tongued and often vicious gossip, the owner of the village post office shop. She has outlived two husbands, and is currently married to Bob Hope. She's the mother of Scott (by her first husband, Reg Dawson) and Donna (with her second, Vic), and was stepmother to Vic's daughter, Kelly. Her marriage to Vic was often unhappy, and she had an affair with Vic's best friend, Terry Woods.

Vic had set his heart on re-creating the rural life he'd enjoyed in his childhood, and the Windsors arrived to view the post office, staying in the holiday village while the deal went through. In many ways, this was Vic's dream, not Viv's, and she sometimes shared the children's view that the move had been a mistake. Within months, the family found themselves right in the thick of the plane crash, although none of them were seriously injured and the post office survived the cataclysm. Viv became a member of the disaster committee.

Viv's had a long-running feud with the Sugdens. Depending on who you believe, this began when the Windsors first arrived in the country and ignored the country code, or when Donna had an accident on a tractor on Emmerdale land.

That said, there are very few

WINDSOR FAMILY TREE

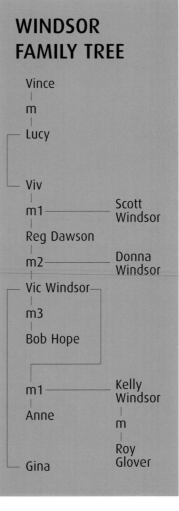

```
Vince
 |
 m
 |
 Lucy
 |
 Viv
 |
 m1————————Scott
 |          Windsor
Reg Dawson
 |
 m2————————Donna
 |          Windsor
Vic Windsor
 |
 m3
 |
Bob Hope

 m1————————Kelly
 |          Windsor
Anne         |
 |           m
 |           |
Gina        Roy
            Glover
```

Viv Hope.

Viv wasn't pleased when Reg Dawson reappeared.

Scott, Donna and Kelly Windsor.

people in the village who haven't either been barred or have boycotted the shop after exchanging sharp words with Viv over the years. Kim was barred for trying to evict the Dingles... and only a few weeks later the Dingles were barred, when Viv decided she didn't want their sort in the village after all. Viv and Shirley Foster stopped talking to each other after Viv refused to accept Shirley's past as a prostitute. Shirley would die a few months later when Viv's ex-husband returned to raid the post office – the irony being that the bullet had been meant for Viv.

Viv was left £30,000 in Reg's will if she divorced Vic, and she seriously thought about it. She chose to stick with her man, although she was soon taking dance classes with Terry Woods and winning competitions with him. She stayed faithful to Vic... for a while.

Viv spent her energies trying to put a stop to things – Zoe's and Emma's lesbian blessing, Mandy's munchbox, Vic and Scott's trip to a gun club, Andy Hopwood sharing a class with Donna.

She started sleeping with Terry, and was soon found out. By the end of 1996, she'd moved into the Woolpack with Terry. Donna joined them, but Viv and Terry fell out when Donna started drinking alcopops. She moved back in with Vic, although she also tried to seduce Paddy Kirk. Her relationship with Kelly was now hitting rock-bottom, and got worse when Kelly found she was pregnant with Chris's baby.

Viv and Sarah Sugden were now used to feuding – Andy and Donna were taking turns to bully each other at school. Vic tried to build bridges by hiring Andy as a paper boy – but this, indirectly, led to his death, as it encouraged Billy Hopwood to think about raiding the post office.

While Viv was cursing Vic for being late for Christmas dinner in the Woolpack, he lay bleeding to death – Vic had disturbed Billy and had received a fatal head wound.

Viv struggled to keep the family together after Vic's death. She remained blissfully unaware that Kelly and Scott were starting to explore their feelings for each other.

Instead she decided to blame everything on Andy Sugden, and tried to get him excluded from Hotten Comprehensive.

Kelly's engagement to Roy Glover seemed to mark a new start for the family, and Viv eagerly embraced it, offering to pay for the wedding. However, she was clearly favouring her children Scott and Donna over Vic's daughter Kelly – she gave Scott the money Vic had provided for Kelly in his will so that Scott could set up a computer company. Viv had befriended Stella Jones, the lottery winner who'd bought Home Farm, purely because she was keen to climb the social ladder. Viv's grasping ways (she expected Stella to help pay Kelly the money) was one of the reasons Stella decided to leave the village. When Kelly found out what Viv had done, she punched Viv so hard it gave her a black eye.

Viv hired Emily Wylie to help in the shop, and had to put up with her somewhat eccentric behaviour, not to mention the almost constant presence of a lovestruck Butch Dingle.

Viv set her sights on Richie Carter, Scott's friend and partner, who was terrified of her but too polite to say anything. Richie was soon having a secret affair with Sarah Sugden, Viv's arch-enemy – he'd discovered that the safest way to avoid Viv was to spend time with Sarah, and their relationship grew from that!

The shop suffered when a new supermarket opened outside Hotten, and Viv seriously considered selling up. Business picked up after the bus crash, though, and Viv was able to carry on. Her old friend Carol came to stay, and annoyed Viv by starting to date Terry. Viv finally found true love with Bob Hope, and they were married after a whirlwind romance. Viv and Carol fell out when Carol bought the bed and breakfast.

Viv was horrified to find Donna in bed with Marc, worried that her daughter would make the same mistakes as Kelly.

Viv and Bob are now settled in the village, and Viv has opened a tearoom, Cafe Hope.

SCOTT WINDSOR
(played by Ben Freeman,
originally Toby Cockerell)
Born: 20 July 1980
First Appearance: 10 August
1993 (Ben Freeman:
9 April 1998)

The son of Viv Windsor and her first husband Reg Dawson. Scott hated the country when the Windsors first came to Beckindale to run the post office, and was badly affected by the death of his father, a violent criminal who resorted to raiding the Windsors' post office. Joining the Army changed him – on his return Scott had become a ladies' man, bedding (amongst others) Lyn Hutchinson, Paulette Lewis, Tricia and even his stepsister Kelly. While officially discharged from the Army on medical grounds, it transpired he'd been sleeping with the medical officer's wife, Cass Linton, and her husband had forced him out of the service. Scott tended to love them and leave them, and other

Scott Windsor

aspects of his life tended to show the same selfishness and cynicism. Recently, though, he seems to have settled down – he now works as a car mechanic (he owns the village garage) and is living with Chloe Atkinson.

Young Scott was a tearaway – bored and frustrated by leaving all his friends behind and moving to a tiny village. He ran away a couple of times. He was badly psychologically affected by both the plane crash and his father's death, and went into therapy. His unhappiness manifested itself in crime, and he stole fireworks, pension books and even the odd car. He was usually caught. His most public crime was daubing 'Lesbean' on Zoe's and Emma's new house. A couple of months later, he'd become fascinated with guns, borrowing Ned Glover's shotgun. This proved to be a bonding experience for him and Vic – they secretly went to a gun club together.

In 1996, he got four GCSEs, and decided to leave school and join the Army. He left the village.

Scott returned briefly in April 1998 on leave, then returned for good in August. Scott persuaded the other village lads to do odd jobs around the village to pay to repair an old car. It soon became clear to the others that they were doing the work and Scott was having all the fun driving.

Scott soon realised he was attracted to his stepsister Kelly – Kelly was horrified, and explained to Scott that he only had those feelings because he knew she was the one girl he couldn't have. They ended up kissing on Christmas Day. Kelly was repulsed by what she'd done – and before they could come to terms with

Scott and Chloe.

it, they learned that Kelly's dad, Vic, had been murdered.

Scott left the village for a couple of weeks to sort himself out – on his return, he discovered that Kelly had got engaged to Roy. Scott began suffering from impotence with Tricia, and knew this was because he wanted to be with Kelly instead. He split up with Tricia, blaming her. He was the best man at Kelly's and Roy's wedding, and let it pass uneventfully.

Scott began working for ThinkTank Logistics, a Hotten computer firm, and, despite having almost no knowledge of computers, found he could charm people into buying. He contacted an old friend of his, Richie Carter, who did know about computers, and they set up a computer sales and repair business, DaleTech, in the village – using £5000 from Viv, which had been left to Kelly in Vic's will. He claimed it was for vital start-up costs, but used it to put the deposit down on a sports car. He intended to poach customers from his real job at

ThinkTank – but when his boss, Miss Winters, discovered his plan, she sacked him, and he was forced to come clean to Richie.

When Roy was sent to prison, Scott took Kelly out for a meal to cheer her up, and they ended up sleeping together again. This time it was Scott who regretted it. He started seeing Lyn again, giving her a computer for college.

In early 2000, Kelly tried to kill herself. Scott found her, but was at least as concerned with destroying the letters and tapes she'd left saying they'd slept together – he was naturally worried about the village finding out. Lyn discovered the truth, and left him.

Meanwhile, Richie went behind Scott's back and persuaded Chris Tate to buy into DaleTech – but Chris's condition was that Scott had nothing to do with the business. Scott felt betrayed, but could do nothing about it. He would soon discover that Richie was having an affair with Sarah Sugden, but failed in an attempt to blackmail them.

Scott started working for Lisa in the garage, and soon took over the business for himself, with Roy helping him. The two argued constantly, and Roy soon walked out. Scott had clearly put his homophobia behind him as he replaced Roy with Frankie Smith.

Donna announced to a crowded Woolpack, including Viv, that Scott and Kelly had slept together. Viv threw Scott out, and he ended up living with Richie. The two were friends again, and Scott provided support to Richie in the aftermath of Sarah's death.

Chloe Atkinson's arrival has softened Scott – they quickly fell for each other and now live together. While still not on the best of terms with Viv, he's helped Donna – talking to her after she slept with Marc, and about joining the Army.

DONNA WINDSOR
(played by Verity Rushworth, originally by Sophie Jeffrey)
Born: 1986
First Appearance: 10 August 1993 (Verity Rushworth: 25 February 1998)

The daughter of Vic and Viv Windsor, half-sister to Scott and Kelly and stepdaughter to Bob Hope. A typical teenage girl, who's recently emerged from the shadow of her older siblings.

Donna was upset to see Viv and Terry cuddling, and affected badly by the subsequent temporary break-up of the family. She had an early bad experience with alcohol – drinking cider in the Woolpack led to her getting sick on whisky and alcopops, and having to go to

hospital to have her stomach pumped. She was excluded from school for having her nose pierced.

She got into a cycle of bullying with Andy Hopwood. He hit her, and they would get involved in a number of fights over the years. Andy was very insecure about being fostered, and Donna knew she could get under his skin by teasing him about it. He hit her again, and she broke his Playstation. The two continued to have a troubled relationship – and their mothers, Viv and Sarah Sugden, did nothing but fan the flames with their own feud. In May 1997, Andy was excluded for three weeks for accidentally hitting a teacher when he lashed out at Donna.

A year later, Donna turned the tables. She'd fallen in with a gang of bullies led by her friend Chelsea, and they would routinely trip Andy up, steal his money and lunch. Andy got the blame when they got into a fight, and was punished by having to clear up the playground after school. It all came to a head when Robert punched Donna in the face. The

Donna Windsor

Bob and Viv Hope.

truth about the gang of bullies came out, and Miss Strickland had Chelsea sent to a school for children with behavioural difficulties. Donna was chastised, and began to mend her ways. When Andy's father killed Vic in a raid on the post office, she was naturally heartbroken, but blamed herself more than Andy.

Donna developed a bit of a crush on Marc Reynolds, but she was a couple of years younger than him and he was a little wary about pursuing her.

Donna found it difficult to deal with Kelly's suicide attempt, and started to hang around with Ollie. She finally got her man after the bus crash, when Marc was slightly injured and she rushed to make sure he was all right. They slept together, and Donna was mortified when first her mother caught them and then

Viv stormed into her classroom to lecture her about it. Marc soon got a little bored with Donna, and became more interested in Eve. But Donna proved far more of a friend following the hit and run incident.

Donna felt left out as Viv and Bob started spending more and more time together. When Viv and Bob married, she was livid when Viv tried to get her surname changed to Hope on the school register.

BOB REGINALD HOPE
(played by Antony Audenshaw)
First Appearance:
19 September 2000

Bob first arrived in the village as a travelling lingerie salesman. Viv was taken with him, bought a great deal of stock from him… and the next morning, Donna caught him coming downstairs in Viv's dressing-gown.

Kelly was disgusted by the relationship. She made a point of flirting with him, but Bob made it clear he wasn't interested. Viv saw this, and asked Kelly to leave home. Viv asked Bob to move in, but Bob was reluctant, suggesting Viv sort out her family problems first.

Bob disappeared for about six weeks, returning just before Christmas, acting like he hadn't been away. Viv was delighted. Bob was rather less happy to find himself mediating between Viv and her friend Carol. They organised a Christmas party, and that night Bob accepted Viv's offer to move in. Donna wasn't too happy, feeling there was no room.

Donna was suspicious of Bob – he was endlessly putting off moving his stuff into the house. He tried to buy Donna's trust by taking Donna shopping for a new ski jacket, but

she became suspicious again after finding hotel toiletries in his car.

Viv grew annoyed with Bob going away for long periods, and kicked him out. Bob shinned up a drainpipe to deliver her chocolates and underwear, but fell off the roof. Viv let him back in – but threw him out again when she discovered he'd been boasting about their sex life to Cain.

Viv wouldn't take Bob back. In desperation, he proposed – and was surprised when Viv accepted. Bob quickly had second thoughts, but they married just a few weeks later.

Viv wanted Bob to work with her. He really didn't fancy helping to run the shop, and wasn't that much happier when Viv announced she was going to bid for the bed and breakfast. Viv kept pressing him to leave his job and spend more time with her, but he continued to fob her off. When Carol outbid Viv for the B&B, Bob was

Bob proves to be a dark horse - here are his secret wife and kids

relieved – but this soon turned to annoyance when Viv banned him from seeing Terry, 'the enemy'.

Viv became convinced that Bob was a bigamist after an old friend of his seemed to suggest as much. Carol and Viv tracked down Bob and found him talking to a young woman with children. Bob came clean when he was confronted – he'd been married before and was having to pay a great deal in maintenance. He couldn't afford to take Viv on honeymoon.

Bob did come up with a way they might get a holiday – Viv could enter the Naughty Nylons Lovely Legs competition. Viv won, but Bob lost his job with the company when they realised he was married to the winner. Viv wasn't impressed when the catalogue appeared with another model's head pasted on her body!

Bob became the new manager of the Tat factory after Gloria's departure. They finally got to go on honeymoon when Seth found them a cheap holiday on the internet.

Bob frequently finds himself mediating between Donna and Viv, who has caught her daughter in bed with Marc, argued with her over applying to join the Army and clashed over Donna's involvement in the hit-and-run on Miss Strickland.

CHLOE ATKINSON
(played by Amy Nuttall)
First Appearance:
4 December 2000

When Marlon opened his Chez Marlon restaurant, he found it difficult to hire staff. Betty was keen on septuagenarian Alfred, but

Chloe Atkinson

Marlon wasn't. Late in the day, Chloe appeared and Marlon, clearly charmed, hired her on the spot.

Marlon's girlfriend Tricia was openly hostile to the new arrival, sacking her behind Marlon's back and provoking a huge row. Marlon couldn't cope without Chloe, and rehired her. He refused to sack her despite constant pressure from Tricia.

Chloe moved into Pear Tree Cottage with Charity, not understanding why so many people in the village disliked her. She was often Charity's only shoulder to cry on.

Chloe took a shine to Scott when he ate at Chez Marlon. She chatted to him about buying a car, and he bought her a drink. When she picked up the car, Scott moved to kiss her, but she pushed him away. Soon afterwards, though, they were going out together.

THE BLACKSTOCKS

BERNICE MARIE THOMAS
(née BLACKSTOCK,
formerly BINNS)
(played by Samantha Giles)
Born: 29 December 1968
First Appearance:
November 1998

Bernice first appeared in Emmerdale as the temporary barmaid brought in by Alan to cover for Mandy. She was an instant hit, especially with the men of the village, but also built up a good relationship with both Turner and Betty. Her public smile and calm efficiency concealed a complicated and troubled personal life.

Early in 1999, she returned as the bar manager of the Woolpack. She saw the job as an attempt to bring direction to her life. Something of a control freak, she infuriated Tricia and Mandy by insisting they

Bernice Blackstock.

do things 'the proper way' – suggestions included getting Mandy to dress more conservatively, telling them 'a smile costs nothing' and even giving Tricia elocution lessons. She also got Mandy to cook 'Woolsnax', pub food. Fed up with her, Tricia and Mandy broke into Bernice's room and found shelves full of self-help manuals and a diary with a life plan marked out – every detail planned, down to the names of her future children, with ticks next to the aims she'd achieved. There were, though, four years missing from the diary... she was behind schedule, and lying about her age to get back on track. She'd married a man (Tony Binns) whom she'd then found in bed with another man. It had been an experience that made Bernice more than a little homophobic.

Now, though, Bernice had found a man – Gavin Ferris, an oil-rig worker. They'd met and got engaged in the same week. Bernice eagerly waited for him to join her.

Bernice took against Tricia, and wasn't above rearranging the pub roster to ruin her social life. That way, she managed to get herself invited to the Vets' Ball as Paddy's companion, a valuable event for any social climber. In the event, she spent the evening bored stiff.

However, Bernice made a good friend in lottery winner Stella, whom she recognised as her hairdresser from Leeds – she'd once modelled at a hair fair for her.

Gavin showed up, and while he spent a lot of time smooching with Bernice, Tricia could see he wasn't as

Bernice does not suffer fools gladly – here she humilates Tricia.

besotted with her as she was with him (one big clue being that he slept with Tricia the day after he arrived). Gavin liked Bernice, but was a little overwhelmed by her devotion to him – he'd only half-meant to propose to her. However, when the chance to buy the pub came up, he realised he was on to a good thing, and stuck around.

Bernice organised a Camelot theme night, and Tricia (whom Bernice had dressed up as the jester to her Queen), had had enough and for her 'act' she brought Bernice's diary down and read out extracts. Many villagers felt it was spiteful, but Tricia had proved Bernice to be barmy.

Bernice's plans to buy the Woolpack seemed doomed when it became clear that her ex-husband's

bad debts meant she was refused a loan. At the same time, she valued her friendship with Stella, and turned down her offer of the money. She confided in Ashley, who had long been secretly smitten with her. Just as she admitted to Gavin and Alan that she didn't have the money, Stella left the village – and as a parting gift, she gave Bernice the £75,000 she needed for the deposit. Bernice was so happy that even the misspelling of her name on the pub's 'licenced to sell' sign as 'Blockstack' couldn't dampen her mood.

Bernice soon hired Marlon to hold gourmet nights, which proved very successful. But her attempts to Feng Shui the Woolpack (insisting, for example, that everyone came in through the back door) were less popular.

BLACKSTOCK FAMILY TREE

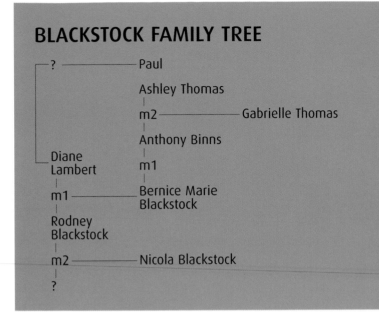

```
? ──────────── Paul

               Ashley Thomas
                 │
               m2 ──────────── Gabrielle Thomas

               Anthony Binns
                 │
Diane          m1
Lambert          │
  │            Bernice Marie
m1 ──────────  Blackstock

Rodney
Blackstock
  │
m2 ──────────  Nicola Blackstock
  │
  ?
```

Ashley and Bernice get married.

Her mother Diane arrived in the village, and backed Gavin into beginning to plan his and Bernice's wedding. However, this was called off at Christmas when she found him kissing Jason Kirk. Bernice was shocked by the betrayal, and didn't want to hear Gavin's explanation of his bisexuality. Gavin left – and Bernice realised she was in financial trouble, as the mortgage was in his name. Diane agreed to take it over.

On her birthday, 29 December, Bernice agreed to Tricia's idea to burn her 'plan'. At the news, Ashley was ready to declare his love, but Diane warned him that Bernice was too emotionally fragile. Bernice and Ashley became best friends, and he helped her get over her loss of Gavin.

It was months before Ashley plucked up the courage to tell Bernice how he felt – only to discover she'd fallen asleep. A couple of weeks later, he tried again, and Bernice was initially annoyed. Soon afterwards, though, they kissed, and the next morning Betty was scandalised to come to the vicarage on her cleaning rounds and discover Bernice there wearing nothing but one of Ashley's shirts. A number of traditionalists in the village wondered if Ashley was right to have a sexual relationship, especially with a divorcee. The Bishop of Hotten received complaints, and offered Ashley the chance of running a prestigious project in Damascus Street, Leeds, which would mean him leaving the village. Ashley was torn – and Bernice forced his hand by asking him to marry her.

Bernice moved to calm the waters by asking the Bishop to perform the ceremony. He could now see that she was good for Ashley, and agreed. Meanwhile, though, Ashley wrestled with the dilemma – he knew he could do good work at Damascus Street, and wondered if he should put his own pleasure before that. He compromised by taking the job at Damascus Street, but formally becoming engaged to Bernice and announcing it. The bishop eventually agreed to let Ashley return to Emmerdale.

While Bernice was visiting her cousin Paul in Sorento, Ashley secretly contacted her father, Rodney. Diane was furious, and Bernice was shocked, and unsure if she could trust Ashley any more. The new Woolpack chef, Carlos, had become good friends to them both, and engineered a reconciliation.

After a raucous hen night, Ashley and Bernice married on Christmas Day 2000.

They began trying for a baby almost straight away. With a lot of talk about families, Bernice decided to invite her half-sister to the village. Nicola arrived, and the two got on very well – enough to make Tricia jealous and eventually quit her job at the Woolpack.

Diane catches Bernice and Carlos together.

Bernice thought she was pregnant, and got her hopes up, but it was a false alarm. By the end of February, though, she was expecting.

When Nicola got together with her friend Carlos, though, Bernice was surprised at how jealous she felt.

Tricia went to Bernice asking for her old job back, and Bernice turned her down. This quickly turned into a slanging match – and Tricia finally told Bernice she'd slept with Gavin. Bernice was shocked. A few days later, Bernice realised she'd suffered a miscarriage. Tricia blamed herself, and fled the village.

The loss of the baby made Bernice cold and withdrawn, particularly towards Ashley. She admitted to Nicola that she found her marriage unfulfilling. Around that time, she was comforted by Carlos, and they ended up hugging. By the end of May, they had kissed for the first time. Bernice was guilty and confused, but ended up having an affair with him.

Diane quickly became suspicious, and soon caught the two in bed together. Diane suggested that Bernice leave the village for a few weeks to think things through. When she returned, Carlos had also had time to think and tried to end the affair. Bernice fired Carlos – but they were soon sleeping together again.

In August, Bernice discovered she was pregnant. She had no idea who the father was. Ashley was delighted at the news – and convinced that Bernice's unhappiness was just her worrying about another miscarriage. Bernice drew the line with Carlos, telling him their affair was over. He ended his relationship with Nicola… but then discovered she was pregnant, too, and agreed to marry her.

On her hen night, Nicola confided to Bernice that she wasn't really pregnant – it was her way of keeping Carlos. Horrified, Bernice told Carlos on his wedding day. Carlos, in turn, told Nicola that it was Bernice he really loved. And Nicola revealed the whole mess to a stunned congregation and Ashley.

Bernice moved back into the Woolpack, with Carlos, and faced the anger and disapproval of pretty much everyone in the village. Bernice soon realised she wasn't meant to spend her life with Carlos, and asked him to leave.

Alone and heavily pregnant, Bernice tried to make amends with Ashley, but he refused. She gave birth to a baby girl on her wedding anniversary, Christmas Day. Carlos returned to the village, offering Bernice a new life away from the village, whoever the baby's father was. When tests proved it was Ashley's baby, though, this proved enough for the reconciliation between her parents to start.

GABRIELLE BLACKSTOCK
(played by Jemma Giles)
Born, and first appearance: 25 December 2001

Bernice's and Ashley Thomas's little girl.

Gabby Blackstock and family!

DIANE BLACKSTOCK
(played by Elizabeth Estensen)
Born: 21 June 1947
First Appearance:
23 November 1999

Bernice's mother, Rodney's first wife.

Diane Lambert fell for Rodney Blackstock, and has never fully forgiven him for walking out on her. She is intensely protective of Bernice, but she's not afraid to criticise her daughter when she thinks she's making a mistake. Diane is completely unable to cook. She professed to preferring chunky men ('I have a penchant for a paunch'), but apart from Turner, the men she's been involved with haven't fitted that bill.

On her arrival in the village, Diane quickly proved to be the life

Diane Blackstock.

and soul of the party, flirting with both Turner and Pollard, shamelessly playing them off against each other. She also soon realised that Gavin wasn't keen on Bernice, and warned him against hurting her. Diane's visit to the village ended – but on her next one, Gavin had just left, and Bernice was feeling wretched. Diane tried to cheer her daughter up, and warned Ashley not to make his move too soon.

Diane could also offer practical help, and the Woolpack mortgage was transferred from Gavin to her.

Diane had a dark secret – her hair was actually a wig. She tried to keep this secret from everyone, and was very sensitive about it. Only Kathy knew the truth.

Diane was friendly with Jack Sugden, and was a shoulder to cry on as his marriage to Sarah collapsed. She also lent him the money to send his children on school trips. Neither was ready for a serious

relationship – but they did spend furtive nights together. When Jack lost custody of Victoria, it was Diane who snapped him out of his depression. And after the arson attack, it was Diane who told Richie that Sarah had died. Richie told her Jack started the fire – and Diane found herself believing it.

The arrival of Rodney irritated Diane – she had thought he was out of her life for ever. Bernice's natural interest in her father and half-sister made Diane very jealous, but Bernice moved to reassure her that she still loved her mother.

When Diane started telling people she was seeing Jack, Jack called off the relationship – he was a friend, but he didn't love her.

Diane was aware of Carlos's and Bernice's affair from early on, and tried to impress on them that it would end in tears.

Holding baby Gabby made Diane very proud, though – and delighted to be a grandmother.

NICOLA BLACKSTOCK
(played by Nicola Wheeler)
Born: 1978
First Appearance:
10 January 2001

Rodney's daughter from his second marriage, half-sister to Bernice. Nicola has grown up with her father around, so is far closer to him than his eldest daughter, and Rodney spoils her rotten. As a result, Nicola's used to having a safety net and to being the centre of attention. She's her father's little girl, and hasn't quite grown up.

Bernice was wary of Nicola's arrival, but they soon hit it off. At

Nicola Blackstock.

the time, Nicola had a boyfriend, a ski instructor called Darren. Bernice intercepted a postcard from Nicola's friend saying she was having an affair with Darren. Nicola was heartbroken to discover the news.

The first person Nicola met in the village was Emily, and they get on very well, despite being like chalk and cheese.

Nicola had a brief relationship with stud manager Andrew Fraser, but he didn't want it to continue.

Nicola didn't get the message until she saw him kissing another woman. Her response was characteristic – she sent for her father, who arrived and punched Andrew.

Soon afterwards, Nicola started seeing Carlos Diaz, the new chef at the Woolpack. Everything seemed idyllic, but Carlos and Bernice had started an affair. When Carlos tried to break off his relationship with her, Nicola, unused to not getting her own way, pretended she was pregnant and Carlos offered to marry her. But the truth came out on her wedding day and, despite her scheming, Nicola was devastated. Her relationship with Bernice was ruined.

She picked herself up by helping her father run the holiday village, frequently coming to blows with Maggie Calder, the woman Rodney had appointed as the manager.

RODNEY BLACKSTOCK
(played by Patrick Mower)
Born: 1949
First Appearance:
24 October 2000

The ex-husband of Diane, father of Bernice and her half-sister Nicola. Rodney has made his money selling cheap bulk wine.

His parents were fairground folk, and Rodney met Diane Lambert in 1965, when he was sixteen and she was seventeen. They had a wonderful week together, before the fair moved on. They met up the next year, this time deciding to marry. Bernice was born in December 1968.

Rodney Blackstock.

Marriage to Diane was rocky, but intensely passionate. Rodney soon had an affair, which Diane forgave him for. He then had a second affair with a girl called Rita, leading him to walk out on Diane when Bernice was five (in 1973).

Rodney left Rita and met – and married – a young woman called Maureen. They had a daughter, Nicola, who was born in 1978.

After his departure, Bernice didn't see Rodney until 2000, when her husband to be, Ashley, invited him to reconcile with his daughter in time for the wedding. Diane was horrified, and Bernice – who served him a pint without having a clue who he was – was shocked enough to feel betrayed by Ashley, and to almost call off the wedding. She learnt she had a half-sister, Nicola. Rodney left the village, returning for the wedding on Christmas Day (he also organised the stag night, which ended with Ashley stripped and tied to a lamppost).

Nicola arrived a month later, and Rodney returned, this time settling in the village. He struck up a business relationship with Chris Tate. Diane found his presence difficult to cope with, especially as Rodney was stirring up trouble between Jack and Alan. When Bernice became pregnant, her parents tried to out-do each other buying presents. When that pregnancy ended in a miscarriage, Rodney was very upset and angry, and made it clear to Tricia that he thought she was to blame, leading her to leave the village.

Chris suspected Charity of having an affair with Rodney, speculation fuelled by Lady Tara.

Now a firm part of the village, Rodney decided to take a room at the bed and breakfast, advised Nicola about her relationship with Carlos, and bought shares in Chez Marlon and entered a partnership to buy the holiday village with Chris Tate. He also found love with Louise Appleton, the new Woolpack barmaid, 20 years his junior, although the relationship didn't last.

ASHLEY MICHAEL THOMAS
(played by John Middleton)
Born: 1961
First Appearance:
5 December 1996

Ashley Thomas.

Ashley is the vicar of Emmerdale and surrounding parishes. For his first few years in the village, his role was confined to conducting weddings and funerals, but this soon changed when he became smitten with Bernice Blackstock. Although it would be over a year before Bernice realised, it was love at first sight. A man of principle, Ashley does

Ashley on his stag night.

nevertheless have something of a ruthless streak, particularly when dealing with crooks like Eric Pollard.

Ashley's first duties as vicar were to marry Biff and Linda Fowler – and to bury Linda's brother Dave a few days later. He officiated at Frank Tate's funeral, as well as Linda's, and tried to keep order at the farcical wedding attempt of Lisa Clegg and Albert Dingle. He has officiated at every church wedding, christening and funeral in recent years.

He became good friends with Zoe Tate (she was the 'best man' at his wedding to Bernice), and was always involved in village business. He was the stooge in Kim's and Steve's horse robbery – the unimpeachable alibi they set up to cover their activities. Always the mediator, he helped Mandy, Paddy and Butch sort out their problems after the eviction in 1998 and Mandy's marriage to Butch.

THE REYNOLDS

ANGIE REYNOLDS
(played by Freya Copeland)
Born: 1965
First Appearance:
23 March 1999

Ex-wife of Sean Reynolds, mother of Marc and Ollie, daughter-in-law of Len Reynolds. Angie is a sergeant (No. 1304) with the Hotten Police.

When Chris Tate called the police to arrest Sean Reynolds for threatening behaviour, he was shocked that they sent Sean's wife to do it. Chris suspected that the police's lacklustre response to the break-ins and vandalism he'd been suffering was down to Angie covering her husband's tracks. Angie, though, proved more sensible than either of them and suggested that, rather than fight for a tiny market, they should join forces.

Angie was sent to Hotten Comprehensive to deliver a lecture on the evils of drugs – she brought a sniffer dog... which discovered cannabis in Rachel Hughes's handbag. Unknown to anyone, it had been planted by Graham, Rachel's boyfriend, who wanted her to leave her job. Angie took a fairly lenient line, but the school sacked Rachel.

Sean and Angie had been together since they were teenagers, and neither had had previous lovers (and, at least until they moved to Emmerdale, neither had been unfaithful). They married young, and Angie had her first child, Marc, when she was 18. Olivia (Ollie) followed a little under two years later. It was clear they'd outgrown the tiny house in Hotten they'd bought as newly-weds, but Sean was reluctant to move. When the merger with Tate Haulage gave Sean security and a fair amount of cash, Angie forced him to move – handcuffing him to the bed until he

REYNOLDS FAMILY TREE

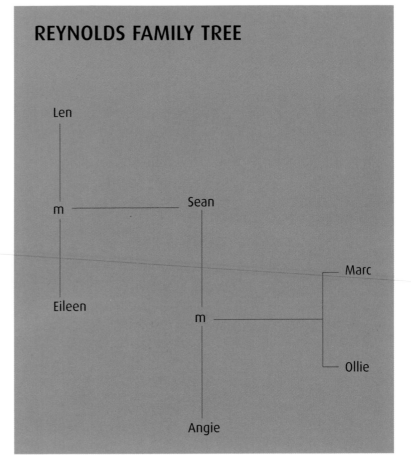

signed the contract to buy Holdgate's Farm in Emmerdale.

Angie quickly came to regret her haste, when she discovered her new neighbours were the Dingles. Zak and Butch had already robbed the removal lorry, not realising Angie was a policewoman. Angie pursued them out of the village in the family car, enjoying the car chase ('This is better than sex!'), but ran out of petrol and the Dingle van made its getaway. Angie vowed to get revenge, and achieved this shortly afterwards when Mandy accidentally hit Stella at the summer fair (she'd been aiming for Pollard). Mandy was sent to prison for three months. Zak redeemed himself a

little by saving Ollie's life after an electrical fire in the Reynolds's basement, although, it was a fire started by a dodgy cable Zak had installed to steal electricity.

Angie befriended Sarah, advising her about her problems with Jack.

Keen to transfer from uniform to CID, Angie took a step towards this when her local knowledge proved useful in the wake of Chris Tate's kidnapping. But DI Spalding wasn't impressed when it became clear that Sean was a prime suspect. She risked her career, hiding evidence of a grey market scam Sean had organised, and fell out with her husband as a result. Things hadn't improved by Christmas, when Sean turned up

The Reynolds family.

Cain and Angie.

late for dinner, which Angie tipped over him.

Ollie was beginning to cause problems – mischief at first, like writing a sketch for a village panto that insulted Bernice and Ashley. It was a classic cry for attention, which Angie and Sean were too preoccupied to deal with. They were even too busy to make it to parent's evening at Ollie's school. Ollie progressed to shoplifting at the post office shop. When Angie found out, she offered to pay Viv for the goods, but Viv insisted on going through the proper police channels. Angie decided the shock should be good for Ollie and she even got the police to pick up Ollie when she bunked off

school. Ollie broke down in tears as she was interrogated at the police station.

Shortly after this, Sean and Angie decided to make a fresh start.

When Marc was slightly injured in the bus crash, Angie was one of the first on the scene.

But the arrival of Cain Dingle quickly started causing problems. Sean and Cain fought in the Woolpack.

Sean and Angie were shocked to be called to the school to be told that Ollie was the leader of a gang that was stealing from other pupils. Ollie was excluded, and found herself having to accompany Sean to work. She enjoyed herself, flirting with the

truckers. Shortly afterwards Ollie ran away. Angie was worried, but Ollie soon reappeared.

Angie tried to spend more time with Ollie, but it didn't work. Meanwhile, Sean and Angie were both guilty of neglecting Marc – they assumed he would pass his exams with flying colours, and become the first Reynolds to go to university. But Marc deliberately failed his exams.

Slimy vet Dan Dean tried to chat up Angie at one of Tara's parties and was kneed in the groin for his trouble. Sean was impressed, and they hurried upstairs to christen one of Tara's bedrooms – however they were discovered by Tara, Zoe and Frankie, and Tara threw them out.

Angie was shocked when Cain started showing an interest in Ollie, not least because she found herself drawn to the swarthy young Dingle herself. Angie came to realise Cain was attracted to her, and was using Ollie to get at her. She tricked Cain into admitting it while Ollie was in earshot, which seemed to end Ollie's crush. Cain started to flirt with Angie around the time Sean and Tara were beginning to flirt. Angie was unsettled by her feelings for Cain. Cain began insisting that Angie search him.

Angie was devastated by Sarah's death, and spoke at her funeral.

When Angie discovered that Sean and Tara had been having an affair, she threw him out of the house, then struggled to keep the family together. She confronted Tara in the Woolpack, slapping her. Angie was confused about her feelings for Sean. She wanted him back, but couldn't forgive him or trust him.

Angie sought solace from Cain, who proved surprisingly sensitive. Their paths kept crossing, and within a few weeks they'd kissed, and began arranging to meet secretly. Before long they were sleeping together, often narrowly escaping being caught together.

Angie decided to end the relationship, and was scared when Cain threatened her. But Angie was rebuilding her marriage to Sean, and the family appeared to be getting back on track.

Cain blackmailed Angie – he was seeing Ollie again. They hadn't slept together, but if he couldn't have Angie, he'd have her daughter. Angie agonised, and decided to sleep with Cain – but was late to their rendezvous. Cain went straight over to the Reynolds house, and seduced Ollie. Len caught them together, and fell down the stairs after a struggle. Angie managed to keep Len quiet, convincing him that it would keep the family together. But Cain told Sean he'd slept with both his wife and his daughter – and the moment he did, the Reynolds family collapsed. Cain even went to the police, seriously damaging Angie's career. Sean and Tara became a couple, and they left the village together in 2002.

Over the months, Angie managed slowly to rekindle her bond with Ollie but things were difficult for her children. When they were involved in a fatal hit and run on 10 September, Angie realised that her children desperately needed her support. And as Marc's court hearing loomed, she realised he would not escape going to a Young Offenders Institute.

MARC REYNOLDS
(played by Anthony Lewis)
Born: 12 December 1983
First Appearance: 17 June 1999

The son of Sean and Angie Reynolds, older brother of Ollie. Marc was a quiet, intelligent, studious teenager, who was badly affected by the break-up of his parents. Marc felt left out when Ollie's rebellious nature got her a lot of attention from her parents, but his steady progress and good sense was taken for granted. His birth certificate spells his name 'Mark', but he thinks spelling his name with a C makes him more interesting.

Marc made an immediate impact on village life by beating Seth in the vegetable competition at the summer fair. He suggested some menu ideas to Marlon, and forced him to employ him in the evenings to help out.

Marc fell for Donna Windsor, and the two first kissed on a camping trip organised by Ashley

Marc Reynolds.

and Bernice. But when his parents blamed him for Ollie's bad behaviour after a party, Marc himself started to rebel, taking a job at the Woolpack, and barely revising. He finally asked Donna out – but before things could go too far, he was mildly injured in the bus crash. Marc was ready to sleep with Donna, but she was hesitant. When they did sleep together, Viv discovered them in bed. She tried to keep them apart, but the two found ways to meet.

Fed up with his parents ignoring him, Marc deliberately failed all his GCSEs, despite a prediction of straight As. He moved out, first to Annie's Cottage then (after Terry threw him out when he caught him with Donna), into the Sugdens' farm. Donna had a pregnancy scare, which made Marc realise some of his responsibilities. Donna dumped him when he boasted to his friend Johnny.

Marc set his sights on Tara, even inviting her to his birthday party, and was encouraged by how keen she seemed: she even gave him driving lessons. Tara, though, was doing this to wind Sean up. Marc's father was firmly of the belief that Tara was a 'parasite', and hated working with her. But contact between the two led to an affair – and when Marc found out, he told Angie. Ollie accused Marc of splitting the family, but he was a great comfort to his mother. He also started seeing Donna again. It would be a long time before he spoke to his father again.

Marc eventually passed his driving test, with the help of his grandfather, Len. Very soon

Marc & Eve realise someone knows what they did last summer.

afterwards, he knocked over Danny Daggert, but he wasn't injured. Marc dumped Donna when Eve Birch arrived in the village. The two dated, and kissed.

On 10 September 2001, the village teens went out to a Hotten nightclub, but missed the last bus home. Andy suggested they 'borrow' a car – and as the only person who'd passed his test, Marc was nominated driver. Marc accidentally hit someone on the road – and when they investigated, they found it was their headmistress, Miss Strickland, who had been killed instantly.

The teens agreed to keep quiet, and burned the car. The tragedy drew Marc and Eve together, and they slept together.

However, the police caught up with the group, and while the others were sentenced to community service, Marc, as the driver, was sent to prison for 12 months. It remains to be seen whether he can get his life back on track.

OLIVIA REYNOLDS ('OLLIE')
(played by Vicky Binns)
Born: 11 August 1985
First Appearance: 17 June 1999

Ollie is the daughter of Sean and Angie Reynolds, Marc's younger sister. Ollie is a typical teenage tearaway – much more feisty than her older brother Marc. In something of a break with tradition, Ollie was one teenager who was very excited about moving to Emmerdale – she even persuaded Marc to bunk off school so they could go have a look at their new home. She was doubly pleased when she discovered they would be living next door to the Dingles.

Ollie very soon got in trouble in the village, getting so drunk at the summer fair that she passed out. For most of her first year in the village, she was responsible for a lot of this sort of mischief, and her parents did little to rein her in. When Ollie wrote

Ollie Reynolds.

a scurrilous sketch about Ashley and Bernice for the village panto, causing it to be cancelled, Ashley told Angie he was worried about her, but Angie told him to mind his own business. Ollie began to feel neglected as Sean and Angie started rowing.

Ollie was starting to have a love life, of sorts. Andy Hopwood had a crush on her, and bought her cheap perfume for Christmas. Viv caught Ollie shoplifting, and wanted her prosecuted. Angie and Sean scared the life out of her by taking her through the proper police channels. Sean undermined this a little by apologising afterwards. Meanwhile, Ollie started running a gang at school that stole from other students, and was excluded from school.

She ran away from home – Marc thought she'd gone to London, but she'd only made it as far as Jack's barn, where Andy looked after her, and made sure she phoned Childline to let her parents know she was safe. It was Ollie who first discovered

Sarah and Richie's affair, when she saw them kissing in the barn. She told Andy.

Robert found out and told the Reynolds – but before they caught up with her, Ollie had hitched a ride with Mike Blake, one of the Tate Haulage truckers. Their truck was blocked by villagers protesting about the bus crash – and Sean discovered Ollie in the truck. He was all for killing Mike for abducting a minor, but Ollie told him Mike was giving her a lift home.

Angie took time off work to be with Ollie, but this just led to more arguments. Ollie told Angie about Sarah's affair.

Ollie was readmitted to school for the summer term. In all the fuss about Ollie, Marc started to feel neglected – it was an exam year for him, but Ollie seemed to be getting all the support.

Ollie became a 'class traitor' according to Sean when she took a summer job at the stud farm. He was more angry when a horse she was controlling lashed out and knocked Paddy out – she must have been in danger herself. Sean became suspicious when he found a bracelet in Ollie's room, thinking she must have stolen it from Home Farm. In actuality, Cain Dingle had left it there. Ollie was flattered by the attention, and developed a serious crush on him.

When Seth was mugged, Angie was suspicious how quickly Ollie got to the scene. Ollie was outraged at the insinuation she did it. Seth told Angie it wasn't Ollie, and Angie apologised to her daughter.

Cain continued to fascinate Ollie, and he invited her for a weekend in Blackpool. Ollie asked

Ollie was the first to discover Sarah and Richie's affair.

Angie if she could go with some friends, but Angie discovered who was really going with her and warned Cain to keep away. Cain assured Angie that he thought Ollie was a silly little kid – Ollie overheard and was very upset.

Ollie, against expectation, passed all her mock exams in early 2001. But this period of family happiness

didn't last long – Marc told Ollie he'd found out their dad was having an affair with Tara. When Marc then told Angie, Ollie blamed him for breaking up the family. She insisted that Angie give Sean another try, and missed her father when Angie kicked him out. She invited Len, her grandfather, over to support her.

Donna confided in Ollie that she

Cain and Ollie.

was thinking of sleeping with Marc. Ollie told her to go ahead. Donna did, and assumed that Ollie was more experienced than her – leading to Ollie having to admit she was a virgin. She tried to rectify that with a schoolfriend, Johnny, but got cold feet. A few weeks later she fancied Marc's friend Ben, but he was just trying to sleep with her for a bet. When Cain found out, he comforted Ollie, and they ended up kissing. Ollie wanted to go to bed with him, but he insisted her family know they were seeing each other before then. Ollie's parents were predictably shocked.

It was all part of a game on Cain's part to get at Angie. He warned Angie he was going to sleep with Ollie, and did just that. Len discovered them in bed together, and after scuffling with Cain, he fell down the stairs. Ollie was terrified that he'd been killed, but he recovered. Cain fled the village.

Cain's return saw the end of the

Len Reynolds.

Reynolds family unit. Cain bragged to Sean, comparing his daughter's and wife's performances in bed. Sean attacked Cain. This brought Ollie and Sean closer, but drove a wedge between her and Angie, and Ollie moved out to the Daggerts.

On the 10 September 2001, Ollie joined the other kids in the village on a night out which ended in tragedy. When they missed the last bus home Ollie went along with the plan to steal a car to take them home. They ran over Miss Strickland, their head teacher, and were forced to burn the car and keep a guilty secret. Ollie found this particularly nerve-racking.

> **LEN REYNOLDS**
> (played by Peter Martin)
> Born: (unknown)
> First Appearance:
> 21 February 2001

Len is the father of Sean Reynolds, grandfather of Marc and Ollie. He was married to Eileen who died a few years ago, and they used to live in Liverpool. His social life and friends were tied in with Eileen, and since her death he finds retaining contact with them quite painful. Despite his bravado and bluster, Len is, in fact, quite lonely. He doesn't get upset, preferring to put the kettle on and do something practical when problems arise. He dotes on his grandchildren, especially Ollie. The kids like having him around because he's a laugh and, like most grandparents, he indulges them. He's still fit and able and resents being on the scrapheap. He's direct and says what he means. He enjoys the village community, which offers him a new start with fewer reminders of his late wife.

THE DAGGERTS

The Daggerts

> **CYNTHIA DAGGERT**
> (played by Kay Purcell)
> Born: 1967
> First Appearance: 6 June 2001

Cynthia is the young mother of two teenage children who has moved to Emmerdale from Bradford to find a better home for them. She found work at Eric Pollard's tat factory and within a few weeks, she'd organised a strike over Eric's terrible working conditions.

At first she stayed in the B & B with her son Danny, but she was made to feel most unwelcome by Carol, who thought Danny was a thief. Ashley invited them to stay in the vicarage with him until they found somewhere else. When Bernice returned, and Cynthia's daughter Latisha arrived, they moved out, deciding to squat in Jacob's Fold, a small cottage. Carol got the authorities to investigate, but the Daggerts were soon living there officially.

The rest of the village tended to share Carol's suspicion at first, but Cynthia has also made some good friends – Ashley, Terry and Lisa in particular.

DANNY DAGGERT
(played by Cleveland Campbell)
Born: 1984
First Appearance: 25 June 2001

Cynthia Daggert's 17-year old son. He worshipped his dog Naz, who was unfortunately shot on farmland shortly after arriving in Emmerdale. Danny does a series of odd jobs around the village, like cleaning windows. He quickly fell in with the youngsters of the village.

LATISHA DAGGERT
(played by Danielle Henry)
Born: 1983
First Appearance: 9 July 2001

The daughter of Cynthia, the sister of Danny and the mother of baby Kirk (born on 9 July, the day she first came to Emmerdale).

Latisha wanted to become a beauty therapist, perhaps on cruise ships, but those plans ended when she got pregnant at 17 to her boyfriend, Paul. Her mother was furious – she'd had Latisha at 16, and, while she loved her, knew having a baby that young had closed doors to her. Latisha is sweet-natured

but rather fatalistic – she knows not to expect what she can't have.

She gave birth to her baby in the back of Jason Kirk's van, with Jason's help, after he'd picked her up as a hitchhiker (and, of course, named him after Jason). She'd been coming from her home in Bradford to see her mother on a surprise visit – and certainly surprised her by making her a grandmother at the age of 34. Latisha confided that she'd left Paul, who had started to hit her.

Latisha started work at the B & B.

Jason and Latisha had a special bond from that moment. Jason was gay, but to all intents and purposes the two were going out together. But an attempt to sleep together ended frustratingly for both of them. When Paul arrived to attend Kirk's christening, Latisha thought hard about getting back together with him. She eventually chose to live in Emmerdale.

Alan Turner.

OTHER VILLAGERS

ALAN JONATHAN TURNER
(played by Richard Thorp)
Born: 5 August 1935
First Appearance:
18 March 1982

A local businessman who's been the estate manager of Home Farm, a councillor and the landlord of the Woolpack. Now ostensibly retired, he runs the bed and breakfast. Twenty years in the village have seen Alan Turner change from being a pompous, arrogant, troubled man into someone far more mellow and genial.

Turner has a turbulent family history. He had a brother, William, who died young. His brother was always much cleverer than he was and made a lot of money out of cheroots. He had an unhappy

marriage to Jill (which ended in 1985), and lost touch with both his children, Terence and Mary. Terence appeared in the village in the early 1980s, and was arrogant, patronising and unpleasant. Turner lost touch with Mary altogether, so much so that he never met his granddaughter, Tricia Stokes, until she was in her early twenties, and turned up in the village out of the blue. Tricia is now the apple of his eye.

Early on, he had drink problems (and was twice banned for drink-driving in the 1980s), gambling problems, and was guilty of using his position of power to seduce women. Alan made a move on four secretaries in less than a year when he moved to NY Estates. After Denise came Pat Merrick, who was actually the cleaner at Home Farm, but Alan mistook her for a secretary and then decided to offer her the job anyway. Then he took on Barbara Peters, the daughter of the local vicar. She refused all his offers of a date, preferring Joe's company, and Alan seriously embarrassed himself trying to seduce her. Finally, Sue Lockwood had been working for him for a few weeks when he offered her a lift home from the Woolpack. He made a move on her, but she got out of the car and ran away. He has blamed many of his problems on being bullied at boarding school.

He is overweight, and has been on a diet for health reasons a number of times – usually putting on more weight. On various occasions, he developed a rash after being put on a diet of pears and mashed potatoes; gave up on a diet after Seth kept altering his scales; smuggled chocolates into a health farm. One brewery man, looking to modernise the pub, once described him as 'an overweight garden gnome'.

He's proved an extraordinarily unlucky driver – he was caught drink driving in 1983. In April 1985, he knocked Jackie Merrick off his bike, and Jackie was on a life support machine for many weeks. He ordered an illegal stubble-burning on a Sunday, but parked his Range Rover too close to the field and it blew up. One accident that wasn't his fault was the bus crash in 2000, although he was the driver of the (stationary) bus and had to be cut from the wreckage. However, for all his faults, Turner is a pillar of the community. He became a parish councillor in 1985 when he beat Seth Armstrong by two votes – although he had taken all his ideas for his manifesto from Mrs Bates. A few years later, he won the local council election by one vote. He served selflessly as councillor (uniquely for Hotten Council, as far as we know). He's generous to his friends and especially to Tricia. He's a connoisseur, and an excellent cook.

Turner, as an authority figure, has always been something of a figure of fun, particularly for Seth Armstrong. Seth's protégé, Archie Brooks, always called his boss 'Tubby' or 'Fatty'. Terry Woods, who worked with Alan at the Woolpack, preferred the slightly more affectionate 'Big Al'. More than once as estate manager, he stomped around looking for Seth and ended up falling flat on his face

Alan frequently argued with Joe Sugden over how best to run Home Farm

in the mud. His hobby, riding motorbikes, has also led to a good deal of mockery – and he can look ridiculous in leather gear or on the back of a Harley Davidson. But Seth and Turner share a deep affection, though – Alan cried when Seth turned up safe after the plane crash, and each have held bedside hospital vigils for the other over the years.

Alan moved to Beckindale in 1982 when he became Estate Manager for NY Estates. He beat Joe Sugden for that position, and although Joe worked under him, he was never entirely happy about it. Turner showed himself to be disorganised, untrustworthy and lazy in his first few months in the job. Indeed in May of 1982, he was accused of mismanagement by Jack Sugden when

NY Estates crop-spraying caused Emmerdale Farm cattle to stampede. In his usual manner, he blamed someone else – Joe.

A couple of months later, the first shoot he was in charge of was a disaster – in front of his managing director. There were very few birds,

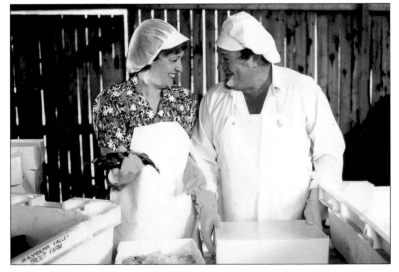

Alan and Mrs Bates at the fish farm

Tricia can wrap Turner around her little finger.

and a dog was let loose.

Once Joe left Beckindale for a job in France, Alan was left to cope on his own and it was not long before his boss noticed that NY Estates was in chaos. Alan was given an ultimatum by his boss to sort himself out in the next three months or else. Jill, his estranged wife turned up the next day demanding that he pay family bills. She ended up helping to sort out his office and tried to get him to sort out his career. Help came in the form of Caroline Bates who started as his secretary

Alan was responsible for Mrs Bates's dog, Bundle, being shot. He would not accept that Bundle was responsible for worrying sheep and insisted on letting him loose. Jackie shot it and Alan lied to cover up his involvement.

Over the course of a number of years, friendship turned to romance – Turner had tried bringing her flowers almost straight away, but had been scared off by Mrs Bates's teenage children. Their first meal together ended in disaster when a gas bottle exploded at Home Farm. Turner got very jealous whenever Caroline seemed to be dating another man.

He joined a dating agency, and had a very boring date with Rosemary Gray, who turned out to be a naturist.

Alan turned to desperate measures to win Mrs Bates's heart, dressing as Clint Eastwood, who, she said, was her ideal man. It was 1989 before the two spent the night together – and they were both terribly embarrassed afterwards. A few months later, though, Alan proposed and Caroline accepted. The wedding plans were called off when Caroline's mother, Alice, tried to split them up. Caroline eventually moved to Scarborough to be with her mother – and Turner was surprised how relieved he felt.

He spent the next few years being quite lonely, even resorting to inviting Rosemary Gray to the Home Farm Hunt Ball - but he pretended that he still owned the place, because he wanted to impress her. He also went out with Dolly Skilbeck a couple of times.

In April 1986, Alan found out that Joe Sugden was applying for the position of NY Estates Regional Manager, and applied for the job himself. He was shocked when Joe beat him to the job, becoming his boss. The two became allies, though, when senior NY Estates management began insisting on higher targets and cost-cutting.

When NY Estates pulled out of Beckindale, Turner was offered a lowly post as publicity assistant to the general manager. It was a humiliation, but within a couple of weeks Turner and Joe had put together an offer to buy Home Farm and the fish farm.

In September 1988, Alan was approached by ruthless businessman Dennis Rigg. He was pressuring local landowners to sell out to him so that his company could build a quarry. Joe was appalled when he found out that Alan had sold his share in Home Farm. Turner became the farm manager for Rigg, but received his comeuppance when Rigg threw him out of Home Farm shortly afterwards

In July 1989, Alan went into partnership with Mrs Bates when they rented the fish and game farm from Rigg's company. He hired Seth as gamekeeper, but wasn't pleased when Seth demanded director's perks. Mrs Bates eventually left the partnership when she moved to Scarborough to look after her mum. Alan made sure that he came off better than her out of the deal and later pretended to her that the fish farm wasn't doing well so that he did not have to pay her a share.

Frank Tate became Alan's landlord when he purchased Home Farm. Alan also sold the fish farm to him in September 1992, but made sure that he kept on Elizabeth Feldmann and Seth Armstrong.

Alan had decided to buy the Woolpack on Amos's retirement in early 1991. He kept Henry Wilks on, but caused bad feeling by asking his advice but not always following it. Turner had an ambitious plan to take the Woolpack upmarket, something which alienated some of the old-timers. Turner opened a wine bar and a gourmet restaurant.

One of the best things to happen in Alan's life was meeting Shirley Foster at a drop-in centre. He was taken there by Mrs Bates who wanted to show him another side of life after telling him, 'You really are one of the most self-centred men I've ever met.' He helped out at the drop-in centre, but thought that all the girls were themselves really self-centred. Shirley and Alan didn't hit it off at first because of this. He spent the night as a down and out in order to appreciate their problems.

He began a relationship with Shirley, but was shocked by the revelation that she had been a prostitute when she was younger. Turner overcame his prejudices and they married, but within four months, she was caught up in the post office raid and was shot.

Alan hit the bottle, and nearly lost the pub to Eric Pollard, who schemed against him while pretending to console him over Shirley's death. Pollard told Alan that Shirley had been embezzling money. Once Turner came to his senses, he kneed Pollard in the groin, telling him, 'That's from Shirley.'

The brewery insisted that Turner needed help running the pub, and Turner appointed Terry and Britt Woods bar managers. Turner was wary of them at first, but it proved to be a fruitful partnership, and Turner was very upset when Britt left. To keep Terry in the village, Turner offered him a profit-share deal.

Alan found love again when he least expected it after meeting a young, blonde biker at a village jumble sale. Jo Steadman surprised everyone when she fell for Alan and not Terry. They enjoyed bike rides together and Alan even went out and bought a Harley Davidson. Alan was embarrassed before and after spending his first night with Jo. He told her he loved her and was upset when she announced that she was giving up her job and going to ride around America. Alan decided to sell up and go with her. He seemed determined until he started to get cold feet and backed out.

In 1998, he invested his life savings in Steve Marchant's phoney business ventures, and was devastated when Steve lost it all.

Some good news finally arrived though in the form of Tricia Stokes, his long-lost granddaughter. He loved Tricia unconditionally – so much so that when she blew up the Woolpack, Turner blamed Terry and sacked him. Terry's replacement, Bernice, proved a good bar manager, and Turner was more than happy to sell her the Woolpack when a mild heart attack led him to retire.

Since then, Turner has kept himself busy and he now runs the bed and breakfast in the village.

PATRICIA SUSAN STOKES
('Tricia', formely FISHER)
(played by Sheree Murphy)
Born: 1975
First Appearance:
16 September 1998

Alan Turner's granddaughter – the daughter of his daughter Mary Stephanie. Alan Turner has had trouble with his family over the years, and had clearly lost touch with Mary. Tricia turned up in Emmerdale out of the blue, and Alan didn't even recognise her – he knew he had a granddaughter, but it's unclear if he'd ever seen her, even as a baby. Tricia needed a place to stay, and Alan quickly took her to his heart, delighted to find a relative who loved him and was grateful for his help.

Tricia combines the ability to wrap men around her finger with the inability to see that's what she's doing. She's eager to please people, and doesn't think too far ahead to the consequences of her actions. Within days of moving into the Woolpack, Terry Woods was hooked. Tricia, who served Terry breakfast in bed wearing a skimpy nightie, and who got him to help her shop for sexy dresses, was surprised when he made advances on her. She was more interested in Scott Windsor. In the event, she ended up sleeping with both of them.

Within a month of arriving, Tricia managed to blow up the Woolpack. She bought some illegal fireworks, planning a Guy Fawkes display, but didn't store them properly, and a candle fell into the box. Terry managed to get her out of

Tricia Stokes – long lost granddaughter of Alan Turner.

the building, but the ground floor was gutted. Turner, unable to believe Tricia capable of wrongdoing, sacked Terry.

Tricia set her heart on becoming the new bar manager, as did Mandy Dingle. The two began undermining each other's work. In the end, tensions boiled over into a cat-fight, and Turner rejected both of them, hiring Bernice Blackstock instead.

Tricia and Bernice became great rivals, then great friends. As Bernice gained more of a grip on the Woolpack, Tricia felt threatened by Bernice, whose hard work, efficiency and organisational skills (and her poor luck with men) made her Tricia's polar opposite. It was Tricia who uncovered Bernice's 'plan', evidence, as she saw it, that her new

boss was mad. Bernice insisted she had a fiancé, Gavin, but after several months of him not showing up when Bernice was expecting him, Tricia

Tricia leads Terry on.

began to suspect that she was deluding herself about her 'perfect man'. Gavin did indeed show up – and within 24 hours Tricia had slept with him.

When Turner decided to sell the Woolpack, Tricia and Bernice joined battle to buy it. Bernice began a series of sensible negotiations with banks. Tricia – after failing to charm Chris with an indecent proposal – began a war on two fronts: trying to organise a 'village bid' to buy the pub, and to charm Turner into selling it to her for less. The former failed when it became clear that people like Zak and Seth couldn't come close to clubbing together to pay the £450,000 asking price. The latter failed when a Marilyn Monroe impersonator she'd hired as a surprise at a theme night (Monroe being a particular favourite of her grandfather) turned out to be a female impersonator. Turner was not best pleased.

Her bid to buy the pub in tatters, Tricia set about sabotaging Bernice's hopes. At the summer fair, she set up a rival beer tent and hitched Bernice's tent to Jack's Land Rover, making it collapse. She kept her job by blackmailing Gavin. Finally though, Tricia came to accept life under Bernice.

The prospect of Turner marrying Stella and becoming lord of the manor (a prospect that only existed in her and Turner's minds), excited Tricia, who even took up riding lessons. Tricia's presumption was one of the main reasons Stella turned against Alan.

Tricia attempted to find a man, and was worried there was something wrong with her when Scott suffered a bout of impotence. When Scott's friend Richie became a Woolpack regular, and she realised he was brainy, she set about pretending to be interested in intellectual pursuits. It wasn't terribly convincing (as Bernice said, 'The last book she finished was probably *Stig of the Dump*') and Richie lost interest. Paddy's cousin Jason seemed like a good prospect – but was keeping the secret he was gay from the village (specifically Zak). Tricia and Bernice discovered this when they caught Jason kissing Gavin.

This shock brought Bernice and Tricia together, and Tricia convinced Bernice to burn her 'plan'. From then on, the two became good friends – and all the time, Tricia had the guilty secret that she'd slept with Gavin and known he was wrong for Bernice.

LOUISE APPLETON
(played by Emily Symons)
Born: 29 December 1968
First Appearance: 20 June 2001

Louise was born in England, but moved to Australia with her family in her early teens. She worked as an air hostess on long-haul flights after graduation. She met a man on a flight to Johannesburg, and after a whirlwind romance, they married. The marriage collapsed soon afterwards, though, and Louise booked a flight home. Until then, she worked as a temp barmaid, ending up at the Woolpack.

Louise struck up a relationship with Rodney Blackstock, a man old enough to be her father. Indeed, she is exactly the same age as his eldest

Louise and Ray.

daughter, Bernice, a fact that disgusted Nicola. Louise convinced Rodney that as she was returning to Australia in a few weeks, they should both enjoy a short, fun, relationship.

When Diane fell ill, and Louise proved well able to cover for her, she was offered a permanent job. She faced a dilemma, finally deciding to stay in Emmerdale, and see if there is a future for her and Rodney.

RAY MULLAN
(played by Seamus Gubbins)
Born: 1956
First Appearance:
26 September 2001

Ray is a 45-year-old, successful and well-respected criminal. He owns a string of nightclubs, along with various other ventures, providing a legitimate front for much more sinister and lucrative dealings.

The golden rule of a criminal is, 'If you can't do the time, don't do the crime.' To Ray, this doesn't apply. Ray doesn't believe in getting his hands dirty – he's got a reliable team raised on fear and respect to do the business for him. He's a man that gets what he wants, when he wants. His Jekyll-and-Hyde personality generates an unnerving aura whenever he's around. A true gent, he has a short fuse, and his temper is nothing short of awesome.

Ray was first seen beating up Cain for jeopardising a counterfeiting ring Ray was running. When he arrived in Emmerdale he was unaware that Cain lived in the village, and was quick to warn him off. He also put Rodney's nose out of joint by buying Mill Cottage, which Rodney had wanted to buy. Ray began buying up property in Emmerdale, including Emmerdale Farm. When he bid for the holiday village, Rodney paid to see the sealed bid, and he and Chris were able to put in a better offer. Despite this setback, Ray began to take an interest in almost every aspect of village business.

Pollard catches Betty snooping.

BETTY EAGLETON (née PRENDAGAST)
(played by Paula Tilbrook)
Born: 22 January 1934
First Appearance: 12 April 1994

Betty is the village busybody and gossip, knowing everyone's business, and never afraid to give advice (or deterred by how unwanted or useless that advice may be). She means well, although most people in the village have had occasion to agree with Kelly's view that she's 'a nasty-minded old cow'. Betty married Wally Eagleton, choosing him over her childhood sweetheart, Seth. She never had children, but has – or at least had – a sister called Elizabeth. Her father was alive as recently as 1994 – he turned up to give Seth the once-over. After Wally died, she and Seth rekindled their romance and now live together. She spends much of her life, when she isn't gossiping, giving Seth a hard time. She works at Pollard's tat factory, as well as being a cleaner.

Betty grew up in Beckindale, lived there during the war and was courted in her teens by both Seth Armstrong and Wally Eagleton. In the early fifties, Betty Prendagast, as she was then, went down to London, and worked as a tiller girl at the Windmill Theatre – appearing naked on stage. While working there she met Reggie, and they started an affair. She discovered she was pregnant, and went round to tell Reggie – finding him in bed with another woman. She had an abortion (at a time when the procedure was illegal and dangerous) and this left her unable to have children. She returned to Beckindale, keeping events in London a secret. They only came to light in 2000, when Reggie turned up in the village and planned to blackmail her.

Back in Beckindale, Seth courted Betty, but Wally Eagleton proposed first, and they married (apparently in 1954). Wally was the local scrap merchant for many years. Betty is something of a dark horse – she's the only villager, for example, who was at Woodstock.

In 1986, Betty told Wally she wished he spent as much time and effort on her as he did on his horse, and gave him an ultimatum – it was the horse or her. He chose the horse, and Betty stormed out and went to live in Filey. In 1994, Wally died (he remained undiscovered for four days). Betty decided to return to the village.

Seth and Betty were quickly reunited, with Seth staying with 'the widow Eagleton' in the aftermath of the plane crash, which had destroyed his house. Betty inherited a lot of money from Wally, but Pollard, who was after her land, made sure she lost it, so she had to sell up. She thwarted Pollard's plan by selling to Frank Tate. Seth and Betty moved into Keeper's Cottage, renting it from Home Farm estates. Seth eventually proposed, and they planned to get married – Betty entertaining the notion she could have a double wedding with Kim and Frank – before deciding marriage was silly at their time of life and opting for a 1944-style knees-up instead.

Betty's job as a cleaner allowed her the perfect opportunity to nose around the village. She got herself into all sorts of trouble – seeing Dave Glover naked, killing Butch's beloved pet rat, hitting a policeman with a frying pan. She was also not backward in publicly denouncing people she felt had behaved badly, like Tina Dingle did in dumping Luke. Although she cleans for Zoe both at home and at the vet's surgery, Betty's been vocal in criticising her lesbian lifestyle. Sometimes her antennae let her down – she was practically the last person in the village to know that Kim and Dave were having an affair, and didn't realise that Tom, a teacher and her lodger, was sleeping with under-age Kelly Windsor. She became a very close friend of Biff Fowler, who became her new lodger, and she was a comfort when his wife Tina died.

She took part in village protests – manned the Dingle barricade and was knocked unconscious during the quarry demonstration.

She also started working as a waitress in Kathy's tearooms. She didn't like its revamp into an American-style diner, but was soon the only person still wearing the baseball cap as part of her uniform.

1998 saw Betty and Seth threatened with eviction when Tara sold off most of the Home Farm estate. She and Seth were too old to get a mortgage, but Biff sold his motorbike to pay the deposit and took on the mortgage himself. Betty took in Mandy and Lisa when the

Betty Eagleton.

Dingles were evicted.

Betty was fascinated by Kim's and Steve's trial, and was the only villager to attend court every single day. She also became fast friends with Bernice Blackstock. She was upset when Stella sacked Seth (at Pollard's suggestion), and – much to Seth's chagrin – quickly fixed him up as caretaker of the village hall. She acted as a matchmaker for Butch and Emily, inviting them both to tea so they got to know each other better.

SETH ARMSTRONG
(played by Stan Richards)
Born: 12 November, most probably in 1926
First Appearance: 16 May 1978

Poacher turned gamekeeper, Seth is the oldest person in the village, and knows everything about the local community, its wildlife and the countryside. He has no enemies in the village, and everyone is usually willing to listen to his advice (or they are foolish to ignore it). Over

Seth hates his false teeth.

the years, Seth has taken a number of youngsters under his wing.

Seth now lives with Betty Eagleton, his wartime childhood sweetheart, but the two aren't married, and they were only reunited in the mid-1990s. He has two sons, Fred and Jimmy, by his late wife, Meg. Seth met Meg when she was working as a barmaid (but not in Beckindale, because Amos was unaware of this until 1980, when she volunteered her services at the Woolpack). Jimmy would now be in his mid-forties and Fred in his late thirties. Seth may well have a grandchild, born in early 1980, as Jimmy's wife Susan discovered she was pregnant in May 1979. Seth possibly has other grandchildren (and maybe even very young great-grandchildren by now), but Seth has lost touch with both his sons – he didn't even have their addresses to tell them their mother had died, so they didn't attend her funeral. He has a sister on the Isle of Wight, whom he went to stay with for a few weeks when she fell sick in 1998.

Over the years, Seth's discovered that he's distantly related to both the Sugdens and the old lords of the manor, the Verneys.

Seth is reticent about his age. Seth's birthday is definitely 12 November, but it's unclear in which year he was born. In 1987, Alan Turner's records showed that Seth was 60 (meaning he was born in 1927), but Seth avoided retirement by claiming he was younger (but not saying how much younger). Character notes drawn up in 1990 say he was born in 1932, making him 58 at the time, but he

Seth skives off, but Turner catches him.

celebrated his 74th birthday in 2000 (so he would have been born in 1926). He gave a strong hint that he'd had a 'very close' romantic relationship with Grace Tolly before the war. He once reminded Amos that he had been a regular in the Woolpack since before Amos became the landlord (in 1948). The knees-up he and Betty had was very specifically a 1944-themed night, as that was the year Betty might have married him. Perhaps surprisingly, given that it was free money, he was reluctant at first to collect his pension. It was 1992 before he opened a bank account – which came with a credit card he was so enamoured with that he bought a round at the Woolpack.

Before his retirement, Seth was ingeniously work-shy, and while he's almost always propping up the bar in the Woolpack, he rarely pays for his pint himself. The Woolpack is important to Seth. It's his idea of

heaven on earth, give or take, and he's been very keen over the years on resisting changes and innovations. That said, he's quite happy to take his custom to the Malt Shovel, if needs be.

He was originally the school caretaker, but supplemented that income with a spot of poaching on Home Farm land. When NY Estates took over, they quickly realised the wisdom of hiring Seth as their gamekeeper – not only did he have unrivalled knowledge of the area and wildlife, but he did the vast majority of the poaching. Paying him a salary not to made sense to both parties. Seth met his match when Alan Turner arrived as a new estate manager at Home Farm. Turner was keen on making the estate more commercially successful – and that meant working people harder and making changes, the two things most hated by Seth.

The Home Farm shoot was

Seth and Betty

traditionally managed by Seth, who resented both the 'amateurs' coming in and not cleanly killing his birds and the hunt, which roamed over shoot land, disturbing the wildlife, all to catch foxes he could shoot without anything like the fuss. Seth is unsentimental about wildlife and hasn't hesitated to shoot a dog that's worrying sheep, but he can't stand cruelty to animals. He has raised the alarm over illegal hare-coursing and badger-baiting over the years.

For many years, Seth had a dog called Smokey, whom he once claimed he'd trained to run to the Woolpack and fetch him a can of lager. Smokey was killed in the plane crash. He had a horse, Samson, and a donkey who ran amok at the summer fair. He's also kept ferrets. He now has a dog called Charlie.

Seth has no teeth of his own, and hates to wear dentures.

Seth is a stalwart of the horticultural club, supplying vegetables to the harvest festival, and winning prizes at summer fairs and shows. He was an eager participant in the amateur drama group, going as far as learning every line of Amos's version of *Dracula* even though he was just the understudy – he ended up playing Dracula... and forgetting his teeth.

Seth was proud he contracted cryptosporidium – it meant two weeks off work. He was less pleased to discover it meant he couldn't drink beer in that time. Other excuses for skiving have verged on the feeble – 'losing his hat' (two days off work) being perhaps his all-time weakest excuse.

Seth is the only person in the village who still likes Kim Tate – he gave her away at her second marriage to Frank and at her marriage to Steve. He continued to support her even after it became clear she'd been involved in the Home Farm robbery and the subsequent murder attempt on Kathy.

When people have gone missing, Seth has been on hand to provide information about the lie of the land to the authorities. He found Sarah when she went missing, and helped find Rachel's body.

His marriage to Meg was long, and she was long-suffering. She was rarely seen in the Woolpack, usually surfacing only after a particularly long absence on Seth's part. Seth was heartbroken when she died.

Betty Prendagast had been his

SETH'S FAMILY TREE

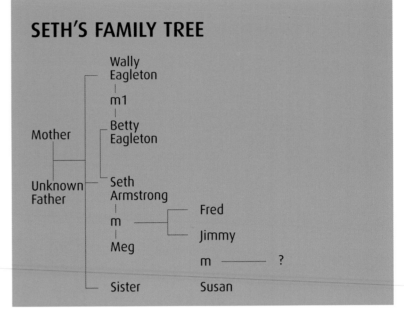

childhood sweetheart, but had married his friend Wally Eagleton instead. After Wally's death, Seth and Betty became close. After Seth's house was destroyed in the plane crash, Seth moved into Keeper's Cottage on Main Street with Betty, but soon grew restless as she started to talk about decorating all the time. The two have huge affection for each other but (quite rightly) they don't entirely trust each other. Seth has shown a keen interest in strippers in recent years, first seeing one at a sportsmen's dinner, booking one for the Woolpack and arranging one for Roy's stag night. This might explain his interest in the internet, which he gained after Zoe gave him her old computer.

Seth finally retired from his job in 1999, when Stella Jones was the owner of Home Farm. She felt guilty about it, and gave him £1000. He told Betty it was £200. Since then, Seth has spent retirement doing exactly what he did when he worked – drinking pints and dispensing wisdom at the Woolpack. His rivalry with Alan Turner long ago turned into mutual respect and, although neither would admit it, real friendship. One of Turner's last acts as landlord of the Woolpack was to mark Seth's regular place at the bar with a small brass plaque.

> **TERRY WOODS**
> (played by Billy Hartman)
> Born: 1957
> First Appearance:
> 2 February 1995

Some people always fall on their feet. Terry never does. He's a nice guy, if perhaps a little too unambitious. His life has been a series of unlucky breaks and great hopes which have never quite come off. He's the definition of unlucky in love. Currently he works as Chris Tate's security advisor – which sounds great on paper, but which tends to mean he runs errands for his boss.

Terry Woods.

In his twenties Terry was a sportsman – a footballer (with Barnsley) and rugby league player (at Farsley). He was good, and could have been rich... but an injury put an end to his playing days.

He arrived in Emmerdale in 1995 with his wife, Britt. They had been appointed by Alan Turner ('big Al' as Terry calls him) as bar managers of the Woolpack. The villagers found them a little brash compared to Amos and Mr Wilks, and they weren't immediately popular. Terry quickly proved a little more down to earth than his wife – flirting with Tina Dingle, getting involved with Vic's and Seth's moonshine scam. That got him sacked by Alan as manager, and demoted to barman and dogsbody. Terry soon got fed up with Britt bossing him around.

He discovered that Britt had been abused by her father, and tried to be supportive, but it put their marriage in trouble. When they were offered a pub of their own by the brewery, Britt left to run it. Terry was left alone in the Woolpack with Alan Turner – but quickly moved Tina in when Alan was away. He tried to reconcile with Britt, but discovered she was having an affair with Gerald Taylor, the brewery manager. Terry was taking ballroom dancing lessons with Viv Windsor, and pressed her to start an affair, but she turned him down. Vic and Kelly both suspected something was up.

His efforts to liven up the social life in the village were bearing fruit – he arranged a dinner for sportsmen, and a 'friendly' rugby match featuring Martin Offiah (where Terry ended up seriously losing). He joined a band with Zak, Vic and Lisa. He met up with an old flame, Elaine, who had a child he suspected was his. He got divorced from Britt in 1996, and couldn't afford to take up Turner's offer of becoming a partner at the Woolpack. Tina and he had a casual relationship, which he found a little frustrating. He finally launched into an affair with Viv, but the family found out and – against his wishes – Viv and Donna moved into the Woolpack. Terry found 'family life' stifling, and cheated on Viv with journalist Helen Ackroyd. Viv found out and ended their affair. He buried the hatchet with Vic, and they ended up getting arrested in an Amsterdam brothel.

When Alan planned to move to America, Terry once again failed to raise the money to buy the Woolpack. Alan eventually decided to stay. Terry broadened his horizons by volunteering to help at the Cairns' activity centre, but he wasn't as fit as he'd thought he was. One good result was that he got to know Will Cairns, and encouraged him to have a trial for the local rugby club. He also had a brief relationship with Heather Hutchinson.

Things started to go wrong with the arrival of Tricia Stokes, Alan's granddaughter. Terry was smitten, and thought Tricia was equally keen. It was an easy mistake to make – Tricia soon ended up in bed with him. Terry let Tricia talk him into organising an illegal lock-in while Alan was away. When that was over, he followed Tricia upstairs, eager for another night of passion... but failed to extinguish a candle on the bar.

Terry and Britt

That fell into a box of fireworks Tricia had failed to put away. As Tricia let Terry into her room they heard the first explosion. The public rooms of the Woolpack were completely gutted. Turner blamed Terry, refusing to accept Tricia could have had anything to do with it. Terry kept his job, but when he discovered Tricia was sleeping with Scott, he announced to the whole village that Tricia was a tart. Alan sacked him – after flooring him with a savage punch. Terry left the village for a few weeks.

He returned on Christmas Day, trying to reconcile with Tricia and Turner. Before he had a chance, he discovered Vic's body in the post office. He did his best to help Viv in the aftermath.

He got a new job as 'head of security' at the new Tate Haulage – in reality, as he was the only security man, he was just a night-watchman. To earn extra money, he started to do more dangerous work for Chris – infiltrating the rival Reynolds Haulage pretending to be a customer to steal floppy disks, going round to debtors demanding they settle their accounts. This did little for his self-esteem and the extra money was fairly pitiful.

Terry moved into Annie's Cottage with Marlon, Biff and Will, convinced he was 'one of the lads', but soon realised he was old enough to be their dad.

When Chris disappeared, Terry was convinced Sean was behind it, but wasn't in a position to shop his boss. He helped Zoe track Chris (and his kidnapper Liam) down – and was promptly sacked by Chris, who felt that if Terry had been doing

his job properly, he wouldn't have been kidnapped in the first place! Terry was soon reinstated.

Terry helped the Windsors, particularly Donna, after Kelly's suicide attempt. This finally convinced Chris that Terry was worthwhile, and he started to confide more in him. Terry got another boost when he threw a nosy reporter out of the Woolpack for hassling Kathy in the wake of Graham's death.

A familiar pattern soon recurred – Terry fell for Claudia, the Tate nanny. She slept with him, but was really interested in Chris, and soon moved on. He couldn't believe his luck when he successfully chatted up Virginia at one of Tara's parties.

Terry learned to tolerate Chris paying Charity for sex – Terry was the one who had to ferry them around to their meetings. His love life had a brief moment of stability when he met and started dating Carol, one of Viv's friends. He helped Carol buy the bed and breakfast, and was disappointed when she left. He was a witness at Viv's and Bob's wedding.

Eric Pollard.

> **ERIC CHARLES POLLARD**
> (played by Chris Chittell)
> Born: 11 June 1945
> First Appearance:
> 30 September 1986

Eric is an antiques dealer, a swindler and a crook who's conned just about everyone in the village over the years. He's also a charmer and a connoisseur, with – by his account at least – a distinguished army career behind him. Eric's the archetypal big fish in a small pond.

Eric has been married four times, but doesn't have any children of his own (he does have stepchildren). His first wife was Eileen Pollock and he never divorced her, a fact that only came to light some years after his marriage to Elizabeth Feldmann. There is extremely strong circumstantial evidence that Eric killed Elizabeth (she died on the night of the plane crash). His third marriage, to Filipino Dee de la Cruz was short-lived. He is now married to Gloria Weaver.

Eric was the manager and auctioneer at Hotten market, and worked with Sandie Merrick, who quickly came to suspect him of doing private deals on the side. His attempts to cover his tracks were fairly crude, and he was sacked. He launched a hate campaign against Sandie, slashing her tyres and threatening her.

A year later, he was back in the village, trying to steal antique prints from Marian Wilks and Paolo Rossetti. Paolo discovered him, and chased him with a gun, but

accidentally shot himself. Pollard was put under police surveillance, and lay low for several months, but no charges were ever brought.

Pollard returned in 1988, involving Phil Pearce in making fake antiques for him. He was beaten to an auctioneer's job by Sandie Merrick. He also blackmailed Nick Bates when he found out he'd taken money left behind by the robbers after the post office raid.

For once, Pollard was accused of a crime he didn't actually do, when the village suspected he'd stolen grain from the Home Farm harvest. By now, Pollard was the new auctioneer at Hotten market. He also fell for a beautiful woman called Debbie who conned him out of £2000 (although he'd 'borrowed' it from the Hotten market account). He was forced to sell his car to clear the debt, and his action led the market to centralise the accounting procedures, effectively making it impossible to fiddle any more money. He resorted to stealing Seth's bicycle to get around.

Pollard and Mr Cuddles

Pollard fell for Elizabeth Feldmann, sending her roses. She was slow to respond, but eventually they started dating. He promised to go straight, but was soon up to his old tricks, arranging side deals on market antiques with crooked councillor Charlie Aindow.

Pollard's money problems continued, with his new car being repossessed. He even had to forgo his whisky in favour of bitter, which was cheaper. A series of cons helped reverse his problems – selling a Roman bracelet found on Home Farm land that was rightfully Frank's, stealing cheques from the fish farm. Pollard even stooped to stealing Robert Sugden's fruit-machine winnings!

On 30 December 1993, Elizabeth told Eric she intended to tell the police about the cheque fraud before going off to babysit for her granddaughter. That night a plane crashed on the village. Elizabeth was among the dead, but some, especially Michael, suspected Eric had done away with her when he insisted she be cremated. After the funeral, Eric reverted to his old ways. He robbed Briardale Hall and sold goods worth £150,000; sabotaged the Home Farm Classic Car Rally by moving all the road signs, and attempted to bully Alan Turner out of the Woolpack. He even defrauded the disaster fund by selling a donated oil painting for £175,000, donating just £1500 to the fund. Also in this year, Pollard's past caught up with him when his first wife, Eileen, turned up and tried to claim some of Elizabeth's life insurance money from him. Eric's scheme to have the Woolpack backfired when Mrs Bates discovered what he'd been up to and Frank Tate crushed his car outside the pub. Once again he was fooled by a woman. He fell for WPC Barbara Metcalfe, and seemed actually willing to give up his dodgy lifestyle for her, but was devastated when she admitted that she had been using him to get back at her husband.

Eric found a useful – or, more typically, use*less* – new helper in Sam Dingle, using him as cheap labour as part of Sam's community service.

Pollard went into partnership with Kathy at the tearooms, opening a wine bar. He spent much of the next couple of years trying to win the rest of the business, by foul means more often than fair, from Kathy.

In 1997 he went on holiday to the Philippines, and returned with his dream woman, Dee. They married in May – he had to resort to having Sam as his best man. Eric found it tiring keeping up with his young wife and asked Marlon to get him a herbal tonic. Marlon happily sold him a mixture of pig steroids, vitamins and laxatives.

Pollard and Dee split up when

Pollard offers free (stolen) pies as a bribe on election day.

her mother died, and it turned out Pollard had been hiding letters from home explaining she was ill. Pollard had suspected Dee of having an affair with Will Cairns (she hadn't), and the marriage was already on the rocks. Pollard was devastated, and hit the bottle. He'd lost all interest in the wine bar, and had his licence withdrawn after allowing alcohol to be sold to minors. He didn't help his case by trying to bribe the magistrate. He planned to kill himself by burning down the diner, but Marlon talked him out of it.

Pollard picked himself up and bought Farrars Barn, selling antiques from it. He attempted to sue the Woolpack when he sustained a cut from the explosion started by Tricia (against lawyer Laura Johnstone's advice – she couldn't even see the cut). He concocted an elaborate scam to get his hands on a valuable teddy bear, Mr Cuddles, that used to belong to Linda Glover, which Ned was holding on to for sentimental reasons. Unknown to Ned, it was a Steiff bear, worth more than £10,000. Pollard sold it at auction for £13,000 – then turned round to see Ned Glover in the auction room. He was forced to hand over the cash.

He landed on his feet when Stella Jones, a lottery winner, arrived in the village, looking to buy antiques. He persuaded her to buy Home Farm, and got carried away at the auction in a bidding war with Chris Tate. He ended up paying a million pounds more than the estimate. Stella was charmed by Eric, and let him take her on antique-buying weekends. She made him her estate manager. Pollard set about fleecing her of money, and had great long-term

plans for her. When villagers started to warn Stella about him, he vandalised her car, blaming the 'barbaric' locals, suggesting she stick with him. In a position of power, a job where one of his duties was to set his own salary, Pollard was in his element. He decided to settle every petty score, and enjoyed sacking Seth. To his credit, though, Pollard suspected Graham of murdering Rachel and his first wife. A clear case of taking one to know one.

Pollard turned his attention to Mandy, winding her up so much she hit him… or tried to. She ended up hitting Stella instead, and going to prison for three months. Pollard started to use Home Farm money to buy items for himself. He spent tens of thousands on dodgy fitness equipment, hoping to persuade Stella to turn Home Farm into an executive health farm. Stella had enough of the grasping ways of the villagers and left, but not before publicly sacking Pollard and ordering Butch Dingle to literally throw him out of the front door of Home Farm.

He started to help Kathy in her custody battle for Alice. By now Kathy was seeing Graham, and Pollard was terrified she was in danger. When Graham tried to drive Kathy off a cliff, Pollard was on hand with Marlon to save her. Feeling slighted that the villagers didn't congratulate him enough, he sold his story to the papers – and once again became the village pariah.

Eric was more popular that Viv Hope, though, and as she was the only other candidate, he won the council elections, representing the Emmerdale ward at Hotten Town Hall.

Eric befriended new villager Gloria and loaned her an antique

Edna Birch and granddaughter Eve.

necklace. When Cain stole the necklace Gloria was forced to buy it from Eric at an abominable price. This contributed to Gloria's depression and she attempted suicide. Eric got to her just in time and saved her. Overcome with guilt, Eric tried to help Gloria and she moved into his cottage. She helped run Pollard's 'factory' in the barn that used to belong to the Dingles, dedicated to producing tatty painted wooden objets d'art for gift shops.

In 2002, Pollard became Mayor of Hotten. Most people are put off local politics by the sleaze and corruption - Pollard's eyes light up at the thought

he could get some of the action…

EDNA BIRCH
(played by Shirley Stelfox)
First Appearance: 25 May 2000

A village busybody and prude.

Edna is widowed. She has at least one child, a son Peter who lives in France with his second wife. He has a daughter, Evelyn.

The love of her life in recent years was her dog, Batley, who won the best in breed at the 1998 Hotten Show. Batley died in 2002, and is buried in Edna's garden.

Emmerdale

BEHIND THE SCENES

CHAPTER FOUR

Making any TV programme is hard work and a
team effort – making one that goes out five times a
week, every week, to BAFTA-winning standard is
unprecedented.

BEHIND THE SCENES OF EMMERDALE

If, for one moment, you think they are doing a good job, then they aren't doing their job properly.

Like pickpockets and spin doctors, the best work of people who make television is completely invisible. Everyone watching *Emmerdale* knows deep down that it's made up, that the people on screen are actors walking around sets, performing lines from a script while someone points a camera at them. But it's very important to maintain the illusion that *Emmerdale* is a window on to a world where real people go about their lives, saying and doing what comes into their head. At heart, the twelve million or so people who tune into *Emmerdale* every weekday evening do so because they care about the characters, they want to see what happens next to them, what the consequences of their decisions and their actions are. And there are hundreds of very talented people behind the scenes whose job it is to make the viewers come back for the next episode.

SCRIPTS

Emmerdale never starts from a blank page. There are 30 years of history and dozens of ongoing, interlinking, evolving stories. There are sets, actors and a whole production team in place, a few of whom have been around since the first episode.

But the best place to find where the process starts is with the writers. Everything that happens depends on the scripts.

When the show started, and for the next 15 or so years, individual writers would script blocks of episodes – four, six, sometimes even eight episodes at a time. There were rules – writers knew how many characters they could have, and which locations and sets were available, but writers had a lot of autonomy within their episodes. The advantage was that a writer could develop the themes and dramas he or she thought were important, and they weren't constrained by a 24-minute length of an episode – eight episodes gave them more than three hours of screen time to tell their stories.

The disadvantage of that system was that stories tended to be quite stop and start, and all the various storylines tended to stop and start in the same episodes. Watching early episodes, particularly the ones from the 1970s, it's striking that, instead of a large regular cast, there are far more casual characters that come and go after a couple of weeks. A new farmer would be introduced, they'd have a problem, talk about it in the Woolpack, and then Joe or Matt would help them out, and that farmer would go away happy, never to be seen again. A mysterious woman

The crew set up a shot.

would turn up in the village, catch the eye of a couple of the men then leave, and after that she wouldn't even rate a mention. Writers would rarely have the opportunity to develop the work of the other writers. It was also a lot of work – nowadays, writers are given three weeks to write one script. Writing eight in a row would be months of work.

In the mid-1980s, facing rivalry from new soaps *EastEnders* and *Brookside*, ITV found themselves outdone in an area that had always been their natural territory. Although it's hard to believe it now, even *Coronation Street* was in trouble, as many of the old guard of actors left the series, and it looked very creaky compared with the new opposition. Another mainstay, *Crossroads*, had been running since 1964, but it had been in terminal decline since the departure of Noele Gordon in 1981. The last episode was shown on Easter Monday 1988.

From the beginning of 1988, *Emmerdale* was networked by ITV, and the way the series was written soon changed to match the newer soaps – a larger team of writers than before would each write individual episodes. At the instigation of new producer Stuart Doughty (who'd previously worked on *Brookside*), the number of scenes per episode was also increased, making the series a little faster-paced. Big stories would be planned, and would be allowed to develop over weeks and months, with all the writers working on them.

Nowadays, with the programme on five days of the week, there are eighteen writers, four storyliners, two story editors and two script editors.

Seth comes face to face with his stunt double

The first part of the production process is to gather all the writers together at conference. Every three weeks, the writers and story and script teams attend a two-day meeting in the Emmerdale production office in Leeds, chaired by the producer. At this stage, writers are discussing episodes that are still five or six months in the future as far as the viewers are concerned. The first order of business is checking the storylines from the previous block – ironing out problems and answering questions.

The next item on the agenda is the future. Three or four times a year, the writers have a long-term conference to discuss months, even years into the future. It's usually here that the big stories that will run for many months and the new regular characters are thought up. Usually, though, conference is concerned with the immediate future, the next three weeks of stories.

The course of many of the stories has already been decided, but it's often only when writers get to grips with scripts that they see new twists or implications, or it becomes clear that there's a danger a story might become repetitive or far too complicated.

In February this year, one conference found itself with an unusual problem. A couple of the episodes in question fell on the Queen's Golden Jubilee. How should the programme reflect that? In 1977, there was a street party in Beckindale. But so far, in 2002, the real-life public response to the Jubilee seemed far more muted, and – with five months before the episodes were due to be broadcast – it was hard to imagine that there would be widespread street parties in 2002. At the same time, there were going to be special bank holidays, and it was likely that some enthusiasm for the Jubilee would build as the day approached.

In the end, the decision was made to run a story where the village celebrated the Jubilee, but in a way which reflected something of the ambivalence that people seem to be feeling, and which showed a spectrum of opinion about it. The stalwarts of the village were going to organise a Jubilee celebration, but not all motives will be patriotic – Viv will be keen, for example, for her daughter Donna to be queen of the Jubilee pageant, and will be spitting nails when Katie wins the honour. Elsewhere in the village there was dissent with the Dingles having discovered that the same day is Jesse James' birthday, and so they were holding a celebration in honour of that instead.

The Jubilee also offered a good focal point for a couple of big developments for long-running stories. For example, what better place for the news to come about Katie's pregnancy than when she was the queen of the Jubilee pageant, and the whole village's attention was on her? The episode saw a number of times where the secret almost came out - and then the episode ends with the revelation.

Emmerdale has 'core characters', ones that have been in the series for a long time and who have a lot of relationships with other characters. Jack Sugden is an obvious one – the only character still there from the first episode, he's the father of Andy, Robert and Victoria, but also works for Chris Tate, he's been in a relationship with Diane Blackstock and the Sugdens have frequently feuded with Viv. Just about everyone has some sort of connection with him. The audience expects to see a lot of Jack, they care about what happens to him and his family. So it's important that the writers make sure that he – as well as the other core characters – is always in the thick of an important story.

Sammy Winwood, who plays Katie Addyman.

With a large cast, there's always a risk that some characters could be sidelined. This is often a particular danger with new characters, who haven't had time to set up a network of relationships in the village and who might end up out on a limb.

The storylining team take the notes from conference and spend the next couple of weeks preparing three weeks' worth of storylines. A storyline document is five pages long, breaks down an episode into individual stories and is a detailed guide to the script writer, telling them what happens in their episode, where they are picking up from and where they have to leave the story and tells a writer which characters they can use.

Each of the four storyliners takes a couple of the story strands and it's decided how far each story will progress in the next three weeks. They prepare the stories, spelling out each 'beat' – each separate element of what happens. It's here that the ideas that

came out at conference are translated into a practical plan of action.

There are logistical limits on the storytelling. It's an ensemble cast, and while only around half the cast are in each episode, all the regulars should be appearing at least a few times each block. As part of their contracts, actors are guaranteed to appear in a certain number of episodes over the course of a year. For most characters, reaching this minimum is not a problem, but it's something the storyliners have to bear in mind. At the same time, actors are paid for each episode they are in, regardless of how many scenes or lines they have – it's usually not very efficient to have a character in an episode just to deliver one line (and the actors find it very frustrating).

At the other end of the scale, if a character is involved in more than one big plot, there might not be enough hours in the day for the actor to appear in all the scenes. A character like Chris Tate, for example, has many connections in the village, and could legitimately appear in most of the stories that are running. So a storyliner has to make sure that the best use is made of him.

Mostly, though, it's creative work. The storyliner comes up with the structure of a story, and thinks through the implications of what the characters are doing. The storyliners work together to discuss 'plot logic' – asking questions about why a character would do what they want them to do, or checking that it's the simplest solution. If someone is threatened, for example, why don't they just call the police? Would the character have the time and money to do what the story demands?

Often it's about getting information across to the audience – a storyline might read, 'Viv is worried that she has bet the housekeeping money on the horses, but assures Bob that nothing's wrong.' But how will the audience know what she's thinking when she can't come out and say it? Some American daytime soaps use voice-overs, flashbacks or even dream sequences to tell their audience what a character is thinking. *Emmerdale* is more 'realistic' and almost without exception it doesn't use flashbacks, or montage sequences. The action is linear, there's no incidental music. So a storyline writer has a choice – it's easy enough to get an emotion across by showing Viv looking worried at a point in the scene when Bob can't see her face, or hurriedly hiding a copy of the *Racing Post*. But if it's more complex or specific, then the storyliner makes sure that there's a scene in the episode where Viv confides in someone and spells the problem out to them, and the audience.

The story editor oversees this, and works out how everything will fit together. Every episode is a set of balancing acts – there has to be the right mix of comedy and drama, between big dramatic

A location shoot.

Once the storylines have been edited and approved, they are sent out to the writers, who are allocated a script each and get a degree of latitude in how they interpret it – if they can come up with a better way of telling a story, they are encouraged to do so. They can also – after checking it first – use a slightly different line-up of characters if they prefer.

The writers prepare a scene breakdown – structuring their episode to show who is in what scene, where it takes place and summarising what happens. They then flesh that out to a full script. Writing an episode takes about three weeks – there's a strict deadline. The writers submit their scripts to the script editor. On *Emmerdale* there are now two script editors, to cope with the workload that five scripts a week demands. They edit a block each.

Writers can also call on the researchers and archivist to check up with details of both *Emmerdale*'s past, and what would happen in real life. The series is currently running a story about Zoe Tate suffering from schizophrenia, a subject that requires a lot of sensitivity and detailed knowledge. But every episode has questions arising – often points of law, or medical information. How would Angie, a serving policewoman, normally deal with such and such a situation? Would Turner be able to do what the storyline says, given that he once had a heart attack?

The script editor checks for a number of things. A lot of these are practical: every episode of Emmerdale has to be 24 minutes long, to within 10 seconds. They check that all the beats from the storyline are included, and which characters are used. The script editor also makes sure that the writers' portrayal of stories and characters is consistent both within the block and the series as a whole. While writers talk to each other, they are all writing their scripts at the same time, and co-ordinating every part of that process can be tricky. Often two writers could come up with the same joke, or one might accidentally include some information that shouldn't come out for a few more episodes.

moments and quieter scenes that explore a story, between established characters and newer ones, between scenes set in the village set and those in the studio.

The stories are divided up into A, B, C and 'business' strands. The 'A' story is the most important in the episode. The previous episode will probably have ended on a cliffhanger leading into it, and as the most dramatic story, the writer will probably use it as either the 'ad tag' that leads the programme into the advertising break in the middle (to make sure no one changes channel during the commercials) or as the 'end tag', the cliffhanger that makes people want to tune in the next day and hopefully talk about it at work. There are usually about 21 scenes in an episode of *Emmerdale*, and the A story should feature in about half of them. The B and C stories are important, too. Over the course of a block, different stories will be the most important in different episodes. There are also items that keep a plotline bubbling away, which will be paid off later. These 'business' scenes are there to remind the audience of running stories – Tricia will complain she's short of money, Louise will suggest to Ray that they go on holiday together. Those stories will be more important later on, but need to be set up before they can be run.

Night filming.

PRODUCTION

Once the script editors are happy with a script, and the producer has read them and approved them, the episodes go into production.

This is overseen by Tim Fee, the line producer, who explains the layout of his half of the production office. 'We have six groups of desks – there are two groups of four prepping, and two groups of four are out there shooting, and then two groups of four editing and dubbing (although that's not strictly true, because some of those people are back prepping). So there are about 20 production people in a constant cycle. It might seem like overmanning – that's what I'm told all the time – but I still maintain it's the leanest crew on the network'.

Prepping involves a careful reading of the scripts to see what's required – which actors are in which scenes, what sets and locations are needed, what props and costume requirements there are. Each block of five episodes is assigned a director, and *Emmerdale* always tries to have a mix. Tim Fee explains, 'It would be really easy to employ the same six directors to shoot the programme week after week, but I suspect that after a while the programme would become boring. We like to introduce new directors, always supported by more experienced ones. They all get through, and really show their colours if they're talented and successful.

'There are two crews all the time – sometimes three. Having two crews is like having railway lines – they can never meet. It's

the actors that move from one unit to the other. And the poor actors sometimes never know where they are, they have to flit between the two crews, and there are days where some of them do scenes for one director in the village, then get in a fast car to the studio, do some scenes from a bunch of different episodes in a different week, then go back to the village for more scenes in the afternoon. And we have to tell them which episode they're in, what scene. The actors have to be spot on all the time, and they are, they're really tremendous.'

A call sheet, a detailed document saying who needs to be where, when and what scenes they will be shooting, is prepared. All sorts of things have to be taken into consideration – actors can't be in two places at once. But what an actor is doing in a scene is also important – if it's more complex or emotional than normal, more shooting time is needed. Also, actors have to sleep, and travel from home to the Leeds studios.

There are practical considerations for the designers, prop buyers, costume designer, gardener, even the stuntmen. Each is allocated a budget to bring the script to life.

The director on a soap inherits almost every member of the cast and almost every location. That might seem to limit them creatively, but the sets (and actors!) are flexible enough to allow for different directors to make their mark on their block of episodes.

Preparing to shoot Rachel's last scene...

Do not adjust your set – through the windows of the studio are realistic backdrop paintings

'bitch', but every time she was, the office would receive letters of complaint. Zoe's lesbianism is also a source of contention. Zoe has been shown kissing women a number of times, but – unlike the heterosexual characters – has never been seen in bed with another woman. It's always tricky, drawing the line of what a 'reasonable' depiction is – even mentioning that she's a lesbian can cause complaints from some quarters.

Studio footage is edited as it's recorded by the vision mixer, working in the studio gallery. Location footage, including material shot in the village set, is edited later. The *Emmerdale* studios have their own editing suites, and –

What the directors lack is time. The director of a big feature film would be delighted to get two minutes of usable footage a day – legend has it that *The Bridge on the River Kwai* averaged about 18 *seconds* worth. A typical television drama would expect to get eight or nine minutes 'in the can' every day. *Emmerdale*, broadcast five times a week, has to record and edit the equivalent of 24 minutes' footage a day. There is little or no time to rehearse – actors are expected to know their lines. They run through scenes a couple of times on set, then it's recorded. On such a tight schedule, there are almost no opportunities for retakes.

Other limitations are imposed by the ITV network, which has a number of standards. Many of these are technical, and there are rules against product placement – brand names are allowed, but can't be given 'undue prominence'. There are also taste and decency issues – *Emmerdale* goes out at seven in the evening, so has to be suitable for that audience. Everyone making *Emmerdale* is aware of these, and it's easy enough to recognise that there's a limit to the depiction of sexual or violent situations. But the line isn't always clear – is it acceptable to use the phrases 'bloody hell' or 'the old bugger' at that time in the evening? For some people, it's offensive language, for others it isn't. Kim was often called a

Behind the scenes - literally.

working with the director and producer – the editors put together the available footage, choosing the best takes, deciding to the frame where scenes start and end.

The producer has overseen every aspect of the making of an episode. Finally, he watches a completed episode and signs it off. In the meantime, another two blocks are in studio filming, and another two are being prepped, there's another block of scripts being edited, another being written, another being storylined...

STEVE FROST

Steve Frost has been the Producer of Emmerdale since early 2001. When asked what a television producer does, his predecessor Kieran Roberts probably put it best: 'Everything'. The producer has the final say on the casting of actors and the appointing of staff. Steve is responsible for the artistic direction of the show – and making sure the finished episodes are as good as they can be.

I'm the same age as Emmerdale – just a little bit older, I was 30 in September. I don't really have any childhood memories of it. I came to it very late, but I was watching it for two or three years before I joined the show as the story editor. I'm that classic viewer who never watched it but saw it as a slow countryside thing that lots of people watch but I don't. I assumed it was far more of a rural thing than it is.

I think the appeal of the show has changed over the years. It didn't start off as a soap, and it wasn't dreamt up as something that would last a long time. I think *Coronation Street* was set up with much more of a long-term view, and if you go back to the original year of Corrie it hasn't moved on that much. *EastEnders* was always drawn up as a big, long-running soap.

I think the original appeal was obviously the characters Kevin Laffan created, like Jack Sugden who's always been the heart of the show. There's always a constant interest in Jack and the family around him, and then as the years go by there's an onion effect, you start moving out to the family next door and the family next door to that, and you get to see the Tates and the Woolpack and they become the focus of interest, too.

But we're still working on the original premise of the class structure – even in the first episode you have the Sugdens from the small Yorkshire hill farm going to the funeral, when Marian Wilks rides past on a horse looking incredibly glamorous. There's always been the levels of society.

I really think the countryside setting is a plus. It's sometimes suggested it's a turn-off for the people who live in cities, but I don't think that's because it's set in the country. I think it's because those people still have this outdated image of the show as slow and old-fashioned, one that probably wasn't even true 15 or 20 years ago, let alone now.

If I was trying to explain why people should watch it, I think essentially it boils down to characters and stories. Well-defined, well-established characters. I think they really are terrifically well drawn, you want to see them react, see what happens to them. I think we've got all types of people familiar to the viewer, but they get to be slightly more extreme. You can identify with them, but they get to do things like slapping someone, or sleeping with their boss or coming up with a funny remark. I think the thing that *Emmerdale* does better than the other soaps is have a mix of comedy and good drama – you can go from one to the other from scene to scene, or even within a scene. The other soaps tend to have clearer boundaries between the comedy scenes and the dramatic ones.

At its heart, I think *Emmerdale*'s about both the comedy of class and the tragedy of class. The people are defined within a class structure, and you have the Tates at the top, who are the powerbrokers and the employers. Charity Tate is great, she has that footballer's wife appeal – no education, no manners, but a

vast amount of money, so she's a bit of a horror. The Sugdens are central to the show, they're the established family, but also the one that's seen the most changes. Then you have younger characters like Marlon and Tricia, who are really trying to make a go of it. And the Dingles are slightly set apart from that. They look like they're at the bottom of the heap, but in a way they're classless – they just get on and live their lives. Then there are characters like Turner and Pollard and Seth - it's difficult to rule anyone out.

Every day as a producer is different. My responsibility is for the editorial content of the programme, and that means I'm involved at every stage. There's a really good team, but a producer oversees pretty much everything so I do script edits with my script editors, discuss stories with my story editors, I sit in on the editor when the tapes are being edited.

I'm only really conscious of the viewers, I'm not too worried by the ITV network or the critics. I'm there to make sure the viewers keep watching, so we have to know what they want. We get letters, and I read them, but I'm always very conscious that there are over ten million viewers, and a letter is just one of those people's opinions. Usually the letters confirm my gut feeling rather than surprising me. We do get letters asking for more farming, like there used to be, but we know that was changed for a reason. But it's a concern I share, and it's why we've got Jack as the estate manager of Home Farm now, and we've got Ray and Chris buying up land. We can tell a dramatic story about land use if we make it about our characters.

Not everything we do is perfect, but when something doesn't work, we're almost always very conscious of that. Remember, too, that we plan episodes six months before they are broadcast, so we're often a hundred episodes ahead of the viewers, with the next couple of dozen already recorded. So if a story's just started being broadcast that isn't working, then it's usually been over for months as far as we're concerned.

It takes the audience a while to get used to new characters – people hated Bernice at first, but when she left this year we got loads of messages saying how much they would miss her. At the moment, the Daggerts haven't gone down very well, but I'm confident people will warm to them.

Going to five episodes a week went well. I wasn't sure how it would affect our storytelling. The stories with a fixed real-life timetable, like pregnancies and court cases, are the hardest – a pregnancy lasts nine months, obviously, but that's nearly two hundred episodes where you have to think of something new to say. There's a balance – when five episodes took two or three weeks, you'd expect there to be real movement in the stories, but would you

One of the busiest characters on Emmerdale, *Jack Sugden.*

really have as much development between just a Monday and a Friday? Sometimes we have to speed things up a bit. We've really researched the schizophrenia story we're running with Zoe, and we've consulted all sorts of people about it, and it'll run for a year, perhaps more. But in real life it would probably take about three years just to get to a diagnosis, and that would be – what? – about seven hundred episodes just to get to the meat of the story. In the end, people wouldn't want to watch that. But some of the time viewers complain about that, but we're right – there was a story last year where Zak had testicular cancer, and he had to have an operation, and we got letters saying that we were giving a rosy picture of the health service because he had his operation in a couple of weeks. But it was an emergency, and it was so serious it could have been done in days in real life.

I don't want to sound too negative: far more works than doesn't, and it's often the case that we'll see a couple of actors in the same scene that we wouldn't usually think of together and they'll spark off each other, and we'll develop that, or something that looked a bit flat on the page is brought to life by the actors and the director. Not everything works out exactly as we planned, but often it ends up better than we imagined it would.

Emmerdale Lists

EMMERDALE BIRTHDAYS

Over the years, the birthdays of many of the characters have been established – some characters have been born on the show, we've seen others getting presents or having a party, or sometimes the date is established officially, as on a birth or marriage certificate... or even a gravestone.

The writers always try to incorporate an established birthday into the show if it falls on a day when an episode is broadcast. Sometimes, though, the episode is already too full or a birthday party would strike the wrong tone, or the actor might not be in the episode.

Some characters are very vague about their age – Seth in particular (see his 'Who's Who' entry p166). Bernice also lied about her age, knocking three years off because she wanted to have achieved more by the time she was 30!

Those were examples of characters fudging the issue. The writers have occasionally contradicted facts established years before. Joe Sugden was 19 in the first episode, but 'over 40' in 1990, less than 18 years later. Jack once celebrated his birthday on 24 February, when his 'official' birthday is 28 November. Seth and Betty claimed to have courted during the War, and nearly married in 1944... when Betty would have been ten years old! Nellie Dingle apparently managed to give birth to Tina in May 1977 and Sam in August of the same year.

Regular characters, past and present, whose ages have been established are included in the list. Babies born in the programme itself are marked with an asterisk.

Bill Whiteley	31 October 1918	Archie Brooks	12 November 1963	Charity Dingle	1978
Amos Brearly	1 April 1920	Chris Tate	11 December 1963	Nicola Blackstock	1978
Annie Sugden	5 July 1920	Sean Reynolds	1964	Linda Glover	5 March 1978
Henry Wilks	2 December 1921	Angie Reynolds	1965	Charlie Cairns	16 July 1979
Seth Armstrong	12 November 1926	Michael Feldmann	30 July 1966	Roy Glover	20 June 1980
Betty Eagleton	22 January 1934	Kathy Glover	29 September 1967	Scott Windsor	20 July 1980
Alan Turner	5 August 1935	Steve Marchant	1968	Will Cairns	15 September 1980
Frank Tate	1 October 1937	Laura Johnstone	29 February 1968	Richie Carter	4 October 1980
Sgt Terry MacArthur	9 September 1939	Zoe Tate	27 April 1968	Kelly Windsor	5 December 1980
Bill Middleton	16 March 1943	Bernice Blackstock	29 December 1968	Lyn Hutchinson	1981
Eric Pollard	11 June 1945	Paddy Kirk	1 July 1969	Samuel David Skilbeck	23 December 1982 *
Elizabeth Feldmann	3 May 1947	Nick Bates	3 September 1969	Latisha Daggert	1983
Diane Blackstock	21 June 1947	Gavin Ferris	1970	Louise Merrick	November 1983 *
Jack Sugden	28 November 1947	Graham Clark	11 July 1971	Marc Reynolds	12 December 1983
Ned Glover	4 September 1947	Rachel Hughes	16 September 1971	Kirsty Hutchinson	1984
Peggy Skilbeck	28 August 1948	Elsa Feldmann	4 February 1972	Evelyn Birch	1985
Rodney Blackstock	1949	Butch Dingle	23 August 1972	Ollie Reynolds	11 August 1985
Joe Sugden	31 May 1949	David Glover	13 February 1973	Donna Windsor	1986
Kate Sugden	13 October 1951	Sam and Sally Skilbeck	10 April 1973 *	Andie Sugden	28 January 1986
Zak Dingle	19 January 1952	Mark Hughes	19 November 1973	Katie Addyman	September 1987
Sarah Sugden	25 March 1952	Lady Tara	1974	William Bates	29 October 1987 *
Ray Mullan	1956	Marlon Dingle	23 March 1974	Peter Whiteley	28 August 1990 *
Lisa Dingle	1956	Dee Pollard	9 October 1974	Alice Rose Bates	14 February 1991 *
Viv Windsor	19 May 1956	Cain Dingle	30 November 1974	Victoria-Anne Sugden	31 March 1994 *
Terry Woods	1957	Tricia Stokes	6 June 1976	Joseph Tate	8 June 1995 *
Vic Windsor	3 May 1958	Biff Fowler	9 August 1976	James Francis Tate	24 Sep 1996 *
Kim Tate	19 January 1959	Mandy Dingle	1 March 1977	Geri Cairns	31 March 1998 *
Tony Charlton	26 February 1961	Tina Dingle	May 1977	Belle Dingle	25 December 1998 *
Ashley Thomas	1961	Sam Dingle	16 August 1977	Kirk Daggert	9 July 2001 *
Stella Jones	1962	Emily Dingle	1978	Gabrielle Thomas	25 December 2001 *

DEATHS

Emmerdale has a reputation for being the soap with the highest death rate, but this seems to be because of its reputation for 'massacring the cast' in the plane crash. Only four regulars died in the plane crash, and disasters in *Brookside* and *Family Affairs* have been far more deadly.

That said, for a village with a population of around three hundred, the rate of accidental death is rather high. Emmerdale is certainly no place to bring up a child, judging by the figures.

KEY
* Character in show, but off-screen death.
** On-screen death.
*** Character not in show, or never/hardly ever seen.

NAME	DATE	CAUSE OF DEATH	LOCATION
Jacob Sugden***	10/10/72	Pneumonia	Emmerdale Farm
Sharon Crossthwaite*	30/01/73	Strangled	Village
Trash (Ian McIntyre)**	20/02/73	Broken neck (suicide)	Mill Cottage
Peggy Skilbeck*	16/07/73	Subarachnoid haemorrhage	Hawthorn Cottage
Sam and Sally Skilbeck*	13/01/76	Hit by train on level crossing	Out of village
Beattie Dowton*	13/01/76	As above	As above
Jim Gimbel*	21/06/77	Suicide (gun)	Holly Farm
Enoch Tolly*	19/02/81	Tractor accident	Tolly Farm
Sam Pearson*	27/11/84	Died in sleep	Emmerdale Farm
Harry Mowlem*	23/01/86	Murdered	Own farm
Pat Sugden**	26/08/86	Car accident	Road in Beckindale
Stephen Fuller*	24/11/88	Killed by tree	Off screen
Denis Rigg**	06/07/89	Killed by bull	Emmerdale Farm barn
Jackie Merrick**	16/08/89	Gun accident	Woods near Emmerdale Farm
Pete Whiteley**	16/08/90	Run over	Robblesfield Road
Paolo Rossetti***	01/01/91	Mysterious death	Italy
Bill Whiteley*	30/07/91	Died in sleep	Whiteley's Farm
Henry Wilks*	03/10/91	Heart attack	Emmerdale Farm
Meg Armstrong***	02/02/93	Possible stroke	6 Demdyke Row
Wally Eagleton***	24/11/93	Heart	Own farm
Mark Hughes*	30/12/93	Plane disaster	Village
Elizabeth Pollard*	30/12/93	As above	As above
Archie Brooks**	30/12/93	As above	As above
Leonard Kempinski**	30/12/93	As above	As above
Raider (Simmy)**	31/05/94	Shot by Reg	Home Farm
Shirley Turner**	07/06/94	Shot by Reg	Home Farm
Reg Dawson*	07/06/94	Shot by police	Home Farm
Ben Dingle**	09/08/94	Heart defect	Betty's land
Alice Bates Sr***	13/12/94	Unknown	Off screen
Joe Sugden*	06/06/95	Car crash in Spain	Spain
Luke McAllister**	01/08/95	Car crash	Country lane
Jed Connell**	11/04/96	Shot by Nick	Home Farm land

Granny Hopwood*	22/08/96	Heart attack	Leeds
Dave Glover**	26/12/96	Burns & lung damage	Home Farm
Ron Hudson**	08/05/97	Huntington's disease	Hospital
Frank Tate**	27/05/97	Heart attack	Home Farm
Kate Sugden*	30/07/97	Brain haemorrhage	Sheffield
Linda Fowler**	16/10/97	Internal bleeding	Village roadside Near Home Farm
Charles Cockburn***	16/07/98	Unknown	Off screen
Lord Alex Oakwell	??/??/98	Fell off a roof	London
Vic Windsor**	25/12/98	Head injury (as result of attack by Billy Hopwood)	Post office
Rachel Hughes**	11/05/99	Pushed off cliff by Graham Clark	Burview Crag
Liam**	11/11/99	Shot	Cellar
Graham Clark**	18/02/00	Off cliff in car	Coast
Butch Dingle **	24/03/00	Injuries resulting from lorry crash	Hospital
Pete Collins	24/03/00	As above	As above
Councillor NSE	24/03/00	As above	As above
Sarah Sugden	16/11/00	Barn fire	Sugden's farm
Ms Barbara Strickland	10/9/01	Hit and Run	Hotten Road

For the record, that's 50 deaths in total, 21 of which were seen on screen.

Thirteen deaths were through illness or natural causes, 20 through accidents (including the plane, bus and car crashes). There have been eight murders or shootings, two suicides and three deaths where the cause was never established.

WEDDINGS

The first Emmerdale wedding was between FRANK BLAKEY (a local blacksmith) and JANIE HARKER (sister of Pat Sugden and school friend of Joe Sugden). Jack Sugden was the best man.
27 MARCH 1973

JOE SUGDEN married CHRISTINE SHARP (who worked for the Milk Marketing Board). Matt Skilbeck was best man. Their marriage only lasted five weeks, and they divorced in 1976.
10 SEPTEMBER 1974

MATT SKILBECK married DOLLY ACASTER. Amos Brearly gave Dolly away and Joe Sugden was the best man. They met after she became the barmaid at the Woolpack.
29 JUNE 1978

JACK SUGDEN married PAT MERRICK who had been his teenage love before he left Beckindale in 1964. She was also the mother of his child, Jackie. They married in Hotten Register Office. Joe and Annie Sugden were the witnesses.
5 OCTOBER 1982

JACKIE MERRICK married KATHY BATES. She wore Annie's wedding dress after her own was damaged in a flood at her mother's cottage. Archie Brooks was best man. They lived in Joe's cottage in Demdyke Row.
3 FEBRUARY 1988

JOE SUGDEN'S second marriage was to KATE HUGHES, a divorcee with two children. Kate was given away by her father and Jack was best man. Joe arrived late on Alan's horse.
12 APRIL 1989

KATHY MERRICK married CHRISTOPHER TATE after a turbulent courtship. Frank provided a lavish reception and helicopter for the couple.
5 NOVEMBER 1991

ERIC POLLARD married ELIZABETH FELDMANN despite serious opposition from her son, Michael. Nick Bates gave Elizabeth away and Archie Brooks was best man. Michael was arrested immediately after the ceremony.
6 OCTOBER 1992

ANNIE SUGDEN shocked her family by getting married at the age of 73 to LEONARD KEMPINSKI whom she met in Spain. Amos gave her away.
28 OCTOBER 1993

ALAN TURNER, landlord of the Woolpack, married SHIRLEY TURNER at Hotten Register Office. They left the ceremony in a horse-drawn carriage. Amos was the surprise best man and Seth gave Shirley away.
10 FEBRUARY 1994

JACK SUGDEN married long-term lover SARAH CONNOLLY. They had been together for five years and had a daughter, Victoria-Anne. Joe was best man yet again.
19 MAY 1994

FRANK TATE remarried KIM TATE. They first married in 1986, but divorced in 1993 after her affair with Neil Kincaid, a local landowner. Chris was best man and Seth gave Kim away after her uncle got drunk.
22 DECEMBER 1994

TINA DINGLE jilted LUKE McALLISTER at the altar.
20 JULY 1995

ANNIE SUGDEN married AMOS BREARLY in Spain. He originally proposed in January 1973, but she turned him down (this happened off screen).
NOVEMBER 1995

RACHEL HUGHES married CHRIS TATE at Hotten Register Office with only Jack and Sarah Sugden present.
7 DECEMBER 1995

ZOE TATE was blessed with EMMA NIGHTINGALE at a local hotel. They exchanged vows and rings, but unfortunately their happiness did not last until the reception.
16 MAY 1996

KATHY BATES finally got her man when she married DAVE GLOVER in secret at Hotten Register Office.
28 NOVEMBER 1996

LINDA GLOVER and BIFF FOWLER had a white wedding on Christmas Eve. The wedding went ahead despite Biff's mum arriving with bad news for Biff. Dave Glover was best man and Alice Bates the bridesmaid.
24 DECEMBER 1996

ERIC POLLARD married his Filipino fiancée DEE MARGHARITA DE LA CRUZ at Hotten Register Office. Sam Dingle was smuggled in to be best man.
1 MAY 1997

LORD ALEX OAKWELL made a lady out of TARA COCKBURN when they married in a lavish ceremony. The reception was at Oakwell Hall.
21 AUGUST 1997

THE DINGLE BROTHERS were involved in a dramatic wedding day when ZAK snatched LISA CLEGG from the clutches of his brother Albert. In the end, Zak and Lisa had their relationship blessed instead.
10 SEPTEMBER 1997

ZAK DINGLE finally made an honest woman out of LISA CLEGG when they married at Hotten Register Office. Paddy Kirk had to step in and donate his grandmother's ring for the ceremony after the ring that Zak provided was reclaimed by its rightful owner.
28 JANUARY 1998

An eventful day was had by all when KIM TATE married STEVE MARCHANT at Home Farm.
7 MAY 1998

LADY TARA OAKWELL broke Biff's heart when she left him to marry LORD MICHAEL THORNFIELD.
16 SEPTEMBER 1998.

MANDY and BUTCH DINGLE gained their family home by tying the knot in a marriage of convenience.
11 NOVEMBER 1998

KELLY WINDSOR and ROY GLOVER married in haste.
26 MAY 1999

KATHY GLOVER failed to make it fourth time lucky when BIFF FOWLER jilted her at the altar.
5 AUGUST 1999

MANDY and PADDY KIRK had to bring their wedding forward to earlier in the day to avoid the police who were after Mandy. Butch tried to distract them by running across a field wearing one of Mandy's dresses. Mandy ran to the church only to find that they had no rings so Sarah kindly gave them hers. The ceremony was then interrupted by Pollard and the police.
13 OCTOBER 1999

BUTCH DINGLE and EMILY WYLIE married in hospital after Butch was fatally injured in the bus crash.
24 MARCH 2000

TRICIA STOKES married Australian JOE FISHER to help him stay in the country.
6 DECEMBER 2000

ASHLEY THOMAS and BERNICE BLACKSTOCK married.
25 DECEMBER 2000.

BOB HOPE and VIV WINDSOR married in haste.
5 FEBRUARY 2001

NICOLA BLACKSTOCK and CARLOS DIAZ, got to the church but not the altar. The wedding never went ahead after Bernice forced Nicola to admit to Carlos that she had lied about being pregnant with his child. An angry Carlos then told Nicola about the affair he had had with Bernice.
4 OCTOBER 2001

CHRIS TATE and CHARITY DINGLE married and had a reception at Home Farm that included a funfair.
27 NOVEMBER 2001

KEITH RICHARDSON

Since the mid-eighties, Keith Richardson has been the Executive Producer of Emmerdale *as part of his role as Group Controller of Drama at Yorkshire / Tyne Tees Television. But his association with the programme stretches back to when he was the Unit Manager on the first episode...*

It was originally commissioned as 26 half hours at lunchtime. We thought that would be it, but of course events have turned out differently. We all enjoyed it, and it was nice shooting up in Arncliffe, because it was fun being away from Leeds and having naughty nights in the hotel. It certainly never crossed my mind I'd be here 30 years on – I'm hanging in to the end, now, so only another 30 years to go!

I haven't been with the programme continuously though. There was a rumour that I'd been offered the producer's job on *Emmerdale* in the early eighties and turned it down, and that certainly wasn't true – it would have been quite helpful to my career at that point. I became Executive Producer in 1986.

By then, **Emmerdale** was all but networked – it was on everywhere but Scotland. The Scottish regions had their own agenda, which was to play Gaelic programmes at peak times to get government money. Despite that, we were up against it – more or less being told that if our ratings didn't improve, we'd be taken off. The programme was changing, but speeding up that process was forced on us.

I think the problem the programme had was that there's a lot of politics involved in television. Although it seems to the viewers that there's just ITV, there are different companies within that. There was a perception, principally put out by Thames Television, that **Emmerdale Farm** was a slow and sleepy programme that nobody liked. This was partly because they resented the fact there were two soaps coming from the North, and they didn't have one of their own, so they would do everything to keep us off the air. That was picked up a bit by Carlton, but it wasn't so extreme, because by then we'd started to change things around. The curious thing is that it's more to do with perceptions than with what you're actually doing. We took a lot of advice – we were told it didn't

matter if we changed the show, because if the opening titles didn't change then people would simply see the old titles and turn over. So that's what we did.

You have to do this comparatively gently, or you frighten off the people that are happily enjoying it. Nearly 15 years on, some people still call it **Emmerdale Farm**, but that can be a good thing, – it means we're firmly fixed in people's affections. Most of the people that still call it 'Farm' are the people who've been watching it for years, we're part of the fabric.

When I started as Executive Producer, there was a perception within YTV itself, never mind outside, that the show was 'just **Emmerdale**' and you tended to find that people were drafted in at the last minute to work on it, and you'd have a cameraman working on **Emmerdale** for two days because he was free. You can't come in for two days work like that and feel that you're a part of what's going on. So the most important change was to create a feeling that people belonged to the programme. Now people work on Emmerdale for at least three months. As people felt they'd contributed, so the internal perception of **Emmerdale** changed. The next stage of that was the move to Farsley, to give the soap its own life, and give it a proper working environment with everyone pulling in the same direction.

It was around then that Kevin Laffan left. Kevin had very clear ideas about what drama is and should be, but 15 years on it was a style of television that didn't hold a modern audience. I fought quite hard to keep Kevin around, and I'd be happy to take suggestions from him today. It was just that the writing style of the show had to be sharper, and more in keeping with what audiences were used to.

When Kevin was the real pushing force behind the show, his ethos was that it was about the characters and that the writers were the key. I actually think we stayed true to that. All soaps are hyper-reality, no-one gets married as many times as they do in soaps. But we do try to keep the characters in some sort of reality. It's a writer-driven programme that stands or falls on the scripts.

The plane crash was a short term gain in terms of the numbers viewing. Sixteen million watched the crash itself, but by the end of the week we were down to 13. A week later the figures were pretty much where they'd been before. But it was a success because it gave us a chance to explain what **Emmerdale** was geographically, how it all fitted together, and what all the relationships were. You can try attracting new people and say that it's different, but it can be quite complex and there's a danger new viewers won't understand it. That week spelled out who everyone was, who was related to who, where they lived, and who their friends were. The show never looked back.

It's much less of a fight with ITV now, we're considered to be an absolutely essential part of the schedule. The reason we went five days a week wasn't that we were desperate to go five days a week – although it's a challenge and we appreciate it – it's that we're the only programme anyone's got that goes out at seven o'clock that guarantees a big audience. The secret of scheduling is to get people in early and try to get them to stay with you all night. So we are pretty essential. We have no problem within the ITV network now, people accept us as a really good… I think they now call it a 'shoulder' for programming. While we're doing well, I don't think that will change.

I think it would be hard for us to do better – that's not to say there's not room for improvement, but in terms of the ratings I suspect we're getting as many people watching as we ever will at seven o'clock. We don't do as well in London as elsewhere in the country, and I think that's simply because people haven't got home at that time. Of the available audience – we can get 16 million when people make a huge effort to watch, but I don't think that's possible five nights a week. Our audience is pretty constant – the others tend to have seasonal changes, not as many watch in the summer when it's nice outside.

Interestingly, whenever we've been pitched head to head with **EastEnders**, we've always won. I'm quite convinced that the reason we win is that when people struggle through traffic on a dark, wet night and they get home and switch on the telly, they don't want to watch instant dark, miserable inner city angst. Even people that don't live in the countryside like to look at it, and it cheers them up. It's our unique selling point, and given a straight choice, people go for it. So we build on that as much as we can.

I've always found it strange about **Brookside** and **EastEnders** that there isn't much humour. Life is full of humour, and the East End of London and Liverpool are both noted for humour. **Emmerdale** has a lot of humour. We don't compartmentalise it, either – we try to give everyone some humour and drama, rather than having comedy characters or comedy stories.

The frustration is that we'll always be considered number three, because of the size of our audience, which I don't think we are. What's interesting is that when **Coronation Street** plays out of its normal slot, it only gets eight million people watching. We tend to get exactly the same as we usually do, often even more. Given the slot we're in, I don't think we'll ever get more viewers than **Coronation Street** or **EastEnders**. There have been rumours recently that we'll go out later – perhaps at eight – I'm not sure it will, I think we serve a fantastic purpose at seven, and on the nights we get followed by **Coronation Street**, it's a difficult line-up for other channels to break. When we were on two and three times a week they tried all the quiz shows and other things on the other nights, but they could never get as many people to watch. The challenge is retaining the audience – asking people to watch five times a week is asking for a lot of their time, and they can always find something else. And with a constant schedule like that, it's easy for Channel 4 or Channel 5 to plan a real alternative.

As Executive Producer, I'm much more concerned with the overall feel of the show. I'm involved with the long-term storylining and key casting. I like to think overall morale is my function. It was a bit depressing not to be represented at all at the Royal Television Society awards, and not to be shortlisted for the BAFTA the year after winning it, so I think it's important to lift people's spirits.

Five nights a week has been good; people know that even if they miss an episode they can catch up. The worry was always whether we could maintain the quality. In some respects, we're actually getting better. We have opportunities now we didn't have before – loads of room to tell stories, to focus down on one thing for a couple of episodes without everything else going off the boil. It gives us a chance to explore the drama. There are production issues, obviously – we're not getting outside quite as much as we used to, and that's obviously always a concern. But we maintain high standards – we won the BAFTA after we'd gone five nights a week.

Winning the BAFTA was a huge surprise and we didn't know until it was read out – if we'd known, I'd have been there at the ceremony! One journalist told me she was sure we'd do well, but I wasn't so sure. I was up in Newcastle that night, and heard we'd won on the car radio. They watched the episodes the different nominees had submitted, and talking to one of the judges afterwards, she told me **Emmerdale**'s was without a shadow of a doubt the best episode submitted. So we won in fair competition, they didn't just decide it was our turn. And the BAFTA is the most prestigious award of the lot.

As for the future… we tend to be commissioned in two-year bursts. In terms of planning the show, we make sure there are strong stories at certain key points of the TV year – the beginning of the autumn schedule, Christmas – this year we've got the anniversary. We decide on the births, marriages and deaths about a year in advance. I'm not sure we have to keep expanding – more episodes, larger casts, bigger sets. In those terms, we can't really get any bigger. We want to keep it unique in terms of the countryside, but village life changes. I can see us adding to the village, there are new areas we could introduce. We'll try to reflect the real situation. At the moment, I wouldn't be surprised if **Emmerdale** was still going in thirty years time. But as long as we keep entertaining people, it'll be there.

Index